THE
QUEST
FOR
HUMAN
UNITY

**1988 Hale Memorial Lecturer of
Seabury-Western Theological Seminary**

Joseph M. Kitagawa
"Religious Visions of the Unity of Humankind"

Recent lecturers

1980 Peter Brown. Culture, Society, and Renunciation in Late Antiquity.

1981 Aidan Kavanagh. Orthodoxy: A Liturgical Theology.

1983 Henry Chadwick. The Originality of Early Christian Ethics.

1986 Jaroslav Pelikan. The Church and Its Continuity in Augustine's Theology.

1986 Stephen Whitfield Sykes. Humiliation and Power of Christ: Kenotic Christology Today.

1988 John S. Pobee. A.D. 2000 and After: Africa and God's Mission.

1989 Robert M. Grant. Jesus After the Gospels: The Christ of the Second Century.

The Hale Memorial Lectures were established in 1900 under the terms of the will of the late Rt. Rev. Charles Reuben Hale, D.D., Bishop of Cairo, Bishop Coadjutor of Springfield, Illinois.

THE QUEST FOR HUMAN UNITY

A Religious History

Joseph Mitsuo Kitagawa

Fortress Press   Minneapolis

THE QUEST FOR HUMAN UNITY
A Religious History

Copyright © 1990 Augsburg Fortress. All rights reserved. Except for brief quotations in critical articles or reviews, no part of this book may be reproduced in
any manner without prior written permission from the publisher. Write to:
Permissions, Augsburg Fortress, 426 S. Fifth St., Box 1209, Minneapolis MN
55440.

Interior design: Karen Buck
Cover design: Patricia Boman

Library of Congress Cataloging-in-Publication Data

Kitagawa, Joseph Mitsuo, 1915–
    The quest for human unity : a religious history / Joseph Mitsuo
  Kitagawa.
        p. cm.
    "Hale memorial lectures"—P. ii.
    Includes bibliographical references.
    ISBN 0-8006-2422-X (alk. paper)
    1. Religions. 2. Religions—Relations. 3. Concord—Religious
aspects. I. Title. II. Title: Hale memorial lectures.
BL80.2.K564   1990
291—dc20   90-31258
                                                               CIP

The paper used in this publication meets the minimum requirements of American
National Standard for Information Sciences—Permanence of Paper for Printed
Library Materials, ANSI Z329.48-1984.   ∞™

Manufactured in the U.S.A.   AF 1-2422

94   93   92   91   90   1   2   3   4   5   6   7   8   9   10

For
Anne E. Carr
Larry L. Greenfield
Martin E. Marty
Delores Smith (+1988)

Contents

Preface

This volume constitutes an expanded version of my lecture notes, "Religious Visions of the Unity of Humankind," for the 1985 Hale Lectureship, which I was invited to deliver at Seabury-Western Theological Seminary, Evanston. My physical condition made it impossible for me to discharge my assignment. However, the faculty of Seabury-Western encouraged me to complete my manuscript and asked—in lieu of giving these lectures—three other scholars to read my manuscript and publicly present their reflections and comments. They did this in March of 1988. I am very grateful to Dean Mark S. Sisk and the faculty of Seabury-Western, especially Professor W. Taylor Stevenson, who took charge of the Hale Lectureship Committee and worked out such a gracious and flexible arrangement, as well as to the three scholars, Professors Robert W. Lynn, F. Stanley Lusby, and Harry B. Partin. (Prof. Lusby's statement is found as an appendix to this volume.)

Personally it is significant that the lectureship in question was established by Bishop Charles Reuben Hale, who passed away on Christmas Day, 1900. He must have sensed that 1900 signified a demarcation between two worlds of experience for many people—the great nineteenth century with its buoyant optimism and enthusiasm for "Man's Western Quest"[1] and the

troubled twentieth century with its deep-seated ambivalence
over the emerging global community. In hindsight it becomes
evident that the year 1900 must have been something of a preg-
nant moment, described by Donald Curless as

> a pause in a symphony, when the great composer brings the fury
> of his music to a stop, a rest so fateful and significant that in the
> silence the listener counts his own loud heartbeats as though they
> were his last—hoping for and almost dreading the beginning of
> the new theme in the next measure. And what will it be, that
> melody?[2]

With the end of the twentieth century right around the
corner, which implies that we have already heard over two-thirds
of its "melody," it may be worth meditating on the contrast and
continuity between the melody of the nineteenth century and
the melody that we have been listening to in our time. Every
melody has within it many motifs that are intricately intertwined,
compelling us to be both sensitive and selective. The motif I have
lifted from the melody, running through the nineteenth and
twentieth centuries, with an ever-accelerating crescendo, is "The
Quest for Human Unity." In this connection it is my opinion that
the intellectual enterprise bearing Hale's name is an appropriate
forum in which to assess the issues of pluralism—religious, cultural, social, economic, and political.

Born and reared in Japan, I came to the United States shortly
before World War II. After being incarcerated during the war in
camps in New Mexico and Idaho, I studied at Seabury-Western
Theological Seminary and the University of Chicago. From 1951
to 1985 I taught the history of religions at the University of
Chicago. I was also privileged to serve as the dean of the University's Divinity School for two terms. Over the years I have had
many opportunities to travel to various continents and meet
people of diverse ethnic, cultural, religious, linguistic, and national backgrounds. These trips, as much as my discipline, the
history of religions, have made it clear to me that people everywhere feel a profound yearning for the unity of the human race
and that they are greatly disturbed by the brokenness of the
human community along religious, cultural, economic, and political lines. I have also watched as the nineteenth century, in

which Westerners' creativity in culture, religion, art, technology, commerce, and international politics had dominated the world, has given way to the gradual but steady advance of non-Western peoples and their worlds. As one concerned with the spiritual welfare of the global community, I have attempted to assess in the present volume, *The Quest for Human Unity*, a religious history of our forebearers in other places and times, hoping to cast our current situation in sharp relief.

I wish to make it clear, however, that this volume was not written as a technical monograph of any of the identifiable academic disciplines, such as the history of religions, philosophy of religion, the social sciences, theology, or the comparative study of cultures and histories. Rather, I wanted to present a straightforward narrative of how humankind, divided into diverse linguistic, ethnic, religious, cultural, geographical, and other groupings, has never ceased its attempts to integrate human communities—very often inspired by religious visions of unity. Little did I realize how difficult and demanding it would be to devise a readable, jargon-free narrative of human experience, telescoping long and complex phases of history and selecting significant items from a mass of data. The scarcity of readable but not too technical literature on this exciting theme challenged me to undertake such a volume.

It is ironic that today many people acknowledge the legitimacy of the idea of a global community, motivated by their respective objectives, for example, economic, technological, military, religious, cultural, without making any serious efforts to enhance the kinds of conditions and atmosphere that might nurture in us, however modestly, a realistic consciousness of ourselves as world citizens, bound to share the burdens as well as the excitements of our common global community. I realize that I may be unduly pessimistic on this point. Perhaps Toynbee is correct when he implies that the framework for one world is already in the making. He thinks that the past histories of non-Western peoples

> are going to become a part of our Western past history in a future world which will be neither Western nor non-Western but will inherit all the cultures which we Westerners have now brewed

together in a single crucible. . . . Our own descendants are not
going to be just Western, like ourselves. They are going to be heirs
of Confucius and Lao-tse as well as Socrates, Plato, and Plotinus;
heirs of Gautama Buddha as well as Deutero Isaiah and Jesus
Christ. . . .[3]

Although I do not share completely Toynbee's optimism regarding the reality of one world, I am as dedicated as he is to working
toward the unity of humankind. It is my hope that the dreams
and visions of our forebears in various lands throughout the ages
might prove to be useful to the would-be world citizens of the
global community and their emerging maps of reality, without
which our future as humankind is bleak.

Working on this manuscript has made me realize how fortunate I have been to have had such excellent teachers, colleagues, students, and friends. I have learned much from all of
them. (I still feel very sheepish, however, about my appalling
ignorance of so many subjects, notably the African and Latin
American traditions.) I also realize that it is nearly impossible
for me to cite all the names of those who have illuminated me.
I humbly agree with Toynbee's feeling that "a scholar's life-work
is to add his bucketful of water to the great and growing river
of knowledge fed by countless bucketfuls of [a great many other
persons]."[4]

It is my pleasant duty to thank Mr. J. Michael West, senior
editor at Fortress Press, and Renee Fall, associate editor, for
seeing the manuscript through the press; Carol Uridil, copy editor; my research assistants and secretaries, Peter Chemery, Jef-
frey Kripal, David Zarate, Karen Pechilis, Stephanie Paulsell,
Nathelda McGee, and Martha Morrow Vojecek, for improving
and straightening out my messy notes; and Jane Marie Swan-
berg-Law, Henry H. Sugeno, and several other friends, for making many stylistic suggestions. Also, I have to express my special
appreciation to four persons who shared administrative responsibilities with me for ten years (1970–1980) at the University of
Chicago. Thanks to their devoted teamwork, I was able to carry
on my research in addition to my administrative and teaching
duties. Thus, with a profound sense of gratitude I wish to ded-
icate this volume to them.

J.M.K.

Introduction

In fairness to my readers, I should depict and explain in this introduction some of the key words and pivotal ideas that have special significance in this volume. I am not referring to foreign words, which inevitably crop up in discussing non-Western traditions, but to familiar terms that have special or somewhat unfamiliar connotations from different perspectives.

1. The first is the notion of "religion." I have no intention of questioning the legitimacy of this concept, although I share Eliade's sentiment that "it is unfortunate that we do not have at our disposal a more precise word. . . ."[1] But since we do not, we are compelled to continue using it. I am inclined to feel, however, that the term has limited relevance. To start with, it is a peculiar Western convention to divide human experience into a series of semiautonomous compartments or pigeonholes, such as religion, philosophy, ethics, aesthetics, culture, and politics. This has been very useful, with the result that many people in the West assume that such a provincial Western mode has universal validity, simply because they have not been exposed to other ways of discerning human experience. It might be pointed out that human beings everywhere live and breathe, not in a series of divided cell-like domains, but in their own seamless

world—a sort of synthesis of what Western convention calls religion, culture, society, and political order. Throughout this volume we are sensitive to the dialectical relationship between what the West identifies as "religion" and the "religious-cultural-social-political synthesis." Within the framework of this synthesis, "religion" plays multiple roles: it constitutes the spiritual or ecclesiastical tradition (often mistakenly understood as the sole feature of "religion"); it serves as the invisible glue holding together the disparate elements of life and the world; as the agent of metaphysical intuition, it defines the kinds and levels of realities, including ultimate reality; and as such, it provides cosmic legitimation for the respective religious-cultural-social-political synthesis. I am not discarding the use of the term because of its ambiguity. Rather, I am shifting the emphasis by focusing on the dialectical relationship that exists between what has been identified as "religion" in the West and the actual synthesis of various compartments *à la* the Western convention, a synthesis that has all the hallmarks of a seamless whole.

2. Secondly, in this volume I want to be sensitive to two related sets of "two-sidedness"—that of our thinking process and that of religion itself. The two-sidedness of our thinking process is evident in our autobiographical and biographical perspectives. Certainly one knows himself or herself better than others, at least internally, hence the importance and legitimacy of autobiography as a genre. What we call faith- or religious-statements are often based on an internal language that looks at the religious experience of one's own community from within. Autobiographically, Gerardus van der Leeuw was right when he stated that

> "community" is something not manufactured, but given; it depends not upon sentiment or feeling, but on the Unconscious. It need be founded upon no conviction, since it is self-evident; we do not become members of it, but "belong to it."[2]

Lamentably, many people have been exposed almost exclusively to autobiographical religious statements, with the result that they feel uncomfortable with such biographical perspectives as those used in this volume. It might be well to remember, however, as Sir Hamilton Gibb (I believe) once said, that to outsiders Islam is a religion of Muslims, but to Muslims Islam is the religion of truth. I am persuaded that the same observation could be made about any religion. Outsiders' views of other traditions, "biographical perspectives," sympathetic or otherwise, are very significant, although they are necessarily very different from insiders' more autobiographical views. Apropos, some people today—following the examples of some politicians and movie stars who write their autobiographies with the help of ghostwriters' biographical sensitivities—hold to the misguided hope of homologizing these two different perspectives.

A person's autobiographical perception of one's own religious or cultural tradition often entails uncritical acceptance of the self-authenticating circularity of the respective tradition. All of us have inherited not only our language but a great many "self-evident" notions of truth, justice, logic, and value. Thus, usually a person not only perceives his or her life and tradition from an autobiographical perspective, but unfortunately tends to view other persons' traditions from the same autobiographical perspective, as often demonstrated in our interreligious, intercultural, and international relationships. Implicit in the autobiographical mind-set is something like a mental prism, which integrates one's notions of the past, present, and future. On the other hand, outsiders—even when they utilize insiders' autobiographical statements for biographical purposes in assessing religion or culture—exercise the principles of selectivity and discrimination according to their own mental prisms.

3. Thirdly, related to the two-sidedness of our thinking process in terms of autobiographical and biographical perspectives is religion's two-sidedness—its "inner" and "outer" meanings, common to various religious traditions. Most religions recognize the existence of other religions. The plurality of religions necessitates and brings about a certain double orientation.

One of the most dramatic examples of this double-edged religious situation is the case of Hellenistic Judaism shortly before the beginning of the common era. This will be more fully discussed in the main text of this volume. I am not an expert on either Judaism or on Mediterranean studies, but I am intrigued by the efforts of the Hellenistic Jews who wanted to convey their autobiographical affirmation of the inner religious meaning of Judaism biographically to non-Jews through the Greek language and Hellenistic thought patterns. The Hellenistic Jews must have realized that their enterprise could not be completely successful. But in that religiously pluralistic Mediterranean world, they wanted non-Jews to understand some aspects of the contours of their monotheistic faith, or mono-Yahwism. Conversely, the non-Jews who could not enter into the "inner meaning" of the Jewish religion at least biographically understood the "outer meaning" of Judaism in terms of a "monolatristic particularism," a special accent on a particular deity within the context of "monolatry" (acceptance of many deities, each one worshiped as the supreme deity by different groups). Parenthetically, I might add that early Christianity also affirmed this double orientation—with monotheism as its "inner meaning" and monolatry as its "outer meaning"—as eloquently stated by the apostle Paul, who dared to say: "although there may be so-called gods in heaven or earth—as indeed there are many 'gods' and many 'lords'—yet for us there is one God . . . and one Lord, Jesus Christ. . . ."[3]

The tragedy of having one established religion was that it made European Christians functional (not necessarily religious) monotheists, who began to operate only with their autobiographical affirmation of the inner Christian meaning, misguided by the self-authenticating circularity common to religious traditions. Then they persuaded themselves that whatever they affirmed had to be objectively true in the eyes of others as well, simply because the "inner meaning" of their religion declared it to be so. For example, the "inner meaning" of Christian tradition regards the Hebrew Bible as the Christian Old Testament that prepared the ground for the New Testament. However, this "inner meaning" that Christians autobiographically affirm no way changes or invalidates the fact that the Hebrew Bible remains normative as *the* sacred scripture for the Jewish tradition.

4. The relationship between the two related sets of two-sidedness (of our thinking process and of religion itself) and the religious-cultural-social-political synthesis always has been intricate, precarious, and subtle. It has often been distorted by a

variety of factors, which include well-meaning but misconstrued perspectives and one-sided or exaggerated interpretations of religion. Bearing this in mind, we might review and briefly compare what took place in medieval Europe and early America. The medieval European form of the religious-cultural-social-political synthesis was referred to as the *corpus Christianum*, as it was given its cosmic legitimation by Christianity, the religion of the Roman Empire. Medieval Europe developed three major establishments internally—(1) the *sacerdotium* (church), (2) the *imperium* (state), and (3) the *studium* (university)—that eventually became three competing, rival institutions. For example, the conflicts between the papacy, the symbol of the *sacerdotium*, and the imperial throne, the embodiment of the *imperium*, are legendary. As Protestant reformers insisted on the validity of the truth claims of the *studium*, claims quite different from those of the *sacerdotium* but nevertheless true in their own distinct order, Rome responded by claiming a monopoly on the *magisterium* (teaching authority) regarding truth, faith, and morals. Understandably, the *studium*, even in the Iberian kingdoms, the bastion of the Counter-Reformation, quickly sided with the *imperium*, then heavily involved in the rising nationalism. Historically, it was the alliance—sometimes cooperative but often antagonistic—between nationalistic thrusts (initially of Spain and Portugal, but later of other, including Protestant, nations in Europe) and the more internationally oriented Christendom that propelled both European colonialism and the Christian world mission. In retrospect, many of the rivalries existing among medieval European institutions developed out of the conflicting claims of the *sacerdotium* and of the *imperium*, both of which asserted their prerogatives through autobiographical affirmations of their own "inner meanings." The *studium*, on the other hand, attempted to keep its "inner" and "outer" meanings in balance and was caught between these two powerful establishments. In its earlier phase the Christian world mission played second fiddle to the transplantation of the Iberian forms of the religious-cultural-social-political synthesis to the non-Western world. This was due largely to the so-called *patronato* (patronage) systems worked out between Rome and the Iberian kingdoms (Spain and Portugal).

Later on, Protestant missionaries, under the inspiration of Continental pietism and English evangelicals, asserted the independence of Christendom from the post-medieval European religious-cultural-social-political synthesis.

In early America people approached the political order (the sphere of the *imperium* in medieval Europe), religion (the domain of the *sacerdotium*), and culture-education (the province of the *studium*) not as competing rival features of life, but as mutually dependent dimensions of the same life, the whole that received its cosmic legitimation from "Providence." Medieval Europeans accepted the hierarchical principle underlying their religious-cultural-social-political synthesis in their view that all important things in life were gifts from above, whether political power, religious grace, or cultural values. But early Americans rejected this hierarchical principle and attempted to hold in balance the upward thrust of political life, the downward movement of religion, and the horizontal approach to culture-education in order to enhance the three necessities of life—morality in political life, piety in religion, and knowledge-virtue in the cultural sphere. Understandably, every Jewish and Christian group in early America aspired to press its own version of salvation. But the slowly emerging religious-cultural-social-political synthesis in early America was concerned with both the spiritual welfare of the individuals and adequate social and political structures for the corporate welfare of its citizens. This dual concern led early Americans to accept both religious pluralism and religious freedom as foundational for their young republic. Through experience early Americans developed their own synthesis of the "inner" and "outer" meaning of religion. "Monolatry," according to which each group accepted one supreme deity while tacitly acknowledging that other groups believed in their own, enabled America's early religious groups to comply with the civil virtue of religious liberty.

Ironically, the principle of religious liberty was not adequately understood or supported by the majority of Christian and Jewish clerical leaders. This novel American solution of religious pluralism was almost universally rejected after the Revolution by various religious groups in the U.S. Accordingly, most pious persons, from the large number of immigrants to the revivalists, agreed in principle with antireligious people in affirming the existence of only one meaning—either the "inner" or the "outer"—of religion. Each religious group aspired to establish its own little America in conformity with the "inner" meaning of its own tradition. However, antireligious people, who knew only the "outer" meaning of religion, attempted to eradicate all semblance of religious symbols, beliefs, and customs from America in the name of the separation of church and state.

5. The role of evangelism or mission in contemporary religion has become a hotly debated issue. This is due to the fact that Christianity, which carried on an extensive overseas missionary enterprise in the non-Western world from the sixteenth century on, seems to have lost much of its evangelical incentive since the end of World War II. Related to Christianity's growing disinterest in world mission is the mystery of a sudden but rather pervasive concern, especially among Western Christians, with interreligious dialogue. It might be helpful to sort out some of the tangled issues involved in evangelism and cross-religious dialogue.

Most genuine religions are inclined to be missionary-minded, as they are imbued with a sort of imperialistic temper. This does not mean that each religion attempts to dominate peoples of other religious backgrounds (although this has happened). But each religion does define the levels and kinds of reality, including ultimate reality, which provide the framework and structure for the cosmic, social, and human orders or the religious-cultural-social-political synthesis. Even the most universal vision is usually anchored in the particular perspective of a religion, which usually gives no option but to view peoples of other traditions from its own self-authenticating circular perspective.

One conspicuous example of the missionary spirit was the Buddhist king, Aśoka, in third-century B.C. India. In the opinion of Sir Charles Eliot, Aśoka was not so much "a pious emperor as an archbishop possessed of exceptional temporal power."[4]

When Aśoka was illuminated by the truth of Buddhism, he became an ardent missionary, sending Buddhist missionaries to other parts of Asia, the Middle East, and North Africa. A Christian example is found in the Gospel of Luke, which portrays two disciples of Jesus on the road to Emmaus witnessing their faith to a total stranger, who, according to the Gospel, turns out to be Jesus himself.[5]

Missionary work usually has not been of a purely religious character. Most often religious insights and tenets have been transmitted as parts of the total religious-cultural-social-political synthesis from one orbit to another. The mystery of missionary work is that something profoundly religious or spiritual is conveyed from one synthesis to the sensitivities of people living in the orbit of another synthesis.

Early Christianity, developing in a pluralistic Mediterranean world, was conscious of its own double orientation, with monotheism as its "inner meaning" and monolatry as its "outer meaning." When Christianity was made the established religion of the Roman Empire, however, the absence of rival religions made Christianity singularly oriented to its "inner meaning." This shift of orientation coincided with Christianity's process of acquiring mores of a this-worldly orientation, even though theologically and liturgically it retained other-worldly and eschatological outlooks. Such a this-worldly character became more accentuated in the seventh century with the rise of Islam, the this-worldly religion *par excellence*. Christian Europe benefitted philosophically and theologically from Muslim scholars, especially in the Iberian peninsula. However, fierce competition between the *corpus Christianum* and the *corpus Islamicum* in trade as in military affairs, exemplified by the Crusades, made European Christians extremely antagonistic toward Islam and also to other non-Christian religions. Thus, European Christians rejected the earlier Christian attitudes toward non-Christians, whereby the latter were no longer regarded as travelling companions through whom Christ might reveal his own nature to believers, but as infidels, living in darkness, ready to be conquered, enlightened, and exploited. Once this bundle of mundane wisdoms and this-worldly aspirations were packaged as divine commandments, Christians (initially in the Iberian peninsula, but later in other parts of Europe) found convenient excuses to condone colonialism and patronize crude forms of overseas missionary enterprises.

Christianity, like other world religions, always carried on some kind of missionary activity, as exemplified by the works of Nestorian Christians or some of the Roman Catholic religious orders. But the conspicuous, well-organized, and pervasive rise of world missionary activities coincided with the gradual disintegration of the *corpus Christianum* under the impact of the Renaissance and Reformation. These were in turn followed by the scientific revolution and the rise of rationalism. For example, among the three medieval institutions, the *sacerdotium* (church) was split between the papal church, upheld by the Counter-Reformation, and the Protestants; the *imperium* (state) propelled not one overarching empire, but a number of ambitious modern nation-states; the *studium* also underwent changes as the traditional dominance of metaphysics and theology gave way to the independence of various academic disciplines that no longer depended on the concept of deity for justification. Following the defeat of the Muslim stronghold in Granada, Spain, at the hands of Christian forces in 1492, victorious Spain and Portugal, both devout supporters of the papal church, embarked on their own colonial paths—Spain following Columbus' route to the Americas (and eventually to the Philippines via Mexico), while Portugal followed the ocean route via the Cape of Good Hope to India, discovered earlier by Vasco da Gama. Both governments agreed to maintain missionaries and church institutions in their respective colonies in accordance with the patronage system, which in turn gave them much say on religious affairs at home and Rome. Thus, the Catholic overseas missionary program began as an integral part of the Iberian kingdoms' colonial expansion and was supported, directed, and supervised by civil authorities.

With the decline of Iberian leadership in colonial matters in the seventeenth century, other European powers, including Protestant nations, started their own colonial activities. The governments of these later colonial powers took their forms of religious-cultural-social-political syntheses as *de facto* "religions of secularized salvation," and were not interested in the Christian missionary programs. It was the Continental pietists and English evangelicals, unhappy as they were with the secularized state of European churches, who formed missionary societies that were independent from colonial governments as well as from the existing Christian churches in Europe for the sake of converting non-Western peoples to the "pure gospel" of (Protestant) Christianity. In time the colonial authorities, who had initially abhorred Christian missionary work, and missionaries, who earlier had been hypercritical of any "secularized religion of salvation," made pragmatic compromises for mutual support, especially regarding educational and philanthropic activities. The combined forces and resources of colonialism and the Christian world mission exerted tremendous influence, bringing about social, political, economic, cultural, and religious changes in many parts of the non-Western world by the end of the nineteenth century.

In retrospect, it becomes evident that Western missionaries in the modern period overestimated their independence from colonialism. They also failed to realize that their message, based primarily on their autobiographical affirmation of the "inner meaning"—without any reference to its "outer" counterpart— did not establish any bridge to the peoples of the non-Western world. On this point, Tillich later pointed out that it "is not so much that they [non-Christians] reject the Christian answer *as answer*, as that . . . they do not ask the questions to which the [Christian] gives the answer."[6] European missionaries tended to transmit their own versions of a singular religious orientation (oriented almost exclusively to the "inner meaning") to new converts; they even expected former non-Christians to adopt their (European) spiritual autobiography as their own (non-Western) spiritual autobiography. (Some new Christians in the non-Western world, however, being literally surrounded by other traditional religions, were compelled to wrestle with the problem of plural religious orientations and eventually arrived at their own dual orientation—"inner" and "outer"—toward religion.) The most ironic dimension of the missionary enterprise was the romantic thinking of some missionaries whose well-intentioned but excessive sentimentality led them to think that Christians in non-Western lands should become carbon copies of Western Christians, with only their skin color remaining different. They should have remembered that, much as the ancient Hebrew community came into being as the congregation (*qahal*) of various tribal groups, the early Christian community had understood itself as the *ekklesia* (the Greek term for *qahal*) of various peoples (*ethnai*) of dissimilar temperaments, outlooks, and traditions. Even today some people tend to think of religion as a sort of cookie cutter that produces the same religious cookie, no matter the culture or the clime.

6. Many of us who have lived through World War II are bound to recognize that the days of Western colonialism are over in many parts of the non-Western world. We are mystified, however, by the curious coincidence at the end of Western colonialism, the noticeable loss of missionary incentive on the part of Christianity, and the sudden interest—especially among Western Christians—in interreligious dialogue. Some people admit that the nineteenth century was the age of Christian world mission, but equally insist that it is no longer fashionable to talk about such evangelism, as we are now living in the period of friendly dialogue. This either/or formula (either mission or dialogue) sends a misleading message to other religions that the idea of "dialogue" is used as a gimmick to camouflage the bankruptcy of the historical missionary approach of the Western churches. This kind of loose talk on the meaning of dialogue often leads adherents of other faiths to wonder whether "they are [being] seduced subtly into a new form of theological colonialism that is far from the ideal of 'dialogue among equals' that it is advertised to be, and in some ways hardly preferable to the outright missionary zeal for conversion they are accustomed from Christianity."[7] Dialogue is not a substitute for mission; both are expressions of genuine religion. All religions, including Christianity, must come to terms with this *coincidentia oppositorum*. In recent years many books and articles on the subject of interreligious dialogue have been written by Christian theologians in Western languages. Some have given the erroneous impression that the main objective of dialogue is nothing but

the theological reexamination and reformulation of Christian so-
teriology and Christology. This impression has led adherents of
other faiths to accuse Christianity of an overinflated notion of
its own importance. Dialogue does compel Christians, as well
as all other religious persons, to reassess their theological and
philosophical resources, but the aim of the dialogue should not
end there. Christianity must first of all retrieve its own original
double religious orientation—its "inner" and "outer" meanings.
Sheer dependence on the autobiographical affirmation of the
"inner meaning" of Christianity, as of any other faith, is not an
acceptable stance for a genuine interreligious dialogue.

Christianity's recent trends in emphasizing the importance
of interreligious dialogue, even playing down its historical orientation to missionary enterprise, generally has been received
favorably by spokesmen of other religions of the world.[8] Some
vocal non-Christian members of the dialogue are bewildered by
the lack of rapport between Western Christians and the members
of the "younger churches," that is, Christian churches in the
non-Western world. The spiritual autobiography of these younger church members includes exposure both to the Christian tradition and to the world of traditional non-Christian religions that
have prominent roles in the religious-cultural-social-political syntheses into which these younger church members are born. Many
have experienced what amount to small-scale, internal religious
dialogues. As a result, they have important insights to offer to
more public interreligious dialogues. But thus far Western Christian theologians have felt that they alone are the legitimate guard-
ians and representatives of the Christian heritage. They regard
younger church Christians as pale copies of their Western counterparts with nothing to contribute to the dialogue. Equally puz-
zling from the perspectives of non-Christian religious traditions
is the inferiority complex of the younger church Christians who
still slavishly follow the insights of such Western thinkers as
Barth, Tillich, Rahner, and Pannenberg, without criticizing the
Western Christian tradition from the perspectives of their own
autobiographical experiences.

As we approach the end of the twentieth century we can
see the magnitude of the religious, cultural, social, economic,

political, and military issues that lie ahead of us, especially those caused by the monumental redefinition of the dignity, value, and freedom of the human person—the bedrock of any future vision of the unity of humankind. Interreligious and intercultural dialogues are the most meaningful and necessary undertakings for our future. Our concepts of dignity, value, and freedom cannot be reformulated from the notions of the West alone. Those who believe in dialogue should discard the happy but misguided illusion that the provincial Western mode of structuring human experience is objectively proven and the most adequate common frame of reference for future dialogue. Even Western experts on the thought, literature, and religions of the non-Western world still see their methods as unbiased (even scientific), objective, and neutral, while non-Westerners see them as grounded in the self-authenticating circularity of the modern Western religious-cultural-social-political synthesis. The "canons of dialogue" that could do justice to both the non-Western and Western under-standings of human experience have not yet been hammered out. Such is the sobering predicament of our time and the un-avoidable solemn challenge to all of us, wherever we may live, in the years to come.

CHAPTER
1
A Vision of Unity

A persistent yearning in today's divided world is for a unified humanity. Throughout the history of humankind, even ethnocentrists and bigots have never seriously questioned that humanity is one, despite differences in language, culture, and religion. Archaeologists and ethnologists may disagree over when the first *homo sapiens* appeared, but they agree that all branches of the human race are, at least physically, one species.

How, then, do we account for and understand the meaning of the division of humanity into various ethnic, linguistic, cultural, and religious groupings? This is one of the most baffling questions that has confronted us throughout the ages. Since the eighteenth century, scholars of various disciplines have inquired into the origins of art, religion, and morality, to mention just a few. They have assumed that things were once much simpler than they are today, and so they have tried to trace religion, for example, to its simplest form. We know now, however, that these quests are metaphysical in nature, and that their resolutions will ultimately reflect individual views of anthropology. Thus, viewing the human being as primarily an inventor of tools (*homo faber*), following Emile Durkheim and Karl Marx, equates the origins of humankind with the origins of technology. Again, viewing the human being as a potentially religious person (*homo religiosus*) suggests that the origins of religion mark the origins of the human race.

COMMON TENDENCIES

Despite numerous scholarly theories, we have no way of knowing just how our ancient ancestors saw themselves, their life, and their world. Yet piecing together the available evidence from various disciplines, including archaeology, physical and cultural anthropology, philology, art, history, and the history of religions, we can deduce two diametrically opposed tendencies among these peoples: settlement and migration. The ancients considered their dwellings, whether rock shelters, caves, or forests, as worlds *in toto* where all activities were directed toward subsistence through simple food gathering, fishing, or hunting. All cultic or magical activities merged to form a single unified whole called life.

Gerardus van der Leeuw, the noted Dutch scholar, went so far as to say that art and religion could have been equated: "Song was prayer; drama was divine performance; dance was cult."[1] Archaic community life was thus a religious act in a religious universe. My mentor, Joachim Wach, also speculated that from the most archaic level human beings had the religious impulse to believe and to worship as well as the intellectual impulse to understand.[2] The prehistoric paintings discovered in southern France and in Spain reveal that our ancient ancestors were trying to decipher the meaning of life and the world from their primitive dwelling places.[3]

Juxtaposed to this tendency to settle was a propensity for movement and migration, often in search of more food and a better climate. Scholars speculate that as early as twenty thousand to thirty-five thousand years ago ancestors of the Native Americans (Indians) of North, Central, and South America migrated from Eurasia over ice bridges and the Aleutian Islands. Different tribes were also moving back and forth on the Eurasian steppes, and in the Mediterranean, northeast Asia, and the Oceanic Islands. About five thousand years ago, the ancestors of modern Europeans, Iranians, and Hindus, the Indo-Europeans, began to migrate from the steppes north of the Black Sea. Some went westward to Europe and north to Scandinavia and Ireland, while others moved southward into Iran and eventually India. Indo-European invaders are thought to have crossed into northwestern India around 2000 B.C., challenging the original inhabitants of the Indian peninsula. Just as certain aspects of the bear cult in arctic Siberia became known to "such remote peoples as the Lapps [in Finland] on the one hand and the Micmac Indians of eastern America on the other," so were cultic practices and beliefs transplanted to other parts of the world by this migration of peoples.[4]

The modern West, in an effort to understand the human experience of either the remote past or of non-Western peoples, categorizes life into discrete areas, such as art, religion, morality, politics, and economics. But we are only now beginning to realize that through such categories it is impossible to know how prehistoric food gatherers, hunters, and fishers conducted their communal, personal, and religious affairs.[5] Let us now examine the early civilizations.

EARLY CIVILIZATIONS

Agriculture and stock breeding developed as early as 8000 B.C. on the Iranian plateau, marking the beginning of the food-producing revolution that led to self-sustaining villages. The first great civilization arose about 3500 B.C. in the alluvial basin of Mesopotamia. Other civilizations followed in Egypt, Crete, India, China, Meso-America, Peru, and Palestine. All civilizations have self-sufficiency; they are coherent, all-embracing, and interrelated in spite of the fact that they can be divided into various cultures and subcultures, stratified social classes, towns, and countries. Whereas tribal cultures depended primarily on mythic modes of thinking, these civilizations attained a certain degree of *logos* or rationality. Most assumed the existence of another realm of reality, while still exhibiting a marked degree of sophistication in theoretical, practical, and sociological aspects of earthly religion. The most important aspect of their religion was the affirmation of the existence of a cosmic order variously known—and very differently understood—as Ma'at, Themis, Ṛta, and Tao. Closely related to the question of the cosmic order was the individual's understanding of his or her own nature and destiny. Out of these various understandings developed the differences in religious traditions. We will consider the cultural milieus of Mesopotamia, Egypt, India, and China.

MESOPOTAMIA

The Mesopotamian civilization was the hub of the subsequent early civilizations of Persia, Greece, and Palestine. Born in the valley between the Tigris and Euphrates rivers, it encompassed what is present-day Iraq. Human settlement here can be traced back to 10,000 B.C., but the Mesopotamian civilization emerged around 3500 B.C., accompanied by the invention of writing and the growth of cities in the area inhabited by the Sumerian people. Surrounded by Persia, Turkey, Palestine, and Arabia, Mesopotamia was historically sensitive to and influenced by these cultures. According to Thorkild Jacobsen, the ancient Mesopotamians saw the universe as a sovereign state governed by an assembly of gods. The national state, made up of city-states owned by individual gods and ruled by their human stewards, was ruled by a king who was guided by the "executive officer," so to speak, of the assembly of gods. Thus, as a part of the cosmic commonwealth directed by the united wills of the divine powers, the earthly national community was considered sacred.[6]

Mesopotamia left a rich mythological legacy, including the creation myth of the Enuma Elish, Gilgamesh's search for immortality, and the epic of Marduk, the god of Babylon. Ancient Mesopotamians lived very close to their deities. In observing the movements of the planets, for example, they looked "for a purposive will committing an act."[7] As Jacobsen reminds us, the Mesopotamian did not believe in an arbitrary world:

> He demanded that it have a firm moral basis. Evil and illness, attacks by demons, are no longer considered mere happenings,

accidents. . . . Thus in human moral and ethical values man had found a yardstick with which he presumptuously proceeded to measure the gods and their deeds.[8]

The Semitic peoples, whose language differed from the Sumerians, had checkered fortunes in Mesopotamia. The Semitic group was divided into many sublanguage units. The Akkadian, Assyrian, and Babylonian peoples belonged to the older East Semitic branch, and the Hebrew, Aramaic, Phoenician, Syriac, and Ethiopic peoples belonged to the West branch. These peoples fared well under the Akkadian king, Sargon, and his grandson, Naram-Sin, whose empire stretched "from central Persia to the Mediterranean and from northeastern Arabia to the Taurus Mountain."[9] The Akkadian rule was eventually overthrown by the Caucasian Gutians, who in turn were conquered by the resurgent Sumerians. When the Elamites and the Amorites came to power, the Amorite king occupied the old Akkadian city of Bab-ilu or Babylon; thus commenced the Old Babylonian period (around 1830–1550 B.C.).

The Babylonian ruler, Hammurabi, was a famous lawgiver and military genius, as well as a superb administrator. His code of laws bears an uncanny resemblance to the later laws of the Hebrews; the history of Mesopotamia has close connections with the history of the ancient Hebrews. During the Old Babylonian period, there lived a people called the Habiru, a name phonetically identical to the word *Hebrew*. Moreover, the father of the Hebrews, Abraham, originally came from Ur and Haran in Mesopotamia. Of Abraham's two sons, according to the Hebrew scriptures, Isaac succeeded his father on the Hebrew side, and Ishmael became the progenitor of the Arabs. Later, Joseph, Jacob's heir, was sent to Egypt, where his descendants remained for over four hundred years until they were rescued by Moses. Finegan believes that

> the patriarchal stories fit with thorough congruity and often with surprising relevance of detail into the historical setting of life in Mesopotamia during the early second millennium B.C. Likewise . . . other portions of the Old Testament reflect intimate connection with both the mythology and the law of Mesopotamia.[10]

The Assyrian and New Babylonian Dynasties. Shortly after the reign of Hammurabi (died 1750 B.C.), the northern boundary of Mesopotamia experienced pressure from various Indo-European tribes. One of these, the Hittites, strongly influenced Mesopotamia through their dominance of the Anatolian plain. Almost equal in power to Egypt, the Hittites eventually fell to the Assyrians around 1200 B.C.

The Assyrians originated in the northeast corner of the Fertile Crescent and the mountains of Kurdistan and took their name from their kingdom's national deity, Ashur. During the Hittite domination, the Assyrian king, Ashuruballit I (about 1362–1327 B.C.), built a great empire through warfare and trade. Under Shalmaneser III (858–824 B.C.) the mighty Assyrian army campaigned against Syria and Palestine, defeating King Jehu of Israel. Shalmaneser III named himself "the mighty king, king of the universe, the king without rival, the autocrat, the powerful one of the four regions of the world. . . ."[11] His line's reign was usurped by a great general, Tiglath-Pileser, whose descendant, Tiglath-Pileser III (744–727 B.C.), invaded Israel and deported many of its people; Ahaz of Judah became his vassal. Again the Assyrian army, this time under Shalmaneser V (726–722 B.C.), defeated the rebellious Israel and invaded Samaria as well (see 2 Kings 17:5); and in 701 B.C. the powerful Assyrian king, Sennacherib (704–681 B.C.), whose line replaced that of Tiglath-Pileser and Shalmaneser V, quelled the rebellion led by Hezekiah of Judah who was aided by the Egyptian army (see 2 Kings 18:13—19:37; 2 Chron. 32:1-22; Isa. 36:1-37). Sennacherib's grandson, Ashurbanipal, assumed the kingship of Babylon. Upon his death, Nabopolassar (625–605 B.C.) established an independent Chaldean, or New Babylonian Empire. One of the Semitic peoples, the Chaldeans are mentioned as "an ancient nation" in Jer. 5:15. It was the combined forces of the Babylonians and two Indo-European peoples, the Scythians and the Medes, that sacked the magnificent capital city of the Assyrian Empire, Nineveh.

The Chaldean rulers of the New Babylonian Empire soon felt the threat of the Egyptian pharaoh, Necho, who in 605 B.C.

pushed his forces close to the Euphrates; but he was defeated by Nebuchadnezzar II, the son of the emperor, Nabopolassar. Nebuchadnezzar then made Jehoiakim, crowned king of Judah by the Egyptians, his vassal. After a series of rebellions, Nebuchadnezzar punished the Hebrews for their repeated uprisings by destroying Jerusalem and taking most of its population as captives to Babylon. The New Babylonian Empire fell to the forces of the Persian emperor, Cyrus the Great, in 539 B.C.

Persian Rule. The two famous Indo-European tribes of the Medes and the Persians had settled very early in what is now Iran, "the Land of the Aryans," and their existence was noted by the authors of the Hebrew scriptures (Esther 1:19 and Dan. 5:28). The Persians moved southward and developed a large empire by 700 B.C. In the sixth century B.C., Cyrus the Great defeated the rich kingdom of Lydia and subsequently captured Babylon. Cyrus felt guided by his deity, Marduk; but Second Isaiah believes that Yahweh sent him to Babylon in order to enable the captive Jewish exiles to return to Palestine. Under his son, Cambyses II (530–522 B.C.), the Persian Empire became the greatest in the world, its domain stretched from the border of India to Egypt. However, this monarch's madness resulted in a significant loss of unity within the empire. The prestige of the empire was restored by Darius the Great (522–486 B.C.), a scion of the Achaemenids and an important name because of his devotion to Zoroastrianism and his unwitting introduction of Greek influence into the Middle East.

Zoroastrianism. Darius I, his son Xerxes (486–465 B.C.; the Ahesuerus of Ezra 4:6), and Xerxes' son, Artaxerxes I Longimanus (465–423 B.C.; see Ezra 7:1), were ardent followers of Zoroastrianism. Little is known about the life of Zoroaster (Zarathustra) except that he lived sometime before or during the Achaemenid dynasty (559–331 B.C.) in the region encompassing the present-day Khorasan, Western Afghanistan, and the Russian Turkmen Republic. He was born into a polytheistic, sharply defined class society composed of chiefs, priests, warriors, husbandmen, and cattle breeders; he was most likely a priest. Rejecting other deities, Zoroaster proclaimed Ahura Mazdah, the

"Wise Lord," the only true god and creator of both the visible and the invisible worlds. This monotheism superseded an ethical dualism based on the acts of his twin sons, Spenta Mainyu (Bounteous Spirit), who chose good, truth, justice, and life; and Angra Mainyu (Destructive Spirit), who chose evil, lies, injustice, and death.

According to Zoroaster's message of reform, people are free to choose between good and evil—just as Ahura Mazda's twin sons were at the time of creation. The world is a struggle between good and evil. Zoroastrian cosmology is based on a world history divided into four three-thousand-year periods; the end of each period is marked by the coming of a new savior, a posthumous son of Zoroaster. The last savior and judge, Saošyant, is expected to appear at the end of twelve thousand years, miraculously born of a maiden and the seed of Zoroaster; he will rehabilitate the whole of creation by casting the devil into hell and purging the human race of the stain of sin. An unsuccessful reformer, Zoroaster finally found a patron in Prince Vishtaspa; with the prince's help, Zoroastrianism was established. Only a fraction of the Zoroastrian sacred book, the *Avesta*, is written in the ancient Iranian language of Avestan. The later texts, written in Pahlavi, do not reflect the monotheistic teachings of Zoroaster.

"The significance of Zoroastrianism," writes R. C. Zaehner,

lies not in the number of those who profess it, but rather in the influence it has exerted on other religions [for example, on all Gnostic religions—Hermetism, Gnosticism, Manicheism], and particularly on Christianity, through the medium of the Jewish exiles in Babylon who seem to have been thoroughly impregnated with Zoroastrian ideas. . . . Christianity claims to be the heir of the prophets of Israel. If there is any truth in this claim, it is no less heir to the prophet of ancient Iran, little though most Christians are aware of this fact.[12]

In the ensuing pages we will note the impact of the savior Saošyant on the Buddhist savior images.

Greek Influence on the Middle East. We will now look at the impact of Hellenism on the Middle East through the policies of Darius the Great. In 512 B.C. the ambitious Darius launched an expedition to the Danube and sent his officers to the Balkans to see to Persian interests in Asia Minor and the rebellious Ionian colonies. After a series of punitive measures against the disgruntled Greeks, Darius resumed his European conquests in 492 B.C., beginning with the invasion of the Bay of Marathon, north of Athens. He was defeated by the Atheneans in 490 B.C. In 479 B.C. the Persian navy was badly defeated at Salamis. Although the Achaemenid dynasty existed until the mid-third century B.C., successive waves of Hellenization infiltrated the Middle East during its tenure, even before the time of Alexander the Great (336–323 B.C.).

The migration of peoples of Greek, Macedonian, Thraco-Phrygian, and Illyrian languages into the Balkans, the Anatolian plain, and the Greek peninsula can be traced back to the Copper and Bronze ages; in time these tribes developed into the Minoan and Mycenaean civilizations. At the same time, a new wave of Greeks speaking an Archaeo-Doric dialect appeared. With the decline of the Hittite empire in Anatolia there developed a series of Greek colonies in that area and in the area of the Aegean Sea. The Greeks were internally quarrelsome, but they maintained an external solidarity based on their

> racial unity, across a hundred modes of dialect, custom, and cult. What mattered most was that all recognized a group of major Panhellenic deities, of whom the great poets sang. They had their great temples . . . and they had their games—great meeting places, in which they got to know one another, where they exchanged ideas, and where artistic production and initiation were fostered.[13]

Unlike many ancient peoples who took kingdoms and empires for granted, several of the Greek colonies developed a new pattern, the *polis*, a common citadel, "a refuge in time of war, and the centre of their political life—of assemblies, markets and magistrates, of their artisans and industry, of their cults and their law courts."[14]

There was nothing unique about primitive Greek religion; however, it typically venerated animate and inanimate objects. The Greek pantheon was comprised of diverse Greek and non-Greek deities reflective of the people's checkered experiences with migration and regionalism. Some deities were syncretized into a single figure, as seen in the "Homeric Hymn to Apollo."[15] There were many divine beings with local cults; some were known for their oracles. For example, the Oracle of Delphi required the services of diviners and interpreters. Among some Greeks, mystery cults like that of Dionysus were popular, offering men and women "ways of removing the stains on the soul, in order to free it from the influence of demons, conquer fate, and in the end produce happiness in another world and the prize of resurrection."[16]

The Greeks excelled in philosophical thinking since ancient times. Such excellence is borne out in the development of the *physiologoi* of Ionia and in the work of such great thinkers as Anaximander (around 615–546 B.C.), Xenophanes of Colophon (around 580–480 B.C.), and the Sophists of the fifth century B.C. Socrates (470–399 B.C.) felt that a voice of a *daimon* within him compelled him to teach men what is truly good. Plato (428–347 B.C.), Socrates' disciple, left philosophical writings on various subjects; and Aristotle (384–322 B.C.), Plato's greatest pupil, wrote in areas including metaphysics, politics, and poetics. From 343 to 342 B.C. Aristotle served as tutor to Alexander the Great of Macedonia.

Alexander the Great.   The Greek peoples' discontent with the tyranny and cruelty of Persia fostered the formation of Greek union against Persia in the fourth century B.C. This league was led by King Philip II of Macedonia, who mobilized the troops and ships of the Graeco-Macedonian League against the Persian forces in 336 B.C. Upon Philip's assassination, his twenty-year-old son, Alexander III (336–323 B.C.), assumed the rule of Macedonia and the generalship of the Panhellenic League. He began his brilliant military campaigns in the Balkans, on the Danube, and in Greece itself, removing all opposition before moving into Anatolia, Syria, Phoenicia, and Egypt.

Of all Alexander's campaigns and accomplishments, three deserve special mention: (1) he consolidated the Middle East, Egypt, and the Mediterranean world; (2) he made contact with India; and (3) he inaugurated a new "cultural" colonialism for unifying all peoples in the *oecumene* or "inhabited quarter" of the world through Hellenistic civilization and the Greek (*Koine*) language and presented to the world the cultural image of savior and benefactor of the human race. This savior or benefactor was different from the religious savior images of Judaism (the chosen people), of Christianity (the incarnated *logos*), or of Islam (the saving book); but it exerted an important influence on subsequent Middle Eastern, Mediterranean, and European religious thought.

In 334 B.C. Alexander initiated his Persian campaign and conquered Asia Minor, Tyre, and Egypt, the last praising him as liberator and pharaoh. In Egypt he established his new capital of Alexandria. In 331 B.C. he returned to Asia and defeated the last Persian emperor, Darius III (335–331 B.C.). In a bid for peace, Darius offered Alexander a sum of money and half of Asia Minor, but Alexander reportedly refused the gift, saying that "the earth could not stand two suns nor Asia two kings."[17] Alexander took countless treasures at Susa, Persepolis, and Ecbatana—according to the Greek historian, Plutarch, at Persepolis "10,000 pairs of mules and 5,000 camels were required to carry away the loot. There at the main capital, with 3,000 of his soldiers occupying the royal terrace, Alexander sealed the conquest of Persia by putting to the torch the palaces which symbolized the power of the Achaemenids."[18] After conquering Mesopotamia and Babylon, he moved into Media and central Asia and overpowered the antagonistic Scythians in 328 B.C.

In 327 B.C. Alexander invaded India and after a long campaign in Bactria (located along the borders of present-day Afghanistan and the Soviet Union), he crossed the Indus River in 326 B.C. and proceeded to Panjāb. His generals feared mutiny if he penetrated further into India, and he was forced to turn back; but he was determined to keep the already conquered territories of India under his reign. He left garrisons and newly appointed governors to protect Macedonian interests. His death in 323 B.C., at the age of thirty-three, prevented further exploration. His Indian invasion left no cultural legacy in India, but the Hellenized colonies in Bactria and central Asia fostered a fusion of Indian, Persian, and Greek religious thought and aesthetics.

Alexander was a man of contradictions. A man of culture, he spent most of his young life in military campaigns. During his brief career, he attained an almost supra-human level of power, claiming to be simultaneously King of Macedonia, General of the Greek League, King of Asia, Pharaoh of Egypt, and King of Kings of Persia. More significantly, he marked the end of the Mesopotamian/Middle Eastern civilization and the beginning of the Graeco-Roman-based Mediterranean outlook with its vastly different religious, cultural, political, social, and economic institutions. He did not behave like most Middle Eastern monarchs and tyrants. For example,

> he put the conquered Persians on a level with the Macedonians, and employed them together in the army and in the administrative services, as well as permitting fusion of religions and mixed marriages. He founded a number of cities in the Persian districts, settling both veterans and immigrants from Macedonia and Greece; and he developed trade between the different regions of the vast new empire, in which he made Babylon the capital but Greek the official language. At the moment of his death he was preparing . . . [for] a still larger empire, a world empire embracing the Caucasus regions, Arabia, and the central and western Mediterranean.[19]

Throughout his life, Alexander considered himself a divinely commissioned "savior and benefactor of the human race." After his time this was not an uncommon belief of religious and philosophical figures or kings and popes in the Mediterranean/Middle Eastern world.[20]

After Alexander's death, it became obvious that his feeble-minded half-brother and his young son could not handle the affairs of the vast empire. In time the most able of his generals, called "successors," assumed monarchical roles and developed their own dynasties, for example, the Seleucid kings of Babylon, Syria, and the eastern provinces, and the dynasty of the Ptolemies in Egypt. The preoccupation of the Seleucids with Syria created a vacuum in Persia where a Parthian Arsacid dynasty arose (around 250 B.C.–A.D. 229). The Seleucids took Judea from the Ptolemies around 198 B.C.; the cruel excesses of the Seleucid king, Antiochus IV Epiphanes, led to the Maccabean War in 168 B.C.

Egypt enjoyed relative peace under the Ptolemies until the rise of Rome. Rome became a major power with the defeat of Hannibal and the Carthaginian army in 202 B.C. Under the great general Pompey (106–48 B.C.), such power was virtually undisputed throughout the Mediterranean world. The Ptolomies' reign ended and Egypt became fully incorporated into the Rome with the fall of Marcus Antonius and Cleopatra.

EGYPT

Egypt, the world's second great civilization, was a younger contemporary of its Mesopotamian counterpart. Here, Neolithic dwellings can be traced as far back as 5000 B.C.. Most archaeologists agree that the earliest people in this part of the world, usually called Bardarians, were succeeded by the Amaritans. Their communities—believed to have been Totemic clans—apparently used copper. The Amaritans were succeeded by the Gerzeans, who evidently originated in Lower Egypt but gradually penetrated the Upper region. The Gerzeans deemphasized clans but developed towns, and continued to view animals and plants as totems. Tension already existed between the Upper and Lower regions; toward the end of the predynastic period, the king of Upper Egypt forged a single kingdom by conquering the delta region of the Nile.

During the First and Second Dynasties, often called the "Protodynastic Period" (around 2900–2700 B.C.), Egypt enjoyed regular commerce with Mesopotamia. Egypt welcomed Mesopotamian trade and technologies, especially techniques for brick-building. With the exception of the Mesopotamians, and later the Greeks and Romans, the Egyptians did not have much commercial or cultural contact with other peoples. As John Wilson states:

> The Nile cuts north out of Africa, surmounts five rocky cataracts, and finally empties into the Mediterranean. These cataracts form the barriers of Egypt against the Hamitic and Negro peoples to the south just as effectively as the deserts and the sea bar Libyan and Semitic peoples to the north, east, and west.[21]

The Nile influenced Egypt in that its annual rebirth and the daily rebirth of the sun were ingrained in the Egyptian psyche.

Wilson also explains that the ancient Egyptian viewed the earth as a sort of flat platter—the bottom of which was the Egyptian plain—floating in the primordial water (*Nun*). Above the earth was the inverted pan-shaped sky, supported by four posts embedded in the earth. Between heaven and earth lived the air-god, Shū, and under the vault of heaven were the heavenly bodies and the stars. The sun-god, Rā, was the supreme god and a divine king believed to have been the first king of Egypt in primordial times. This cosmos, like the Nile Valley, was characterized by regularity and periodicity: "Its structural framework and mechanics permitted the reiteration of life through the rebirth of life-giving elements. The creation stories of the ancient Egyptian were also in terms of his own experience, although they bear loose general similarity to other creation stories." [22]

In sharp contrast to the ancient Mesopotamian, who regarded the whole cosmos as a sort of huge "state," the ancient Egyptian made a clear distinction between the heavenly abode and the earthly state that were linked by the king, simultaneously one of the gods and the representative of the state. Understanding the ancient Egyptian concept of the pharaoh with contemporary Western categories is a tricky and often misleading endeavor. When we read that to the ancient Egyptian the pharaoh was the sky-god, Horus, we tend to think of him as the "symbol" of Horus, distinguishing as we do between symbolism and participation. But Wilson explains that when the ancient Egyptian said that "the king was Horus, he did not mean that the king was playing the part of Horus, he meant that the king *was* Horus, that the god was effectively present in the king's body during the particular activity in question." [23] In addition to being seen as the divine king, the son and successor of the sun-god, and Horus himself, the pharaoh was also believed to be the ruler of the Upper and Lower regions, the herdsman of his people, and the controller of the Nile waters.

Although scholars are divided on the epochs of ancient Egyptian history, James H. Breasted's chronology is highly respected.

The "Old Kingdom" [known as the Pyramid Age], Fourth
Dynasty, ca. 2900 B.C.–2750 B.C.

The Fifth Dynasty, ca. 2750 B.C.–2625 B.C.

The "Middle Kingdom," Twelfth Dynasty, ca. 2000 B.C.–1788
B.C.

The "New Empire," Eighteenth Dynasty, ca. 1580 B.C.–1350
B.C.

The Nineteenth Dynasty, ca. 1350 B.C.–1205 B.C.

The Twenty-second Dynasty, ca. 945 B.C.–745 B.C.[24]

Djoser, the founder of the Third Dynasty, supposedly
marked the first high point of Egyptian civilization. He is buried
in a 190-foot-high pyramid designed by the architect Imhotep,
who was also a priest, a magician, an author, and a physician.
The founder of the Fourth Dynasty, Khufu, and his successor,
Khafre, were also buried in huge pyramids. Khafre's likeness
has been preserved in the Great Sphinx that stands near the
Second Pyramid.

Confusion and chaos followed the decline of the Old Kingdom, but the founder of the Twelfth Dynasty inaugurated the
"Middle Kingdom," the second great age of Egyptian civilization.
Scholars believe the establishment of the Middle Kingdom co-
incides with Abraham's entry into Canaan, around 1935 B.C.,
and his visit to Egypt, although there are no substantiating ref-
erences to the latter in Egyptian sources. The fall of the Middle
Kingdom was followed by a period of disintegration, which resulted in rule by the Hyskos, a foreign tribe, probably from the
Semitic group; the successors were not the Hebrews, as Josephus
assumed.

The Hyskos tribe fell to the forces of the founder of the
Eighteenth Dynasty and its queen, Hatsshepsūt, who dared to
proclaim herself king (she ruled both the Upper and the Lower
regions of Egypt). Thutmose the Great succeeded the throne,
becoming history's first empire builder. His kingdom stretched
from Egypt to the Euphrates: "Never before in history had a
single brain wielded the resources of so great a nation and
wrought them into such centralized, permanent and at the same
time mobile efficiency."[25]

The Eighteenth Dynasty also produced Akhnaton (also called Akhenaten), known as Anemhotep IV (reign 1372–1354 B.C.), whose wife, Nofretete, was a renowned beauty. Akhnaton believed in a solar monotheism based on the sole worship of the sun god, Aton. He was determined to wean Egyptian religion away from polytheism, but his efforts were undermined by the powerful priesthood of the traditional deity, Amon-Rē. After his death his son-in-law and successor abandoned these reform measures, restoring the old religious practice. Akhnaton's religious reform movement was doomed to fail, but his famous "Hymn to the Aton" survived. His neglect of the empire's practical affairs resulted in rebellion in Palestine and Syria. His reign coincided with the rise of the Habirus, identified with the Hebrews.

By the Nineteenth Dynasty, another great period in the history of Ancient Egypt, the country began to experience increasing pressure from the "Asiatics." Rameses II (reign 1292–1225 B.C.) was pressed by these tribes during his long reign. He finally agreed upon a nonaggression pact with the King of the Hittites in order to keep southern Syria and Palestine within Egypt's domain. However, he recognized Hittite rule in northern Syria and Amurru. Many scholars believe that the Israelites entered Egypt around 1720 B.C. and left under the leadership of Moses around 1290 B.C., during the reign of Rameses II.[26]

Egypt's prestige waned steadily from the Twenty-first to the Thirtieth dynasties (around 1150–332 B.C.). A Libyan family founded the Twenty-second Dynasty, an Ethiopian family the Twenty-fifth. The Twenty-sixth Dynasty, however, came from an Egyptian line that began a period of native restoration during which contact was made with Greece. The second ruler of the dynasty, Necho (around 609–594 B.C.), killed King Josiah (see 2 Kings 23:29ff) and after marching to the Euphrates was stopped by Nebuchadnezzar of Babylon. Necho's great-grandson, Amasis, witnessed the rise of Cyrus the Great of Persia. His son, Psamtik, was defeated by Cyrus's son, Cambyses II (around 525 B.C.). From Psamtik's defeat until the end of the Thirtieth Dynasty, Egypt was under Persian domination. Alexander the Great invaded Egypt in 332 B.C.; after his death, the Ptolomies ruled Egypt until it was incorporated into the jurisdiction of Rome in 30 B.C.

Death and Immortality. S.G.F. Brandon states that

the ancient Egyptian evaluation of human life and destiny has a significance beyond that which inheres in the fact of its great antiquity, and it will be seen that certain Egyptian concepts in this connection are unique in that they represent man's first recorded efforts to express certain basic human intuitions and aspirations.[27]

Egyptian religion left a rich legacy to the Mediterranean world. The oldest collection of literature, compiled by priestly scholars of the Old Kingdom, resides in the Pyramid Texts. Beginning in the Middle Kingdom, portions of these texts were copied onto the coffins of kings and nobles; these became known as the Coffin Texts.

Then as early as the Eighteenth Dynasty, which began in 1580 B.C., most of the religious literature of Ancient Egypt, including the Pyramid Texts and the Coffin Texts, was brought together. . . . This we call the Book of the Dead. . . . The last recension of the Book of the Dead was still in use during the Ptolomaic, Greek, and Roman periods, even to the very end of the Egyptian civilization.[28]

Many scholars speculate that the institution of kingship and the belief in the dying-rising god Osiris were united in a cult as early as the predynastic period. The purpose of such a cult was to affirm that the deceased king might attain everlasting felicity; eventually, even people of common blood aspired to some sort of immortality. This theme became an important motif in ancient Egypt.

Egyptian civilization demonstrated very early—as did the old civilizations of Mesopotamia, India, and China in their respective ways—the truth of Mircea Eliade's observation that our ancestors consciously collaborated with nature in order to dominate it. They created civilization with the realization that by conquering nature through civilizing techniques, which facilitate or speed up the processes of nature, humankind could become nature's rival without being the slave of time.

The Egyptians who . . . hated iron . . . considered the flesh of the gods to be of gold. In other words, the gods were *immortal*. That is why, after the models of the gods, the pharaoh was also assigned flesh of gold. Indeed, as the *Brāhmaṇas* repeatedly proclaim, "Gold is immortality." Consequently, obtaining the elixir that transmutes metals into alchemical gold is tantamount to obtaining immortality.[29]

Ancient civilizations such as the Egyptian tell us that humankind, both as *homo faber* (inventor of tools) and *homo religiosus* (religious being), from the very beginning of its existence, has been dominated by the fear of death and has sought to conquer death through civilizing activities and a ritually constructed afterlife.

The ancient Egyptian was incapable of considering an afterlife without the body; hence the importance of physical preservation and the art of the embalmer. Moore realistically describes the process of embalming and the funerary rite:

The viscera having been removed, the body was steeped in natron and asphalt, and when sufficiently impregnated with these preservatives was wound, with various aromatics, in endless coils of bandages, and laid in a sarcophagus. Fashions changed in mummies and coffins as in other things; but the object always was not merely to prevent decay, but to keep as far as possible the form of the man as he had been in life. At the burial, the priests went through the motions of opening the eyes, mouth, and nose of the mummy, reciting meanwhile potent spells to restore to the dead man the use of his senses.[30]

These procedures were followed flawlessly so that the *ba* (soul) and the *ka* (an ethereal alter ego) could live on, provided that the body was properly kept in the appropriate tomb and received sufficient food, drink, and funerary offerings. The deceased was believed to appear before the King of the Dead, Osiris, to have his or her heart weighed against an ostrich feather, the symbol of *maʿat*—originally a term from physics implying evenness or correctness but eventually meaning justice and social responsibility.

The ancient Egyptian civilization attained a high degree of material culture, as demonstrated by the sophisticated scientific technologies of the Old Kingdom, and a high standard of morality, as exhibited by the administration of the Middle Kingdom. In the early days of the Old Kingdom, noblemen wished to be buried close to kings in order to share the continuation of the royal life in the hereafter. Otherwise each man primarily lived for himself, often falling prey to a deep pessimism or to unethical magical practices—or to both. With the coming of the Middle Kingdom, people began to believe that the reward of divinity in the hereafter was open to commoners—every dead Egyptian could become the god Osiris, as both god and judge of the deceased. Such beliefs imply the equality of all human beings in opportunity and a sense of collective responsibility on the part of humankind. To quote Wilson, "the Middle Kingdom continued the physical establishment but introduced a new note: 'Do not be evil, (for) kindliness is good. Make thy monument to be lasting through the love of thee. . . . (Then) the god will be praised by way of rewarding (thee).' "[31]

The movement from the theocratic autocracy of the Old Kingdom to the atomistic, more democratic Middle Kingdom waned with the rise of the New Kingdom under the alien Hyskos rulers. In order to rid themselves of the Hyskos, the Egyptians were forced into a communal solidarity and a new sense of nationalism (as exemplified by the strength of Thutmose II), conformity to a national religion, and a marked sense of fatalism. These characteristics were accentuated by the failure of Akhnaton's religious reform.

The period of the Twenty-first to the Thirtieth dynasties marked the decline of Egyptian civilization. Yet this period produced the remarkable document well known to the Hebrews, "The Wisdom of Amenemope." The Book of Proverbs used passages from this document almost verbatim, and Jer. 17:5-8 and Psalm 1 reflect Amenemope's protrayal of the two trees.[32] In the following we read that a wise man named Amenemope gave his son advice on honesty, integrity, and kindliness:

> As for the passionate man in the temple, he is like a tree growing in the open. Suddenly (comes) its loss of foliage, and its end is reached in the shipyards; (or) it is floated far from its place, and flame is its burial-shroud.
> (But) the truly silent man holds himself apart. He is like a tree growing in a garden. It flourishes; it doubles its fruit; it (stands) before its lord. Its fruit is sweet; its shade is pleasant; and its end is reached in the garden.[33]

But "wisdom," without a strong sense of the interrelation between human being and the god, between the individual and the community, was not sufficient to sustain the Egyptian civilization. And Persia, which dominated Egypt from the Twenty-seventh to the Thirtieth dynasties, had little use for the religious and cultural traditions of its new vassal.

When Alexander the Great conquered Egypt, he was proclaimed a deified pharaoh and the son of the Egyptian god. It was his policy to protect Egyptian civilization, even though Egyptian nationalism ended with his assumption of the throne. His policy was followed by his successors, the Ptolemies; Ptolemy V Epiphanes (around 203–181 B.C.) was honored by the priests of Memphis for his ardent and generous support of the Egyptian temples.[34] During the Ptolemaic era the Egyptian deities remained intact, although a new god, Serapis (the name signifies in Greek a combination of Osiris and Apis) was honored, and eventually gained great popularity in the Roman world as an Egyptian deity.

When Egypt became a Roman province in 30 B.C., Roman authorities continued to protect Egyptian religion while introducing Roman deities. Still, the passion of Osiris and the mysteries of Isis were widespread among the Romans. The edict of Theodosius (A.D. 345–395) reputedly closed the Egyptian temples, but cultural practices such as burial customs persisted for years in Christian guise. In A.D. 642 the Arabs eventually ended Roman rule in Egypt.

The Significance of the Egyptian Civilization. Did the ancient Egyptian civilization that attained such high standards in art, architecture, and government also contribute to the philosophy, ethics, and world-consciousness of later times? "No," says Wilson, "not directly in fields which one may specify, as in the case of Babylonian science, Hebrew theology, or Greek or Chinese rationalism. . . . That culture [Egyptian] had reached her intellectual and spiritual heights too early to develop any philosophy which could be transmitted in cultural heritage to the ages."[35] Wilson's argument is valid, but so is Mercer's that no modern categories and classifications can account for all the peculiarities of ancient Egyptian civilization. It contained elements and aspects of many domains of life familiar to our modern age; "and withal it was symbolical and literal, mystical and pragmatic, conservative and syncretistic, and supremely contradictory and inconsistent at one and the same time."[36] The impressive fact is that the ancient Egyptians had an amazingly rich experience ranging from monotheism to pantheism, from autarchy to democracy, from supreme optimism to severe pessimism, from lofty morality to open selfishness; and pervaded with that sense of justice and futility that underlies all human community and cosmic order. The fact that they recognized that "all men were created equal in opportunity" was a significant discovery for humankind—a principle that we are still attempting to actualize."[37]

INDIA

The world's third great civilization, India, has been alive up to the present day. However, this discussion will be confined to the beginning of the common era.

The Indian peninsula had numerous prehistoric nomadic food-gatherers and hunters; more developed agriculture and permanent villages emerged around 3000 B.C. Many theories have been advanced concerning the identities of the people who dwelt in these communities, but the earliest pages of Indian history remain a mystery. Two main sources are turned to as tangible beginnings of Indian civilization: the remains of the ancient Indus Valley civilization and the religious literature of the Indo-Europeans. Thomas Hopkins states, "The first of these carries our knowledge back to the third millennium B.C. by means of material artifacts; the second presents in ritual hymns the religious life of Aryan tribes that entered India in the second millennium B.C."[38]

Indus Valley Development. Geographically, the Indian subcontinent was isolated from the rest of the world by the ocean and snowcapped mountains, except for the narrow northwest passage leading into central Asia. The first known urban development arose here around 2500 to 1500 B.C.: the Harappā culture, named after the ancient city in what is now the Panjāb. A second city, Moheñjo-daro, located 250 miles from the mouth of the Indus River, followed an identical cultural pattern. These two cities, according to Mircea Eliade, "would have to be considered the first examples of the secularization of an urban structure, which is an essentially modern phenomenon."[39]

Most scholars think that the Harappā culture was not Indo-European in origin but a mixture of other racial groups and that their culture was different than the cultures of Mesopotamia and Egypt. The major crops of the Harappā were most likely corn, wheat, barley, peas, and sesamum; they also raised fowl. A.L. Basham states that "on the basis of this thriving agricultural economy the Harappā people built their rather unimaginative but comfortable civilization. Their bourgeoisie had pleasant houses. . . . Evidently a well-organized commerce made these things possible."[40]

Harappā and Moheñjo-daro were built on similar plans—a citadel, walls, an advanced sanitation system and, among other amenities, an elaborate system for bathing. There were stone structures and enclosures for sacred trees but no obvious temples—much to the bewilderment of archaeologists who expect to see temples in ancient cities. Indus art consists primarily of carved stone seals and clay products, especially terra-cotta figurines of human beings (mostly females) and of animals (mostly males and frequently bulls). Judging from the seals, people apparently conceived of supernatural beings resident in trees and plants and of a pantheon with many deities. Many similar elements were absorbed into later Indian religious traditions.[41] Basham feels that "the Harappā religion seems to show many similarities with those elements of Hinduism which are specially popular in the Dravidian country."[42]

Opinions vary whether the Indus Valley civilization was overthrown by invading Indo-Aryans or declined of its own accord. But by 1500 B.C. once thriving cities such as Harappā and Moheñjo-daro had disappeared, leaving no obvious legacy to the next masters of the Indian peninsula, the Indo-Aryans.

The Penetration of the Indo-Aryans. The Indo-Iranian tribes, who called themselves "noble" (*Airya* in Old Persian and Ārya in Sanskrit), likely originated on the central Asian steppes north of the Black Sea. These tribes belonged to a large language family with many subgroups. They were sturdy, light-skinned nomads who made a living grazing cattle and farming. They were familiar with metals, wheels, and chariots. Some migrated west into Europe, others settled in Persia, and still others moved southward into the northwest part of the Indian peninsula around 200 B.C. According to George Dumézil's lifelong research, the Indo-Aryan societies from Ireland to India were divided into groups according to three functions: priests, warriors, and husbandmen. This tripartite social division is reflected in the deities each group worshiped. The Indian deities Mitra and Varuna are associated with the priests; Indra and the Maruts are venerated by the warriors; and the Aśvins and Sarasvatī are honored by the husbandmen.[43]

The early phase of Indo-Aryan civilization is revealed through collections of the hymns, the four *Vedas* (bodies of knowledge): the *Ṛg Veda*, the *Yajur Veda*, the *Sāma Veda*, and the *Atharva Veda*. These bodies of sacred knowledge were transmitted orally, a practice confined to the priestly (*brāhmaṇa*) class. Thus the knowledge of this culture's early phase is only partial and one-sided, although we have a fairly realistic picture of a people who loved music and dancing and often indulged in intoxicating drinks such as *soma* and *surā*. The Indo-Aryan civilization was firmly grounded in religion, known as Brahmanism or Vedism; it later developed into the major tradition we call Hinduism.[44]

Brahmanism considers the *Vedas* (usually three—the *Ṛg*, *Yajur*, and *Sāma Vedas*—but occasionally adding the *Atharva Veda* to complete the four) as *śruti* (heard) or revealed knowledge, in contradistinction to the literature of later religious tradition based on human authorship (*smṛti*). The term *Vedas* sometimes included such expository literature as the *Upaniṣads*. Of the four *Vedas*, the centerpiece was the *Ṛg Veda*, a compilation of ten books of hymns and litanies in praise of the gods Indra, Agni, Soma, the Aśvins, Varuṇa, and Mitra, dated around 1400 B.C.

The focus of the Vedic tradition is the liturgical use of *mantras* (sacred formulas) collected for use in the *yajña* (sacrifice). The *Yajur Veda* is one collection of mantras and explanatory materials for the instruction and use of priests. The *Sāma Veda* is a collection of chants, some of them taken from the *R̥g Veda*, that accompanied the sacrifice. The *Atharva Veda* is a collection of hymns but also contains folksy spells and incantations recited to avert evil or to promote long life and material prosperity.

In addition to the verses of the *Vedas* (*samhitas*), Brahmanism also produced expository prose that developed in three successive phases. The *Brāhmaṇas*, dated around 1000–800 B.C., comprise a collection of guidelines for and principles of great rituals, the *soma* sacrifice especially. The *Āraṇyakas* (Forest Books), dated around 800–600 B.C., contain both ritual materials and speculative exposition on such topics as the three-way parallelism thought to exist among ritual, macrocosm, and microcosm. Finally, the *Upaniṣads* (literally, "squatting close to a teacher" or "instruction thus imparted") include materials that date as far back as 600 B.C., although some of its contents may date around 300 B.C. The compilation of the *Upaniṣads* overlapped with the founding of non-Aryan religious traditions, such as Buddhism and Jainism; it also reflected the gradual eastward movement of Brahmanism from northwestern to northeastern India. Along this route Brahmanism borrowed new doctrines, such as the belief in transmigration and the notion that all beings must be constantly reborn in an endless cycle, from the indigenous peoples living along the Ganges. With this doctrine of transmigration developed the need for release (*mokṣa*) from the bonds of endless rebirth. Such a concern encouraged the ascetic practices of wanderers and forest hermits whose discussions and teachings are contained in the *Upaniṣads*. These forest hermits affirmed the unity of the individual soul (*ātman*) and the absolute World-Soul (*brahman*). For Indian civilization, humankind's perennial search for unity resided in the unity of all things—not just human beings—in the one Absolute Being.

Religious Movements and Buddhism. In addition to the mystical speculations of the *Upaniṣads*, which provided a path of knowledge (*jñāna*) for the orthodox Brahmanic tradition, a number of religious movements arose in northeastern India around the sixth or fifth centuries B.C., where Indo-Aryan influence began to be felt strongly by the indigenous non-Aryans. The orthodox used the word *heterodoxy* to describe these religious movements. Some scholars believe that Buddhism and Jainism were deviations of orthodox Brahmanism. Of these religious movements, Jainism (followers of the conqueror, or *jina*), a religion of radical asceticism founded around the sixth century B.C., has remained active in India. It affirms the ideal of a triumph over all material existence. Mahāvīra (literally, great hero), the great saint of Jainism, is purported to be the twenty-fourth and last in a series of enlightened teachers. In the course of time, famine drove Jain monks to Deccan. Jainism became divided into two groups: those who practice nudity and those who wear white garments. A movement of other ascetics, the Ājīvikas, was founded by Gosāla, one-time associate of the Mahāvīra of Jainism. According to the Ājīvikas' belief, human effort cannot affect the soul's predetermined path. This religion, very active in the third century B.C., began to decline and eventually died out around the fourth century A.D.

The Buddhists fared better than the Jains and the Ājīvikas, although mostly so in other parts of Asia. Little is known about the founder of Buddhism, Siddhārtha Gautama (Śākyamuni before he became the Buddha), or the "Enlightened One." The canonical accounts of the Buddha's life, which couple dogmatic and apologetic interests with pious imagination, were written centuries after his death. The Buddha was born in Lumbini, located near the Nepal-India border. He was born sometime between the seventh century and fifth century B.C. Pious legends of the Buddha, like those of Jesus, follow the pattern of sacred biography. There is the stereotyped notion of a holy man whose life is marked by a series of supernatural events. He proclaims in his youth his future calling. He seems to have prior knowledge of the death that awaits him and is believed to have overcome physical death. When these legends are analyzed closely, we really only know how such religious figures were remembered by their followers, and so it is with the Buddha. Based on the memories of the early Buddhist community, his father was a minor tribal chieftain and not a king, as portrayed in legends. Gautama was married and had a son. The term *Gautama* indicates that if his family was not of Aryan descent—which is not likely—it had adopted elements of Indo-Aryan civilization.

When Gautama was about thirty years old, he made a decision to forsake the world and become an ascetic. He abandoned this path when various forms of asceticism did not give peace of mind. At thirty-six, while sitting under the Bodhi tree, he gained a piercing insight into the meaning of existence and the way of deliverance from the transitoriness of the finite world. His mind was freed from sensual desires, from the desire for earthly existence, and from ignorance. Buddhism's uniqueness is that while it accepts the Buddha as the discoverer of the true law (*dharma*), it knows no savior or deity in the usual sense. There is no "revelation" or "revealer" behind the Buddha's enlightenment experience; he found the true law by himself.

The Main Tenets of Buddhism. The Buddha's cardinal teachings, the so-called "Four Noble Truths," diagnosed the human problem and posed a method for its treatment.[45] The Four Noble Truths are these: (1) the nature of existence is characterized by universal suffering; (2) the origin of suffering can be traced to a "craving" for mundane pleasures and success; (3) the cessation of suffering is necessary for deliverance; (4) the remedy is the Buddha's Middle Way, also known as the "Aryan Eightfold Path," namely, right view, right aim, right speech, right action, right living, right effort, right mindfulness, and right concentration. The "Eightfold Path" will enable one to achieve saving knowledge, enlightenment, *Nibbana* (Nirvāṇa). Historically, the Buddha never discussed the meaning of Nirvāṇa; for him, religion was not a matter of information but of salvation.

Buddhism does not depend on a sacred scripture as the basis of doctrine. Few clergy and laity know all the scriptures that their tradition has produced.[46] What unites all Buddhists are the "Three Treasures": the Buddha, the Holy Law (*Dharma* or *Dhamma*), and the Buddhist Community (*Saṃgha* or *Saṅgha*). According to Buddhism, the holy and true law was discovered by the Buddha, and it can be realized only in the new type of holy community, the spiritual fellowship of monastics and laity who intend to follow the Buddha's saving path.[47]

King Aśoka. The rise of Buddhism coincided with a period when the outside world was encroaching upon India from the northwest. As noted earlier, Cyrus the Great (around 550–530 B.C.) of Persia absorbed much of the Panjāb into his vast domain. Two centuries later, Alexander the Great subdued the Persian Empire and invaded the Indus Valley; but his sudden death in 323 B.C. resulted in the retreat of the Greek forces, leaving India in the hands of rival principalities. The most able and ambitious of these was Candragupta of the Maurya dynasty, who chose as his capital Pāṭaliputra, on the banks of the Ganges. His grandson, Aśoka, converted to Buddhism and became an energetic advocate of his new faith. He sent Buddhist monks out on religious, educational, and philanthropic missions, to all parts of his domain, to India's neighboring countries, the Hellenistic kingdoms of Asia and north Africa, and to parts of Europe. According to Basham,

> . . . the keynote of Aśoka's reform was humanity in internal administration and the abandonment of aggressive war. In place of the traditional policy of territorial expansion he substituted conquest by Righteousness. . . . It seems that Aśoka believed that, by setting an example of enlightened government, he might convince his neighbors of the merits of his new policy and thus gain the moral leadership of the whole civilized world. He by no means gave up his imperial ambitions, but modified them in accordance with the humanitarian ethics of Buddhism.[48]

Just as Alexander the Great must have had a philosophical vision of the unity of humankind with himself as the savior and benefactor of the human race, Aśoka was evidently persuaded that the unity of humankind must be based on two levels of reality—the historic "Three Jewels" of the Buddha, *Dharma*, and *Saṃgha*, and his own understanding of the new triad: the Buddhist kingship, a greatly expanded and applied *Dharma*, and the Buddhist-inspired state with himself as the universal king and the beloved of the gods.[49]

Aśoka's numerous reform measures are recorded in his *Edicts*.[50] To ensure his policies he created a new class of officials, the "Officers of Righteousness." Under his dominion, Buddhism not only guided individuals but also an entire complex society, nation, and civilization. The Buddhist community was no longer a small segment of Indian society; it was the total nation and, potentially, a total human community.

Ironically, Aśoka was not a popular king. Critics readily point out weaknesses in his policies. Nevertheless, he forged Buddhist religion and morality into the basis and framework for achieving the unity of mankind.

The Two Threads of Indian Civilization. Contrary to a widely held view that Buddhism emerged from within Indo-Aryan tradition as a deviation of it, we suggest that it arose as a result of an encounter between the perception of reality held by the indigenous people and the reality of Brahmanism in northeast India. We hold this position despite the fact that shortly after the Buddha's death Buddhism steadily appropriated the Brahmanic idiom and vocabulary. From a broader perspective, Brahmanism and Buddhism comprise two separate philosophical currents, as T. R. V. Murti observes—"the *ātmā*-doctrine of the Upaniṣads . . . and the *anātmā*-doctrine of Buddha."[51] These currents continued to stimulate each other for nearly ten centuries after the birth of Buddhism.

After the death of King Aśoka, a rivalry was maintained between the Greeks and the Persians in Bactria; both groups frequently invaded northwestern India, at times reaching into the central and northeastern areas of the country. A noted Greek king of the Panjāb, Milinda (Menander), reputedly became a Buddhist and has been remembered for his conversation with the Buddhist philosopher-monk, Nāgasena.[52]

In the second century B.C., Bactria was occupied by the Parthians, who originally came from Persia, thus confining the Greeks to their possessions in India and Afghanistan. Meanwhile, the unification of China by Ch'in Shih Huang Ti (247–210 B.C.) caused a series of chain reactions including the migration of a central Asian nomadic tribe—which the Chinese named

Yüeh-chih—into Bactria, then under the Scyths—called *Śakas* by the Indians—who in turn attacked the Persians in Iran and the Greeks in India, finally reaching Mathurā in north central India. To make matters more complex, the Pahlavas—known for the Iranian names of their kings who ruled northwest India— were conquered near the beginning of the common era by the Yüeh-chih rulers who were succeeded by King Kaniṣka, probably of the Śaka tribe, who controlled the western half of northern India and a vast area in central Asia. Scholarly opinions are divided as to whether Kaniṣka lived in the first century B.C. or the first century A.D., but the close connection that northwestern India enjoyed with the Greeks and Persians in Bactria and central Asia resulted in a fusion of artistic, cultural, and religious forms and concepts shortly before and after the turn of the common era. Illustrating such a fusion are the development of the Gandhāra school of art, the popularity of new savior images in both Brahmanism and Buddhism, and the emergence of the Mahāyāna tradition of Buddhism as represented by King Kaniṣka.

After Aśoka Brahmanism lost its appetite for the great sacrifices of the Vedic tradition. To compete with new religious movements such as Buddhism, Jainism, and the Ājīvikas, the old Vedic gods such as Indra and Varuṇa were replaced by new and more glamorous gods, such as Viṣṇu and Śiva, who had not been prominent earlier. By the early centuries of the common era, Brahmanism—which slowly changed by adopting various forms and concepts from new religious movements and non-Indian sources—developed into "classical Hinduism," embodied in such classics as the *Mahābhārata* and the *Rāmāyana*.

Buddhism, which began as an insignificant religion of mendicants and pious lay people in northeast India, was promoted as the religion of the empire, if not the world, by King Aśoka. It promoted elaborate systems of doctrine, philosophy, and ethics, rich ceremonials and holy days, voluminous scriptures, and elegant art and architecture. Buddhism also accepted an ancient Indian mythical image of a just and virtuous world-monarch, the Cakravārtin (turner of the wheel [*cakra*]), as a paradigm for its speculations regarding the Buddha and the

Buddhist king. Popular piety developed the notion that the Buddha and Cakravārtin shared identical universal principles and a set of thirty-two physical marks. In time, such symbols of the Cakravārtin as the sacred wheel (*cakra*), the divine white elephant, the white horse, and the magic jewel were used on Buddhist altars and in Buddhist relic mounds (*stūpas*); eventually, the image of the Cakravārtin fused with the image of the future Buddha, Maitreya. Many scholars believe that the figure of the Iranian cosmic savior, Saošyant, inspired the Buddhist notion of Maitreya as the future Buddha who will come at the end of the world and establish peace and justice. Popular piety also found the Cakravārtin an appropriate model for the Buddhist king. Although Aśoka never claimed to be Cakravārtin, later Buddhists came to regard him as the Buddhist image of the coming universal monarch.

It seems to be a strange coincidence that the rise of Mahāyāna Buddhism coincided with the beginning of Christianity. Edward Conze finds three important parallels between the Mahāyāna tradition of Buddhism and Christianity: emphasis on love and compassion; focus on the "compassionate being" (Christ and the Bodhisattva); and certain eschatological interests.[53] Further, only one other savior figure, Amitābha, believed to be the lord of the blissful Western paradise to which the sun and departed spirits go, emerged from the cross-cultural and cross-religious milieu in northwestern India and central Asia around the beginning of the common era. Both Maitreya and Amitābha followed the eastward expansion of Buddhism from India to China, Korea, and Japan.

Betty Heimann stated that in tracing the sources of Western philosophy to Plato and Aristotle and still earlier to the pre-Socratics of ancient Greece, she was led to study Indian thought, which both climatically and geographically "was predestined for the full development of cosmic speculation. . . . Here therefore Man was, and ever remained, no more than part and parcel of the mighty whole."[54]

Other scholars, such as the founders of the Harvard Oriental Series, have found the religious thought and civilization of the

Hindus fascinating because the Hindus are "a race akin, by ties of blood and language, to the Anglo-Saxon stock."[55] But even if the Indo-Aryans were not related to the Anglo-Saxons, Indian civilization should be studied because it has offered much to the religious sensitivity of humankind, especially in the cosmic vision that underlies its perception of the unity of mankind—a vision that was embodied not only in Brahmanism (or Hinduism) but in Jainism and Buddhism; and it has informed and guided millions of people through the centuries.

CHINA

China, the fourth great world civilization, actually the Far East in general, is an enigma to many. According to Harold Isaacs, in 1942 40% of Americans could locate China on the map; and in 1945, after direct American military involvement in Asia for more than three years, still only 43 to 45% of Americans could place China geographically.[56] Moreover, India was equally vague in the minds of a similar number of Americans to the degree that an astounding number believed that the Chinese and the Indian civilizations are parts of one amorphous "Oriental" civilization.

There are basic similarities between the civilizations of China and India; there are bound to be by virtue of the human condition. But except for the expansion of Buddhism into China from India, these two great cultures developed independently. Further, Asia witnessed the development of a number of other similar but autonomous civilizations, those of Korea and Japan.

Today, China is the third largest country in the world with one of the longest recorded histories. D. L. Overmyer states that "it is as if the Babylonian kingdom established by Hammurabi in 1750 B.C. were still active today, with its ancient language and social ideas still largely intact."[57] The famous "Peking Man," a Paleolithic creature, is estimated to have lived about four hundred thousand years ago.[58] Scholars are uncertain whether the Chinese Neolithic culture was a part of the ancient culture of West Asia; we do know that there were many tribal groups in northern China, presumably all Mongoloid, and that they merged in the course of time.

These are good reasons to believe that agriculture was practiced in northern China toward the end of the Neolithic period. Chinese legends give accounts of such cultural heroes as Fu-hsi, who taught the people how to domesticate animals; Yu-ch'ao, who transmitted the art of building houses; Shen-ming (literally, divine farmer); and the celebrated mythological Emperor Huang-ti, who is credited with initiating various arts from medicine to government. Later Chinese traditions idealized the "Golden Age"—the so-called period of Yao and Shun—believed to have existed in the second half of the third century B.C.; and, according to a popular but unverifiable mytho-history, a leader named Yu founded the first dynasty, the Hsia, which lasted until around 1751 B.C.

The Early Phase.   Archaeologists are more informed about the early phase of Chinese civilization starting with the Shang (or Yin) period (ended around 1040 B.C.). There were a number of kingdoms or principalities under the Shang rulers. Anyang, an important Shang capital situated near the northern border of the present Honan, has yielded many recent archaeological findings, among them both oracle bones and tortoise shells for divination and an indigenous system of writing with characters. The artifacts and archaeology of huge unearthed tombs, temples, and palaces assist speculation concerning rituals performed by kings, aristocrats, and priests to honor ancestors and deities. Society was sharply divided between the aristocrats and the commoners, with educated officials—the forerunners of the scholarly elite—somewhere between the two in status. People primarily engaged in agriculture, sericulture, and a variety of handicrafts; beyond this, little is known with certainty.

The Shang period's major accomplishments include the discovery of bronze metallurgy and the invention of writing. The Shang technique of metallurgy was superior to that of the European Renaissance. In addition to bronze, stone and especially jade were in great demand. The origin of the Chinese writing system is traced in a legend to the Eight Diagrams, made famous in the West by the *I-Ching* and allegedly invented by Fu-hsi. The distinctive indigenous writing system exerted a decisive influence on Chinese government, education, literature, philosophy, religion, and other patterns of thought and life. It also provided a common written—but not spoken—medium between China and its neighbors.

The Shang rule was followed by the Chou (1040–265 B.C.), the longest dynastic reign in Chinese history. Under the Chou rule, loosely organized political dimensions of the Shang dynasty were systematized into "feudalism" (*feng-chien*). According to Dun J. Li, whereas the Shang had allowed subjugated tribes a degree of autonomy as long as they recognized Shang suzerainty, the Chou imposed a rigid feudal order on all conquered tribes, annexing or relocating many. "A new theory was advanced that 'all land belongs to the king and all men are the king's subjects,' and the king could grant land to whomever he wished."[59] The Chou claimed that the king (*wang*) reigns over each separate state within the realm by the "Decree of Heaven." Interestingly, the most famous Chou ruler was not a king but a regent named Chou Kung (the Duke of Chou) who was idealized by Confucius. He was credited with initiating many things, including the compilation of the *Ritual of the Chou* (*Chou Li*) based on an imaginary utopia in antiquity.

One of the greatest marks of the Chou period was a philosophical creativity that opened a variety of metaphysical options for later Chinese civilization. The emphases of these philosophical schools varied widely, but they shared basic concerns for the salvation of society, about the nature of the human being and his immortality, and about the authority of antiquity.

A major philosophical system regards Confucius (around 551–479 B.C.) as its founder and has taken its name, Confucianism, from him. Confucius believed in righteousness and held that the universe is on the side of righteousness. But he was unsuccessful in persuading any prince to adopt his philosophy of a just society based on the inner sense of ethical commitment, *jen* (humaneness), that characterized a superior person. He became a teacher of philosophical morality, believing in the educability of any human being interested in the true way (*tao*).

According to the Analects (*Lun-yu*), the purpose of education is the cultivation of virtues through four items: literature, conduct, sincerity, and faith. Confucius was deeply concerned throughout his life with *li*, variously translated as propriety, ritual, or etiquette. For him, the family was the model for society and state; the so-called five relationships—the ruler and the ruled, father and son, husband and wife, brother and brother, the superior and the inferior—are based on the principle of the rectification or ordering of names that stand for roles, statuses, and functions.

One hundred-fifty years after Confucius, a second great master of this school named Mencius (371–289 B.C.) graced Confucianism by presenting the original teachings with his own twist, that humankind is innately good and hence capable of performing, and even delegated to perform, political and economic righteous action (*yi*). His ideal society—in which all men are brothers—deeply impressed future thinkers of many philosophical schools. Mencius's younger contemporary, Hsün Tzu (340–245 B.C.), was renowned both for his view that the human being is by nature bad and for his theory that the power of the prince is absolute.

When Confucianism became the state philosophy in the second century B.C., the following works were accepted as the Five "Confucian" Classics: the *Book of Odes* (*Shih ching*), a collection of poems primarily from the Chou period; the *Book of History* (*Shu ching*), historical and semi-historical accounts from the early days of the Chou period; the *Book of Changes* (*I-Ching*), a collection of manuals of ancient diviners; the *Book of Rites* (*Li chi*), a second century B.C. compilation of canonical ritual and protocol; and the *Spring and Autumn Annals* (*Ch'un-Ch'iu*), a history of the feudal state of Lu attributed to Confucius.

Taoism, the second great philosophical tradition, was named after the Tao (the way of the universe) and is presumed to have been founded by Confucius' contemporary, Lao-tzu, whose life is a mystery despite numerous legends. The *Book of Taoist Virtue* (*Tao-te Ching*) is ascribed to him. According to Taoism, the Tao is a formless, shapeless nothingness. This nothingness is the mother of all things, including the universe; and the way of the

Tao is *wu wei* (the principle of inaction). According to Li, Taoism stands for "the negation of all values, religious or otherwise. It was against any efforts, including efforts to attain a better life in the next world. If we have to use an analogy . . . Taoism was a state of drunkenness without being intoxicated."[60] A distinction exists between Taoism as a philosophy (*Tao chia*) and Taoism as a religion (*Tao chiao*).

The Chou produced other philosophical systems including the School of Mo Ti, the advocate of universal love who probably lived between the time of Confucius and Mencius; the School of Legalists (*Fa Chia*); and the School of Names (*Ming Chia*). Also noteworthy was the eclectic School of Yin-Yang, based on the two opposing principles of the Tao—*yin* (negative, dark, female) and *yang* (positive, light, male)—that are related to the five elements (wood, fire, earth, water, metal), to the five directions (east, south, center, north, west), to the five seasons (spring, summer, midsummer, autumn, winter), and to the five planets (Jupiter, Mars, Saturn, Mercury, Venus), to name the most important correspondences. The Yin-Yang School provided sophisticated cosmological theories, but also influenced popular beliefs and practices, such as *feng shui* (a form of geomancy) and calendar-making.[61]

Although some Chou court officials were assigned to rituals and divination, other religious specialists, mainly shamans or spirit mediums, were occasionally consulted, for it was believed that demons (*kuei*) or unhappy ancestral spirits caused illness or misfortune. The Chou period was also known for its search for immortality. Laurence G. Thompson states:

> The search for a magical elixir, known in the West in later times as alchemy, began in China. . . . But there was a basic difference in the purpose of alchemy in the two civilizations. In China the primary motivation was the desire to attain immortality, whereas in the West it was the hope of obtaining gold from base metal.[62]

Imperial China.   With the rise of the Ch'in dynasty (221–207 B.C.)—to be followed by the Former Han (202 B.C.–A.D. 25) and the Later or Eastern Han (A.D. 25–220) dynasties—China entered an imperial era that lasted until 1912. The founder of the Ch'in dynasty called himself Shih Huang-ti, the First Emperor, believing that his line would last forever. He is remembered primarily as the man who began construction of the Great Wall, a massive human monument over three thousand miles long, and who instigated an infamous episode of bookburning. Nevertheless, he was an unusually able, shrewd, energetic, and farsighted autocrat. He was determined to wipe out the feudal residues of the Chou regime and to make China a unified empire of thirty-six administrative provinces with the same language, traditions, and beliefs. He planned to unify China, freeing it from legal and social discrimination based on geographical or tribal background, and transcending the distinctions between Chinese and barbarians. At the same time, in order to consolidate the fabric of the nation based on state ideology (Legalism), he rejected Confucianism, Mohism, and other schools of thought.

The Chinese empire expanded in all directions during this era, extending its boundaries into non-Chinese regions; this in turn drove nomadic groups further into central Asia. However, the downfall of the expanding Chinese empire was its rigid thought control, anti-intellectualism, strict execution of laws (especially in regard to punishment), and overambitious and never-ending public work projects that required an inhuman exploitation of peasants and high taxation, all of which backfired against the regime. The grand dream of the Ch'in ended in 207 B.C. when the son of the First Emperor died at the hands of conspirators.

Han China.   Following the period of civil strife after the downfall of the Ch'in, China was unified by the Han dynasty that, except from A.D. 9 to 23, dominated the political scene for four centuries. The temporary measure of accommodating the feudal practices that had characterized the initial Han rule was reversed by Emperor Wen-ti (179–157 B.C.) in favor of centralized bureaucratic policies.

The most eminent among the Han monarchs was Wu-ti, who consolidated and greatly expanded the Han empire during his long reign (140–87 B.C.). As he moved toward central Asia, he confronted the mighty kingdom of Hsiung-Nu (a pastoral tribe, probably akin to the Huns), who had defeated the Yüeh-chih (who likely spoke an Iranian dialect but lived in western Kansu). Migrating westward, the Yüeh-chih

> ruled the territory north of the Oxus, and in Bactria . . . overthrew the kingdoms established by Greek adventurers in the wake of the armies of Alexander the Great. Later some of them invaded Northwest India, and in the early part of the Christian era, under the Kushan dynasty, experienced important cultural development.[63]

Wu-ti wisely allied himself with the Yüeh-chih against their common enemy, the Hsiung-Nu, whom they eventually defeated. Meanwhile, Wu-ti sent his embassy to central Asia, thus opening the overland route for trade and commerce.

Active trade existed between China and Europe in ancient times. Commercial traffic via the overland route was such that as early as the first century B.C. Cicero warned fellow Romans that if Han China pursued an adverse trade policy, a financial panic in Rome could ensue. Frederick Taggert, who studied the Roman-Chinese relationship at the turn of the common era, suggests that "of the forty occasions on which the outbreak [of war] took place in Europe, twenty-seven were traceable to the Han government."[64] International trade was greatly facilitated by sea routes, which interested the Han rulers as much as the overland routes. Historians believe that the discovery during the first century A.D. whereby navigators took advantage of the monsoon in the Indian Ocean enabled Chinese traders to reach Southeast Asia, Ceylon, India, and the eastern part of the Roman Empire. This extended their commercial interests into the Parthian Empire, the Yüeh-chih communities in Kushan India, the Sarmatians in what is now Russia, and the string of Greek colonies on the Indian border and in central Asia. There is even a nonverifiable account that Emperor Marcus Aurelius Antonius of Rome, named Ta Ch'in by the Chinese, sent his emissaries to China.

Chinese Civilization under the Han. The Han's contribution to China was not confined only to the military, diplomatic, and commercial domains. For example, they devised the civil service examination, one of the most outstanding features of the

Chinese educational and administrative system. Their state ideology and cult was Confucianism coupled with the Five Classics, which remained the standard and backbone of Chinese civilization. What became known as Han Confucianism incorporated insights from Legalism, Taoism, and the Yin-Yang School so that a rather eclectic system of philosophical, ethical, educational, and cosmological teachings with myriad cultic features for state and family occasions emerged. The Han regime was very supportive of the literary and poetic aspirations of men of letters and it encouraged historical speculation and writing, as exemplified by Ssu-ma Ch'ien's *Historical Records* (*Shih-chi*) and the *History of the Han* (*Han Shu*) by Pan Piao, his son, Pan Ku, and his daughter, Pan Chao. The history of the Han dynasty was dotted with bloody struggles among emperors, dowagers, ministers, warlords, barbarians, eunuchs, scholar-gentry, harems, secret societies, and peasants. In time, the once tightly knit fabric of their empire began to disintegrate, especially after a rebellion of the religious sect of the Yellow Turbans in A.D. 184. That rebellion made clear both the weakness of the imperial army and the strength of the local governors and opened the way for the fall of the Han dynasty in A.D. 220 and the new rule of the Three Kingdoms era. Nevertheless, the general tone and framework of Chinese civilization were established during the long Han reign.

Lastly, we recall that Buddhism penetrated China during the Han period. Legend states that a Chinese scholar travelled to central Asia in 2 B.C. and learned about Buddhism. Although in China the introduction of Buddhism was commonly ascribed to the dream of Ming-ti (A.D. 58–76)—who then sent his emissary to India whence two Indian monks returned to China to preach the new Buddhist gospel—this story was probably fabricated by the prestige-conscious Buddhist community. Owing to the international trade that flourished along both the overland and the sea routes, Buddhism was undoubtedly known and practiced by people living on China's borders, primarily foreigners but probably also native Chinese, during the Han period. There is a story about An-shih-kao, a Parthian prince, who came as an early Buddhist missionary and translated the scriptures into Chinese.

Although a vigorous expansion of Buddhism into all walks of Chinese life took place after the fall of the Han, Buddhism already had some pious adherents during that era. From the beginning, Buddhism found its way into learned circles—especially among poets, writers, and artists—through Taoist intellectuals to whom many aspects of Buddhism were very congenial. That was the unique feature of Chinese Buddhism: its "gentrification," as some have called it. Gentry Buddhism was instrumental in transmitting Buddho-Taoist inspiration. In addition, many people have pointed out the strong Taoist influence on the later Ch'an Buddhism, better known in the West by its Japanese name, Zen.

We note two important aspects of Buddhism in China. China became one of the three secondary centers of diffusion for Buddhism: China for Mahāyāna Buddhism; Ceylon for the Southern or Theravada School; and Tibet for the Esoteric traditions. Nevertheless, Buddhism did not attempt to replace indigenous traditions in China. It became a supplement to Confucianism and Taoism, so that these three traditions eventually came to be understood as "three dimensions of one truth" (*dharma* or *tao*).

SOME REFLECTIONS

We have briefly looked at the world's four oldest civilizations— Mesopotamia, Egypt, India, and China. These civilizations and the cultural traditions that they engendered developed unique visions for the unity of humankind by the first or second centuries. All of them struggled with competing claims of religious and cultural traditions, and all of them had proposals—however tentative—for unity. For example, the campaign of Alexander the Great was a complex phenomenon inspired by contradictory motivations—a philosophical, even a religious, vision of Alexander as savior and benefactor of the human race. A parallel vision animated the Buddhist king, Aśoka, in third-century B.C. India. Indian civilization preserved a lofty cosmic vision that enabled speculation about the existence of one Eternal law or principle (*sanātana dharma*) underlying all the contradictions of the phenomenal world. And China, with its unshakable conviction about the existence of one Tao (the way or truth of the universe), affirmed the pattern of a multivalue or plural belongingness system in its Confucian-Taoist-Buddhist traditions. No one tradition in China stands alone; all three were mutually interactive in Chinese history from very early times.

However, now we must look at other visions, especially those advanced by the Hebrew, Roman, and Christian traditions, all of which exerted a decisive influence on Western civilization. In chapter 2 we take a cursory look at their development up to the early centuries of the common era.

CHAPTER
2
Hebrew, Greco-Roman, and Christian Visions

Chapter 1 examined how different "universalistic" religious visions of the unity of humankind were nurtured through the "particularistic" experiences of the Mesopotamian, Egyptian, Indian, and Chinese civilizations. This chapter briefly considers the Hebrew and Greco-Roman civilizations and Christianity and their development up to the early centuries of the common era.

THE HEBREW VISION

According to the Hebrew scriptures, Abraham, the legendary founder of the Hebrew people, felt called by his God to leave his birthplace in northern Mesopotamia to search for the Promised Land. As far as it is known there was nothing that set the Hebrew people apart from other nomadic or seminomadic peoples in Mesopotamia. Biblical accounts portray Abraham both as the patriarch of the Hebrews and as the founder of the Hebrew religious community because his religious outlook was different from that of the pagan religions of the surrounding peoples. His willingness to sacrifice his son, Isaac, attested to this fact. Morphologically speaking, Abraham's sacrifice was no different from the common paleo-Oriental practice of sacrificing the firstborn for the circulation of sacred energy in the cosmos; but since Isaac was the son of the promise, the Hebrew religious community interpreted the sacrifice as a unique event. Abraham did not understand why he must sacrifice his "divinely given" son, but he accepted the deed as God's command. So, as Eliade poignantly observes, "by this act, which is apparently absurd, Abraham initiates a new religious experience, faith."[1] Abraham's faith was rewarded by God's assurance that his descendants would multiply in the Promised Land. The covenantal relationship established between God and Abraham became an important cornerstone of the faith of the Hebrew religious community.

The Hebrew scriptures reveal that the accounts of a religious community often differ from the objective accounts of the same historical events. Any religious history presupposes values that are accepted and shared by the religious community involved. These values are modified by the historical experiences of the community and are interpreted through the community's shared values. Without understanding the way in which meaning is circular, the Hebrew religious community's development—including such features of its development as the suspension of ordinary logic and ethics in the story of Abraham's sacrifice of Isaac—would be incomprehensible.[2] We are also told that Isaac was tricked into giving his paternal blessings to Jacob rather than to Esau. But we would have difficulty understanding the irreversibility of this act if we did not understand the sacrality of the blessing or curse that was a part of the shared values of the Hebrew community. The religious community is the bearer of both value and meaning.

Moreover, like every individual or family, ethnic or national group, every religious community possesses a built-in mental prism that gives community members a way of recollecting past experience, interpreting the meaning of the present, and anticipating the future. A mental prism selects items from a spectrum of data and historical realities, making these available to the religious imagination. It may also produce optical illusions. In other words, religious communities are selective about what they remember (forgetfulness can be a protective device) so that memory and forgetfulness together elicit the meaning of individual events as sacred memories of the community.[3]

Jacob's life exemplifies the characteristic meaning of life according to the Hebrews' faith. After receiving the paternal blessing, he wanders for years, accumulating wealth but not finding the Promised Land that had been assured by the Almighty. Through a dream he learns that the Promised Land might embody a state of mind rather than a geographical domain. He then crosses the river at the fort of Jabbok and experiences fulfillment through reconciliation with his brother, Esau. His character encompasses the two dimensions of the Promised Land that run through the history of Israel, the geographical (or the physical) and the spiritual. With such a dual prism the Hebrew religious community faced the difficulties and ambiguities of interpreting historical events. Both interpretations have been advocated with equal integrity by community members.

The Hebrew religious community, like all religious communities, looks back on a decisive central event that throws light on past, present, and future events. For the communities of the "founded religions"—Buddhism, Christianity, and Islam—the teachings or the life of the founder usually becomes the decisive point of reference. For the Hebrew religious community, which lacks a founder, the Exodus that culminates in the receipt of the Ten Commandments on Mount Sinai provides the central decisive experience. However, scholars disagree on whether the Exodus was a historical, religious, or religio-historical event. To biblical writers the Exodus revealed how the convenantal relationship between God and Israel transcended the order of Nature. Nature was taken for granted as a state of divine givenness; but the convenantal relationship had the dimension of faith unknown to the order of Nature.

Nothing is known of how the two different worldviews of the Egyptians and the Hebrews coexisted. The Hebrew Bible was not concerned with Egyptian influence on the Hebrew views of the world, or vice versa. The biblical writers did not hint at the suggestion of Thomas Mann's "Joseph"—that there is more than one center of the world. From the Hebrew Bible's perspective, Egypt was merely the physical setting for the covenantal relationship between God and the Hebrews; the Egyptians were persecutors and the Hebrews their victims. God came to deliver the Israelites—"I will bring you into the land which I swore to give to Abraham, to Isaac, and to Jacob; I will give it to you for a possession" (Exod. 6:8)—but this one-sided promise of an impartial deity was not immediately actualized. The biblical writers did not omit the fact that the Hebrews' faith was tested by God and that he allowed the Egyptian magicians to compete with his own miracles. God also caused Pharaoh's heart to become hardened, and the spirit of the Israelites was almost broken. But ultimately God led the community out of Egypt, and their deliverance became the cornerstone of their faith.

Integral to the Exodus was the Israelites' wandering in the desert and the delivery of the Ten Commandments to Moses on Mount Sinai. Similarities between some of these commandments and the Laws of Hammurabi notwithstanding, the Hebrew community interpreted the Ten Commandments as a "revelation" and a "seal" of the convenantal relationship between God and the Israelites. At Sinai, God, who called himself "I am/shall be what I am/shall be," made Israel his people and cited the Exodus as a sign of his faithfulness, demanding the Israelites' faithfulness to him in return. From that point onward, the history of the Hebrew community was as two intertwined threads: the jealous God who demanded that Israel offer him an unqualified, exclusive devotion and the fragile, weak Israelites who often resorted to idol worship and apostasy.[4]

The mental prism of the Hebrews required an analysis of both the religious and the secular meanings of events—usually without adequate resolution between, and often with arbitrary and ambivalent fusion of, the two. Thus the emergence of a monarchy implied both a popular demand for a polity and a betrayal of the Hebrew's devotion to the kingship of God. This may account for the ambiguous role of seer-judge Samuel in the tangled affair of King Saul. Equally fascinating is the biblical writers' acceptance of the divine covenant with King David and the Davidic dynasty, which they viewed not as a contradiction to, but rather as a confirmation of, the divine covenant with the chosen Hebrew nation—despite David's moral weakness.[5] The combination of such ambivalence and arbitrary resolution is deeply rooted in the Torah, which began to emerge under the united monarchy prior to the division of the Hebrews into the Northern and Southern Kingdoms of Israel and Judah in the tenth century B.C.

In treating the divided kingdom, biblical writers seem to take for granted the oneness of the Hebrew religious community, despite the historical reality of a politically fractured community. This period coincided with an active prophetic movement—a distinct feature of the Jewish religious tradition—in both the Northern and Southern Kingdoms. For the prophets, purely political or natural events did not exist; everything was governed by God, the creator of heaven and earth and the lord of history. They were especially sensitive to political events, through which, they believed, God ruled the affairs of nations. All of the prophets warned both rulers and ruled to be faithful to their God and to prove their faith through ethical deeds—reminding the Hebrew people of God's faithfulness.

With such sensitivity to the covenant's socio-moral injunctions, the Hebrew prophets, from the eighth century B.C. onward, became advocates of an ethical universalism, although their message was addressed solely to the Hebrew community. For example, they believed that it was God who forwarded the expansion of the Northern Kingdom under Jeroboam II in the eighth century B.C. and that the Northern capital fell to the Assyrian invaders because its citizens trusted only in arms, neglecting to rely on God. According to the Prophet Isaiah the defeat of the Southern Kingdom was also God's doing, as he used Assyria as "the rod of God's anger" (Isa. 10:5) to punish King Ahaz and his people for not trusting in him. Assyria, however, failed to recognize that it was only God's agent and therefore was destined to fall.

Isaiah had a religious vision of the unity of humankind mixed with a particular Hebrew-centered notion of an ideal Davidic king who would enable the nations of the world to gather in Zion and worship the God of Israel as the lord of history (Isa. 2:1-4). His was the precursor of a formula repeated many times in history, based on the fusion of a universalistic outlook and a particularistic orientation regarding the unity of humankind. Isaiah's contemporary and fellow-citizen of the Southern Kingdom, Micah, however, rejected the importance of both the centrality of Jerusalem and cultic practices. His conviction that God expects human beings only "to do justice and to love kindness and to walk humbly with one's God" (Mic. 6:8) left another important legacy for interreligious relations.

In the history of the Southern Kingdom, some religious-minded rulers—for example, King Hezekiah (in the eighth and seventh centuries B.C.) and King Josiah (in the seventh century B.C.)—were determined to reform the nation's religious life. Hezekiah credited Isaiah's prophecy with helping Jerusalem to escape devastation at the hands of the Assyrian king, Sennacherib, even though his kingdom became a vassal state of Assyria. During Josiah's reign, a scroll of the Torah—probably a version of Deuteronomy—was discovered. The king required that representatives of the people renew the covenant with God over this Torah, thus adding national prestige to the cause of the development of a sacred canon. Josiah also purified the national religion of contaminating alien cults.

Meanwhile, the New Babylonian Empire defeated Assyria and King Nebuchadnezzar made Jehoiakim the king of Judah his vassal. He also punished the rebellious Hebrews by sacking Jerusalem and taking most of its population captive to Babylon. The Prophet Jeremiah urged Jews in the name of God to submit to the divinely ordained acts of Babylon. He advocated a spiritual interpretation of the covenant that said God's covenant with Israel should be written on Jewish hearts and that this new covenant was more important than the covenant inscribed on stone.

The Jewish experience of their Babylonian captivity, with its social, political, cultural, and religious dimensions and its far-reaching influences, defies simple explanation. During this period, the classical Hebrew religion came under the strong impact of Zoroastrianism, especially its angelology, demonology, and eschatology. Many new cultic and institutional practices also developed, including fixed prayers, observance of the Sabbath, assembly in synagogues for the study of the Torah, and the beginnings of a sacred canon that later became the Pentateuch. These practices were the cornerstones of Rabbinic Judaism, which emerged after the destruction of the temple in A.D. 70. During this period Jewish monotheism developed a universalistic outlook without rejecting its faith in a national God. According to the prophecy of Deutero-Isaiah (see Isa. 40–66), the God whom Jews called YHWH governed the affairs of all nations and punished the sins of Babylon, anointing Cyrus the king of Persia. Yet God was faithful to the covenant he had made with the Hebrew people:

> But you, Israel, my servant, Jacob, whom I have chosen, the off-spring of Abraham, my friend; you whom I took from the ends of the earth . . . fear not, for I am with you . . . I will strengthen you, I will help you, I will uphold you with my victorious right hand (Isa. 41:8-10).

Thus the Jewish captives hoped to return to their homeland upon the fall of Babylon to Cyrus, who was called by Deutero-Isaiah "my shepherd," who would fulfill all of God's purposes (Isa. 44:28).

Coterminous with the development of the universalistic outlook of Jewish monotheism was a subtle change in the Hebrews' self-identity. They no longer became simply YHWH's "chosen people" but witnesses for him in the world. From this new perspective Deutero-Isaiah was persuaded that Israel's suffering was not so much God's punishment—which was no doubt deserved—but rather a discipline required as preparation for a higher purpose: "I have tried you in the furnace of affliction. For my own sake, for my own sake, I do it" (Isa. 48:10-11). God chose Israel to be his servant, agent, messenger, and witness: "I will give you as a light to the nations, that my salvation may reach to the end of the earth" (Isa. 49:6).

Reflecting on the eschatological orientation familiar to the Zoroastrian tradition, Deutero-Isaiah reminded the Jews that the eschaton—intepreted by the prophet as the fulfillment of God's salvation—was surely to come: "Keep justice, and do righteousness, for soon my salvation will come, and my deliverance be revealed. Blessed is the man who does this, and the son of the man who holds it fast. . . ." (Isa. 56:1-2). He again mentioned the future glory of Zion, his "Promised Land," as the reward: "I will bring forth descendants from Jacob, and from Jacob inheritors of my mountains; my chosen shall inherit it, and my servants shall dwell there" (Isa. 65:9).

The Zion promised to the community of the faithful was not an earthly kingdom, but a new world order: "For behold, I create new heavens and a new earth" (Isa. 65:17).

> For as the new heavens and the new earth
> which I will make
> shall remain before me, says the LORD;
> so shall your descendants and your name remain.
> From new moon to new moon,
> and from sabbath to sabbath,
> all flesh shall come to worship before me,
> says the LORD (Isa. 66:22–23).

As a religious vision of the unity of humankind with a theistic orientation, Deutero-Isaiah offers an attractive option. However, in the context of his spiritual and eschatological hope for universal salvation, moral and social *restitutio in integrum* in this world had only preparatory value. He clearly saw, with a keen historical sensitivity, a hidden meaning in the Hebrew community's suffering in Babylon as the suffering of God's servant:

> He was wounded for our transgressions, he was bruised for our iniquities; upon him was the chastisement that made us whole, and with his stripes we are healed. All we like sheep have gone astray; we have turned every one to his own way; and the LORD has laid on him the iniquity of us all (Isa. 53:5-6).

Deutero-Isaiah no longer understood the significance of the Hebrew religious community, of either its ethnic roots or its achievements and sufferings in connection with an earthly "Promised Land." The Hebrew religious community as a whole, the inheritor of the faith of Abraham and Moses, was to be the servant of the Lord, who had chosen Israel as an instrument to relate the order of nature to the order of salvation.

Deutero-Isaiah's spiritual and eschatological vision of Zion as the Promised Land was ironically ignored by those Jews who were in time permitted by Cyrus to leave Babylon to return to their homeland and rebuild their temple. In their eagerness to literally adhere to the rules of the covenant and to preserve their "ethnic purity," these returnees refused to let the Samaritans, who had intermarried, participate in the rebuilding of the temple. A more exclusive ethno-religious attitude and a rigid adherence to the Torah were advocated by the priest Ezra, who returned from Babylon in the mid-fifth century B.C. The Torah became the law of the land by charter of the Persian king, Artaxerxes I. In order to eliminate Torah inconsistencies, priests developed the art of interpretation, thus preparing the ground for the development of the Midrash. The Hebrew community in Palestine following the exile was (perhaps inevitably) imbued with an exclusivistic spirit that expressed itself in extreme measures at times, such as compelling Jewish men to discard non-Jewish wives. There was, however, a minority of a more rational spirit, epitomized by the Book of Ruth.[6]

Meanwhile, Palestine was conquered by Alexander the Great in 332 B.C., subsequently ruled by the Hellenistic-Egyptian Ptolomies, the Syrian Seleucid dynasty, and Rome. The Hellenistic-Roman period witnessed two important developments. First, the Hebrew community enjoyed a limited form of theocracy because of the tolerant attitude of the rulers—in effect becoming a self-governing community within the larger society. Second, Jewish intellectual life, both in the Jewish diaspora settlement around the Mediterranean and in Palestine, was strongly influenced by Hellenism.

This encounter between Hellenism and Judaism entails numerous and complicated issues. Suffice it to ask, as does Judah Goldin, "why some aspect of Hellenism could almost imperceptibly penetrate Jewish thought and conduct with hardly a murmur of protest. . . ."[7] Hellenistic Jews acquainted themselves with Greek thought and literature, and the Pentateuch was translated into Greek.[8] The Maccabees eagerly assimilated Hellenism also. Thus Goldin quotes E. J. Bickerman:[9]

> "With the Maccabees . . . the internal Jewish reconcilement with Hellenism begins." By strengthening their people, and by appropriating from Hellenism what they could use to enrich Torah teachings, the Maccabees saved Judaism "from the mummification that

overtook the religion of the Egyptians, for example, which shuts itself off from Hellenism completely."[10]

In time, a Judeo-Hellenistic syncretism developed, and the influence of Hellenism becomes noticeable in both the wisdom literature and the apocryphal writings.

With Pompey's entry into the Second Temple in Jerusalem in 63 B.C., Judaea became a puppet state of Rome. King Herod (37–34 B.C.), noted for his pro-Hellenistic sympathies, was sufficiently astute politically to ingratiate himself with Rome. An Idumaean who had been converted to Judaism by force and was not fully accepted by the Jews, he courted Jewish favor by rebuilding the desecrated temple. The real Judaean power, however, lay in the hands of the Roman procurators. One of these, Pontius Pilate (A.D. 26–36), attempted to superimpose the Roman emperor cult upon the resistant Jews. Strong Jewish anti-Roman sentiment resulted in a war with Rome (A.D. 66–70), which dramatically ended with the temple's destruction in A.D. 70 and the suicide of the "Assassins" (the Sicarii) at Masada. Sporadic resistance against Rome continued until around A.D. 125.

Under Roman rule Jews were driven to an intense form of nationalism, aspiring to political independence with the help of a messiah. Moreover, the Jewish population, which had formerly been, in part, a community of faith, became an assortment of many rival religious sects and political parties, including the Herodians, the Zealots, the Essenes, the Pharisees, and the Sadducees—none the sole inheritor of the tradition although all shared in its legacy. Many historians suggest that the origin of Christianity be seen in this light. There is much truth in R.T. Herford's observation that the Pharisees and Jesus, as well as Paul, had much in common. Goldin comments:

> The conflict, Herford feels, was one between two fundamentally different conceptions of religion, viz., that in which the supreme authority was Torah and that in which the supreme authority was the immediate intuition of God in the individual soul and conscience. The Pharisees stood for one; Jesus stood for the other.[11]

It is interesting that following the destruction of the temple, Christianity appropriated the temple, the priesthood, and the lamb among other symbols of biblical and classical Judaism, whereas Rabbinic Judaism discarded them.

Rabbinic Judaism. "Rabbinic Judaism" refers to the Jewish religious tradition that developed after the destruction of the Herodian temple in A.D. 70. Judaism did not die with the emergence of Christianity. There was, however, a distinct rupture between classical and Rabbinic Judaism. Rabbinic Judaism inherited many features of the faith and practice of the Hebrew religious community, but it modified or replaced these with new features that rendered its overall characteristics sufficiently distinct and different from classical Judaism. The difference is explained in part by the fact that under Roman rule the Jewish community was in effect a composite of divided sects, schools, and parties, and lacked the coherence of a unified religious community. Moreover, many active and prosperous Diaspora communities or Jewish settlements outside of Palestine developed in Syria, Asia Minor, Babylonia, and Egypt. Each boasted more than one million Jewish inhabitants, who had developed their own religious dynamics. The Babylonian community was the closest in ethos to the Jewish community in Palestine, whereas the belief and practice in Egyptian Alexandria were considered to be Diaspora Judaism *par excellence.*

Many factors contributed to the gradual transformation of classical Judaism into rabbinic Judaism. For example, the centrality of the temple in Jewish religious life was minimized by the three-year interruption of temple worship under Antiochus Epiphanes (167–165 B.C.) and by Pompey's desecration of the temple (53 B.C.). Judaism increasingly depended on the synagogues, which emerged as the place for worship and study during Babylonian captivity in the sixth century B.C. This dependence promoted the prestige of the rabbis as the interpreters of the Torah and partly explains why the destruction of the Herodian temple in A.D. 70 was not as great a shock as it might have been. After the collapse of Jewish resistance around A.D. 135, Jerusalem ceased to be the religious center of the Jewish community; no longer did Jerusalem serve as the distinguishing feature of Palestinian Judaism over against the Diaspora. Roman officials, concerned to maintain a *Pax Romana*, supported the rabbis, who were politically inactive (and not rebellious) but had prestige among the Jews. Meanwhile, some of the rabbis were eager to replace the traditional temple sacrifice and pilgrimage to Jerusalem with study of the Torah, prayer, and works of piety—activities in which faithful Jews could engage anywhere.

In time, Judah the Prince (reign around A.D. 175–220), head of the Palestinian community recognized by Rome, attempted to standardize Jewish practice in accordance with the opinions of the rabbinate by developing the *Mishnah*, the collection of rabbinic law, and the *Talmud*, the commentary on the *Mishnah*. Two of Judah's Babylonian disciples, Abba Arika and Samuel bar Abba, were instrumental in popularizing the *Mishnah* in Babylon. Both the Babylonian and Palestinian Talmuds, reflecting the views of the rabbinates in the Roman and Persian Empires, respectively, became normative for the mainline Jewish community.[12]

Prior to the emergence of Islam in the seventh century, rabbinic Judaism engaged in energetic missionary activity. It competed with Christian counterparts in the Middle East, especially on the Arabian peninsula. Many scholars believe that Judaism made indelible marks on Islam, including a monotheistic focus, an eschatological outlook, an angelology and emphases on the law, ethics, and the book. The particularistic temper of biblical Judaism was transformed by the influence of the universalistic trends of Hellenism (and thus became Hellenistic Judaism). Then the universalistic ethos of Hellenistic Judaism, in turn, was particularized by rabbinic Judaism, which constructed itself around the supremacy of the Torah, not around the universalistic ethos of Hellenistic Judaism.

Diaspora Judaism. In sharp contrast to the Jewish communities in Palestine and Babylon, the Jewish settlement in Egypt was highly eclectic and thoroughly Hellenized. There is evidence of a sixth century B.C. Jewish military colony with a Jewish temple in Upper Egypt. From the time of Alexander the Great, the Jewish community in Alexandria was reputed to be the most Hellenized

of all Diaspora settlements. The most thorough Hellenizing enterprise of the Egyptian Jewish tradition was the Septuagint, a
Greek translation of the Pentateuch. To Hellenized Jews, the
Greek language was not one among many; rather, Greek symbolized a universal mode of thinking. The Septuagint was an
attempt by Hellenistic Jews to recast their particular Jewish experience into a world of universal discourse.

> The translation shows some knowledge of Palestinian exegesis and
> the tradition of Halakha (the Oral Law); but the rabbis themselves,
> noting that the translation diverged from the Hebrew text, appar-
> ently had ambivalent feelings about it, as evidenced in their alter-
> nate praise and condemnation of it. The fact that such a concept
> as *Torah* was translated as *nomos* ("law") and *tzedaga* as *dikaiosynē*
> ("justice") opened the way to antilegalism in early Christianity and
> to Platonic interpretations. . . .[13]

Egypt's Hellenized Jews produced both prose and poetic
literature, art, philosophical writings, and wisdom literature,
such as the *Wisdom of Solomon*. One of the most famous philosophers of the Egyptian community was Philo Judaeus or Philo
of Alexandria (around 20 B.C.–A.D. 50). Although not an original
thinker, he was nonetheless well versed in Greek thought, especially the philosophical thought of Plato and the Stoics; he
was less familiar with the Hebrew language texts. Born into an
aristocratic family, he had firm faith in the abiding presence of
God. He was strongly motivated to work out a synthesis of the
Torah and Hellenism, identifying the Greek notion of *logos* with
the "Word of God" of the Hebrew biblical tradition and pro-
pounding it as an intermediary between God and the created
universe.[14]

Philo of Alexandria is known for his religious vision of the
unity of humankind. Unlike most biblical thinkers, who located
the basis of the unity of humankind in humanity's search for
justice and law, Philo went much further, positing a cosmos
imbued by a divine *Logos* as one great commonwealth of humankind. He exerted little influence on Jewish philosophical and
religious traditions, but his notion of *logos* and use of the allegorical method left an important legacy for the early Christian
Alexandrian theologians.[15]

In contrast to our knowledge of the communities in Egypt, our understanding of the Jewish communities in Rome is limited. We do know that most of the inhabitants were Greek-speaking Jews and that many participated in the communal and educational activities of Roman society. This was despite the modification of or deviation from traditional Jewish beliefs and practices. Thus some settlers might be characterized as nominal or "secularized" Jews. Records show that many early Christian missionaries began their work in the Diaspora communities and that some settlers were Jewish Christians; but the overall number of Jewish converts to Christianity was surprisingly small. Even the adoption of Christianity as the religion of the empire did not greatly affect Jewish religious life in the Roman world. Nevertheless, the Jews of the Mediterranean basin became fragmented and were harassed by certain hostile gestures, such as the order of the emperor, Justinian (reign A.D. 527–565), restricting synagogue worship and preaching. This was in sharp contrast to the tolerance of the Sāsānian rulers (A.D. 224–651) toward the Jews in Persia.

THE GRECO-ROMAN VISION

The Hellenistic tradition possessed serious reflections on the unity of humankind. The ancient Greeks are credited with formulating the three-pronged Western religio-philosophical schema that embraces theology, cosmology, and anthropology. Of the three, the starting point might most logically be anthropology, a discipline that accounts for man in both the physiological sense, regarding him as a product of nature, and the pragmatic sense, recognizing him as a person.[16]

Many ancient Greek thinkers stressed the unity of humankind on both the physiological and pragmatic levels; and many ancient authors of *materia medica*, beginning with Hippocrates (around 460–359 B.C.), not only discussed the universality of certain symptoms but also the commonality of human bodies— and thus, by implication, of human beings—making light of the division between citizens and slaves. The general concerns of early Greek thinkers and poets surrounded those qualities that made humans different from gods and animals. Further, particularly to the fifth-century non-Athenian Sophists living in Athens, the quest for the identity of human beings was closely connected with the idea of being Greek. Ultimately, the realization that human beings—Greeks and barbarians, citizens and slaves, male and female—have in common their separateness from gods and animals led to the idea of the indwelling *logos*, which in turn prompted the Sophists to affirm the equality of citizens and the supremacy of law in the Athenian democracy. The Sophists were convinced that the actualization of humanity required the proper functioning of the state as a human community. The mathematician-philosopher, Hippias of Elis (around 500 B.C.), is thought to have been the first to advance cosmopolitanism.

Socrates (469–399 B.C.) emphasized *logos* (reason) as the essential component of the human soul. His preoccupation with the city of Athens precluded his pursuing the larger question of the unity of humankind based on his idea of *logos*. With Plato (around 428–347 B.C.), who regarded the human being as a temporary convergence of soul and body in which the former supersedes the latter, the universal existence of the soul might have become the basis for cosmopolitanism. However, his tripartition of the soul into the reasonable, the courageous, and the appetitive and his view of a stratified ideal state made it difficult to affirm the unity of humankind. More biologically oriented than Plato, Aristotle (384–322 B.C.) recognized the physiological unity of humankind within the animal world. For Aristotle, the important human quality, and that which enables humans to live a communal life, was *nous* (intelligence, intellect, or mind), the gift of *logos*.[17] Both Plato and Aristotle acknowledged the physiological unity of humankind but argued against cosmopolitanism advocated by scientific medical writers and Sophists in favor of differentiated human groupings and a stratified society.

Alexander the Great, a disciple of Aristotle, established a vast empire encompassing Egypt, the Mediterranean world, and the entire Middle East from Asia Minor to the Indian border,

introducing a cultural colonialism based on Hellenistic civilization and the Greek vernacular language (*Koine*), with himself the
living symbol of savior and benefactor of the human race. Scholars suspect that Alexander's exposure to the Egyptian ideology
of divine kingship strongly influenced his self-image as a semidivine figure. Thus greatly expanded by his vision of military,
political, and cultural universalism and not in accord with Greek
philosophical and religious ideology, the Hellenistic Persian Empire became coterminous with the *oecumene*, or that portion of
the world inhabited by civilized people. It was Alexander's plan
that after his death thirty-four existing cities named Alexandria
should remain centers of Hellenism. An early death prevented
his goal of world government, but we are told that

> . . . Alexander passed on his ideas to the world that he had con-
> quered. Before him, neither Sparta nor Thebes had been able to
> dominate Greece by arms; even Athens had not succeeded, either
> by force or by intelligence. With Alexander the rule of factions was
> over, the cities were broken, leagues were dissolved, nations cast
> into the melting pot, and races intermingled. . . . While Aristotle
> was drawing up a catalog of the products of earth and man and
> was building up a systematization of the Greek world, his Mace-
> donian pupil was saving the Greek heritage, was opening the Al-
> exandrian Age, and was allowing Hellenism to diffuse throughout
> the world.[18]

Alexander's vision of unity for humankind was not readily
understood by his contemporaries, but upon his death his idea
of the *oecumene* penetrated deeply into the psyches of many.
Charles A. Robinson, Jr., writes:

> In the new Hellenistic Age, man thought of himself more and more
> as a member of a world society, a society in which there might be
> (and were) sharp differences, but in which a common, Greek culture
> nonetheless acted as a natural bond. . . . The great fact of history
> is that for three centuries, until the coming of Rome, this world
> was ruled along western Hellenic lines.[19]

Robinson laments the fact that it was the Romans—and not
the Greeks, with their legacy of the primacy of reason—who
were destined to rule Alexander's unified world, for "had not
Rome intervened, the Greeks might ultimately have given the

Mediterranean not only a common culture, but also a form of government ensuring unity, freedom, and permanence."[20] Conversely, some scholars are convinced that certain pre-Alexandrian Greek philosophers held definite ideas about the unity of humankind and cosmopolitanism.[21] Nonetheless, we must acknowledge that Alexander was the first person who actually demonstrated that the unity of humankind, a world government, and a multiracial society was not merely a dream but a feasible schema that could become a reality.

Alexander's untimely death fractured his unified empire, which was then divided into three main states: North Africa under the Ptolemies, Asia under the Seleucids, and Macedonia under the Antigonies, each with its subdivisions of Greek colonies, petty kingdoms, and tribal societies or cities. Although a vigorous trade developed throughout the Hellenistic states and with China and India, it soon became clear that the *oecumene* was reverting to the Macedonian- and Greek-centered polities. Alexander's idea of a fusion of Macedonians and Greeks with non-Hellenistic peoples died with him. The conquerors allowed the Hellenization of other peoples, but they would not tolerate the "Asianization" of the Greeks: the Ptolemies would not even attempt to speak Egyptian. Athens continued to occupy a supreme cultural role within the Greek world, and the language of the Athenians became the standard Hellenistic language. Thus "a 'cosmopolities' for this generation simply betokened a member of the 'Greek world.' Anyone who spoke no Greek, even if he was a subject of a Greek state, remained in Greek eyes a 'barbarian.' "[22]

However, the Greek world was vastly different from what it had been. For example,

> . . . the Greek found the study of philosophy particularly congenial, because the gods of Olympus no longer satisfied intellectuals. . . . The new forces of the day were weakening the traditional religion, as is amply proved by the growth of king-worship and the increasing appeal of mystery cults, the cult of Eleusis, Orphic cults, astrology, and magic. The Eastern religions, too, made some progress among the Greeks . . . in particular two Egyptian cults appealed to many Greeks: that of Serapis, the guardian of sailors

. . . and that of Isis, who was very popular because of her promise of future bliss.[23]

To generalize about the mental climate of a people scattered over such a vast area is dangerous. Intellectuals followed the philosophical and ethical ideas advocated by the Sophists, Cynics, or Hedonists, while the uneducated and superstitious participated in orgiastic and magical cults along with popular star worship.

Meanwhile, the Greeks began to enter political life in southern Italy and Sicily, with Greek influence in the Roman world reaching its zenith during the reign of King Pyrrhus of Epirus (reign around 307–272 B.C.). Rome became actively concerned in Hellenistic matters, especially at home, after her declaration of war on King Philip V of Macedonia (reign 221–179 B.C.). This war—the Third Macedonian War (172–168 B.C.)—ended the Antigonid monarchy, reduced Macedonia to four separate tribute-paying republics, and established Rome as the ruling power in the Balkans. In 16 B.C. Pompey (Gaeus Pompeius, 106–48 B.C.) was sent by Rome to Cilicia to settle the Piratical War; three years later he entered Syria, taking it for Rome.

The Hellenistic state of Egypt, threatened by conflicts with Syria, Macedonia, and Rome and torn by internal dynastic and territorial disputes, suffered a precarious existence under the Ptolemies. After the death of Ptolemy VII in 116 B.C., the realm was divided among his three sons—Ptolemy IX, Ptolemy X, and Ptolemy Apion. Ptolemy IX offered Rome the right to interfere with internal affairs in Egypt and Cyprus; his son, Ptolemy XII, persuaded Rome to recognize his own kingship. After his death in 51 B.C., Egypt was bequeathed to his two children, Ptolemy XIII, then barely ten years old, and Cleopatra, then seventeen. Ptolemy XIII died during Caesar's invasion of Egypt, and Cleopatra went back to Rome with Caesar. She and her son by Caesar, Ptolemy XV, returned to Egypt as co-rulers upon Caesar's death in 44 B.C. Following the fiasco of the Caesar-Antony-Octavian triumvirate, Mark Antony (83–30 B.C.) and Octavian (63 B.C.– A.D. 14, later Emperor Augustus) sealed their alliance with Antony's marriage to Octavian's sister, Octavia. Now settled in Egypt and in control of the East, Antony soon sent Octavia home to Rome and in 34 B.C. crowned Cleopatra Queen of Egypt; the three sons she bore him were named nominal rulers of the satellite kingdoms. Finally defeated by Octavian's forces in 30 B.C., Antony and Cleopatra committed suicide, ending both the Ptolemaic line and the last of Alexandria's Hellenistic dynasties.

Republican and Imperial Rome. The Romans rebelled against monarchical tyranny as early as the sixth century B.C., after which time a republican constitution slowly emerged with power divided among the senate, the popular assemblies, and the magistrates. In time, the pragmatic Romans devised a collegiate system of two elected consuls who would jointly hold the *imperium* for one year.[24] A people with profound respect for legal rule, the Romans honored good faith and a combination of justice, piety, and pragmatic flexibility that brought many peoples into their sphere of influence.

From the time of Alexander the Romans felt the strong impact of Hellenism. The Greek idea of culture (*paideia*), upholding virtue (*arete*) as the goal of education, was deeply engraved on Roman society. The Romans also learned architecture from the Greeks, erecting magnificent temples, houses, theaters, and public baths. Many citizens, especially those in the upper class, were bilingual; speaking Greek as well as Latin, they introduced Hellenistic philosophy, religion, and literature into Roman culture. The Greek idea of social equality, however, was not a part of the Roman ethic. It is an irony of history that Rome lost her republican form of government as world events propelled her to center stage.

We have noted that upon Mark Antony's death, Octavian, Caesar's adopted son, remained sole ruler of Rome. Although he refused the dictatorship, he had a firm grip on the armed forces and national finance with the able support of his son-in-law, Agrippa (63 B.C.–A.D. 12). In 27 B.C. the senate conferred upon him the title "Augustus." Under him Rome became a full-fledged empire.

As Imperator Caesar Augustus, Octavian was the civilian head of government and the final authority over the armed forces. He was a consul of Rome and head of the colonies and provinces. He was the proconsular *imperium*, or governor and commander of the empire, a title renewable every ten years. In 12 B.C.,

> he became *pontifex maximus* (he had long since been elected to all of the priestly colleges); in 8 B.C. . . . he was designated *pater patriae* ("father of his country"), a distinction which he particularly esteemed because it suggested that he was to all Romans what a *paterfamilias* was to his own household.[25]

In addition to controlling finances and policies, he manipulated senatorial careers, forging Italy into the supreme power of the empire and made it an example to all outsiders.

Augustus intended to instill the traditional values and virtues of the ancestral religions in every Roman heart. Counteracting this intention was the intellectual appeal to the educated of the Greek philosophical schools, including Stoicism, Neo-Pythagoreanism, and Epicureanism, and the emotional appeal to the masses of the Eastern mystery religions brought home by victorious Roman legions. This included the cults of the Magna Mater, Cybele, Dionysis, Isis, Osiris, and Mithras. Mithraism appealed especially to the young and the uneducated, as it

> inculcated [more of the] order and discipline so dear to the Roman heart. Above all it satisfied "the desire for a *practical* religion that would subject the individual to a rule of conduct and contribute to the welfare of the state."[26]

In carrying out the plan for his empire Augustus followed advice given him in his youth:

> . . . do you yourself worship the divine power everywhere by every means, in accordance with the tradition of our fathers, and compel others to honour it too. Hate and punish all who try to introduce innovations in this regard, not only for the sake of the gods . . . but because those who introduce new divinities persuade many to change their thoughts and practices; and from this there spring up conspiracies, revolts, and factions. . . . Do not tolerate atheists or magicians . . . and keep your eye on philosophers too.[27]

Augustus was eager to revive the traditional religion and went to work, renovating eighty-two temples, building countless altars to the Lares, and promulgating the worship of "Dea Roma," or the deified personification of the city of Rome and all she stood for. He was aware that deceased emperors like Alexander the Great were deified by both Greeks and Romans and that after his death, he, too, would be deified. But judging from the homage paid to the living emperor, a practice Augustus had encouraged (in the Asian, Syrian, Spanish, and Gallic colonies but did not dare enforce at home in Rome), historians suspect that Augustus saw himself as trans-human and the new imperial religion as the cornerstone of the Roman Empire.

The precarious relationship between Augustus and the Jews is appropriate to mention here. Rome became involved with the Jews when she supported Jewish anti-Seleucid sentiment and the Maccabean revolt, but even then certain tensions remained, although these were eased with Jewish aid to Caesar's Egyptian campaign against Ptolemy. The Jews resented Mark Antony's giving Cleopatra sovereignty over Palestine, but such anti-Roman sentiment dissolved when Octavian defeated them at the Battle of Actium in 33 B.C. Shortly after the death of Herod of Judea, new tensions arose as the Roman procurator tried to impose the cult of Dea Roma and emperor-worship on the monotheistic Palestinian Jews; but the pragmatic Augustus wisely used restraint. His policies of tolerance at first also protected the Jewish-Christians, but as more Gentiles converted to Christianity and Christianity grew out of Judaism as an independent faith, the issue of emperor-worship became increasingly important to him and his tolerance lessened.

Augustus accepted the traditional Roman premise that divine qualities resided in exceptional humans: Caesar, his adopted father, was regarded by many as *deus similimus*, especially after his death; both Mark Antony and Alexander the Great claimed deification for themselves during their lifetimes. However, unlike Alexander, who passionately felt called to actualize universalism and the *oecumene* by coalescing ethnic and racial groups, Augustus had neither personal convictions nor political leanings toward democratic ideals and universalism. Where both society and the empire were concerned, he was a hierarchical elitist who considered Italy's superiority over other Latin and Hellenistic colonies to be self-evident.

Augustus was simultaneously a religious and a political being. He enjoyed the title of "Augustus" with its implications of sanctity; and as *pontifex maximus*, he was in charge of all religious matters—and these were the foundation of the empire. Politically, he did not want to be a dictator, yet he respected the legality and power of the *princeps* as formulated by Cicero. His political genius lay in his ability to manipulate the complex administrative machine and to build a durable empire on the cornerstone established by Alexander. The Roman Empire would be split in half before its eventual decline, but the *Pax Romana*, supported by law and ably defended, enabled people of different ethnic, racial, cultural, and geographical groups to live together in relative peace and harmony for about two centuries. Moreover, it was the Roman Empire that enabled the Apostle Paul to affirm his Christian vision of the unity of humankind, recognizing "neither Greek nor Jew, barbarian nor Scythian, bond nor free . . ."; and when, rightly or wrongly, Christianity looked for this-worldly prestige, power and wealth, Rome provided two significant models—those developed by Western papacy and Eastern Caesaro-papism.

After Augustus' death in A.D. 14, he was followed by four successors related to him by birth or marriage. Tiberius (reign 14–37), an able soldier but a mediocre statesman, is known primarily because of the birth of Jesus Christ during his reign. Gaius (reign 37–41), whose father was Tiberius' great-nephew, was an inept tyrant. Claudius I (reign 41–54), Gaius' uncle, did much to centralize the government bureaucracy and expanded the empire as far as Great Britain. Nero (reign 54–68) was the son of Agrippina, great-granddaughter of Augustus, by a union prior to her marriage to Claudius I. He is infamous for the cruel murders of his wife, mother, and tutor, Seneca. With Nero's suicide, the Julio-Claudian dynasty that traced its line back to Augustus came to an end. It was about this time that the empire found itself having to defend its borders; moreover, it was facing a religious crisis, stirred particularly by the activities of the Jews and Christians.

The Flavian dynasty succeeded the Julio-Claudian with the ascension of Vespasian in A.D. 69. Vespasian was noted for his stringent economic reforms that included a poll tax on Jews. The short reign of his son, Titus (reign 79–81), was marked principally by the disastrous volcanic eruption that buried Pompei. The Flavian dynasty ended with the assassination of Titus's younger brother, Domitian (reign 81–96). The next eighty-four years covering the reigns of Nerva (reign 96–98), Trajan (reign 98–117), Hadrian (reign 117–138), Antonius Pius (reign 138–161), and Marcus Aurelius (reign 161–180) were relatively calm.[28]

The empire was especially expanded under Trajan, and there was a general trend toward the Romanization of the western part of the empire. Hadrian's policies of granting citizenship and of founding frontier towns did much to civilize the empire. Most of Marcus Aurelius's reign was devoted to defending the empire against barbarians and the Parthians. His son, Commodus (reign 180–192), a pleasure-loving tyrant, was assassinated. By this time, Rome had become a center for freeborn migrants and slaves. Because imperial encouragement of Greek culture restricted Greek learning only to the intellectuals, even Hellenistic towns felt the strong impact of Romanization.

This trend toward Romanization stimulated interest in Latin literature and rhetoric. Stoicism continued to be the most influential philosophy, as evidenced by the writings of Seneca and Marcus Aurelius. Religiously, all sorts of cults and eclecticisms were tolerated as long as people venerated the state gods and the imperial cult as well. Judaism was allowed as an ethnic religion. But Christianity, which severed its relationship with its Jewish roots during the Flavian period, was suspect because of its lack of any racial or national ties.

The early centuries of the Roman Empire marked the beginning of religious queries. The outstanding example was Philo Judaeus (around 20 B.C.–A.D. 50) of Alexandria, who attempted to reconcile the main tenets of the Hebrew scriptures with Platonic ideas. Second-century Christian apologists learned much from Philo's use of the Greek allegorical tradition and attempted to show congenialities between Christianity and Greco-Roman humanism and cosmopolitanism.

The Severian dynasty, in power from A.D. 193 to 235, originated with Septimus Severus, a Romanized Tripolitan from

North Africa married to a Syrian woman. This dynasty saw improvements in adminstration, jurisprudence, and the extension of Roman citizenship to peoples in outlying areas. The most notable event of the period was the establishment of the powerful Persian Sāsānid dynasty in A.D. 232.

With the assassination of the last Severian emperor in 235, the empire entered a thirty-five-year period of military anarchy and disintegration coupled with barbarian invasions in the West and trouble with the Sāsānids in the East. Before this chaos, the Christian religion had been growing, marked by the careers of men with lasting influence: Clement of Alexandria (around 150–215), Origen (around 185–254), and Cyprian (around 205–258). Nevertheless, it is true that

> . . . the disappearance of the great lyric and poetic styles, the fossilizing of education as it came to be completely based on rhetoric (*paideia*), and the growing importance of philosophical and religious polemical literature among both pagans and Christians were the basic traits that, as early as the third century, foreshadowed the intellectual life of the late empire.[29]

Reorganization of the empire was undertaken from 270 to 284 by a group of emperor-generals, although the founder of the late Roman Empire was Diocletian (reign 284–305). Despite the tetrarchy he created, he made all important policy decisions. He increased the number of provinces, grouping them into twelve dioceses, six in the East and six in the West. His policies encouraged the political ambition of power-hungry aspirants so that as many as seven emperors competed among each other by the year 307. Natural death and assassination eventually left two emperors in the East and two in the West—one of the latter was Constantine, who soon attacked and defeated his rival. He allied himself with one of the Eastern kings, Licinius, and together they attacked Licinius's rival, Maximus Dias. In this campaign, Constantine and Licinius gained the help of the Eastern Christians by guaranteeing them religious tolerance under the Edict of Milan. In 316, Licinius and Constantine ended their alliance in a struggle for supreme power. Licinius was executed in 324 and Constantine retained the title of *pontifex maximus* and took it seriously in the manner of a *Caesaro-papist*.

Opinions vary concerning the religious motivation behind Constantine's "conversion" to Christianity. He styled himself as both the "new Augustus" and the "thirteenth apostle," with a mission to Christianize the empire. Combined religious and political interests can be seen in his active role in the Council of Nicaea, although it is doubtful whether he understood the intricate theological issues involved in the debate over the nature of Christ. His greatest moment was the founding of the city of Constantinople, called "New Rome," which was dedicated in 330, seven years before his deathbed baptism. During the last decade of his life, Constantine initiated financial and military reforms, reinforced the defense of the Western front, and at the time of his death was planning an attack on Persia. Fierce power struggles and succession disputes ensued among his children and grandchildren, and with the premature death of Julian (reign 361–363), the Constantinian dynasty ended.

The Roman Empire then faced serious political and religious intrigues at home—the ever-increasing threat of barbarian attacks on the Western borders, and invasions from the Huns, who crossed the Volga in 374. One of the most influential kings at this time was a Spaniard, Theodosius I (reign 379–395). His edict of Thessalonica, confirmed in 381, proclaimed the Nicene Christianity of the Bishop of Rome the religion of the entire empire. On his deathbed, Theodosius willed Eastern Rome to his teenage son, Arcadius, and Western Rome to his ten-year-old son, Honorius, thus endorsing a division of the empire. Aware of this lack of a unified authority, the Visigoth leader Alaric occupied Moesia and Thrace in 395 and Macedonia and Greece in 397. The situation in the West was equally chaotic. As Pareti points out:

In 405 Alaric and his Goths advanced down to Mediolanum. . . . In 405-406 . . . another Gothic army reached Florentia. . . . But in 406 with the Huns who had entered Pannonia pressing at their backs, the Vandals, Alans, and Quadi invaded Gaul and infiltrated as far as Spain, in 407 the Picts and Scots from the island itself, with Saxons from Germany, occupied Britain, and Rome could offer no resistance to them. . . . The lowest point in the history of the Western empire was seen in 410, when Alaric succeeded in storming Rome and put it to sack for three days.[30]

The Roman Empire of the West endured a nominal and insignificant existence for another half-century or more under the hegemony of primarily Germanic tribes, and when the last emperor, Romulus Augustus, was deposed in 476, the official end of the Roman Empire in the West was scarcely noticed.

Unlike the empire in the West, the Eastern empire survived until the Ottoman Turks incorporated it into their empire in the mid-fifteenth century. Because of the Caesaro-papism of the East Roman emperors, endorsed—reluctantly or otherwise—by the majority of Christians in the East, the Eastern empire was not subjected to the constant power struggles between the church and the state that plagued the Western empire. Eastern Rome still had its share of divisive religious controversies, typified both by the Monophysite heresy, which centered around the issue of whether Christ's divine nature altogether excluded his human nature, and by the Iconoclastic Controversy, which centered around the legitimacy of icon veneration. Moreover, the Eastern empire was directly exposed to the challenge of the new religion of Islam from the seventh century on.

The relationship between Eastern Rome, Western Christendom, and the Islamic community as expressed in the Crusades defies simple explanation. One would imagine that the East Roman experience, with its Hellenistic background and rich contacts with Eastern and Mediterranean cults and its direct contact with Islam, might contribute to the discussion of the unity of humankind. However, this history of the Eastern empire did not attract scholars in this area until the modern period, when Russian émigré philosophers and theologians based in Paris began reflecting on the issues involved. Yet we receive from ancient Roman tradition a testimony for the limited viability of the *Pax Romana* supported by an acceptance of the law under a unified authority for the corporate life and well-being of humankind.

THE CHRISTIAN VISION

As we begin the discussion of Christianity, we wish to emphasize that our aim is not to study any particular religion or culture but to reflect on what each of these traditions has to say about the unity of humankind. Although I hope that this book will be read by people of the Christian faith, I hope, too, that it will be read by those of other religious persuasions—since we all, Christians and non-Christians alike, must live together. It is important for members of each religious faith to know how their religion looks to others.

I think that H. Richard Niebuhr was correct in his belief that each religion possesses both an "inner" and an "outer" meaning.[31] It is these two meanings we focus on in this volume. Most Christians will agree with Augustine's definition of the inner meaning of Christianity: that the history of Christianity is as old as the history of the human race and that only its nomenclature was added with the advent of Jesus Christ. Many devout Christians are tempted to think that the outer meaning of Christianity—if such a thing exists—ought to parallel the inner meaning. Moreover, they often compare the inner meaning of Christianity with the outer meaning of other religions or superimpose their own understanding of the inner meaning of Christianity upon other faiths as the only "gospel" truth.[32]

How do we begin to explore the inner and outer meanings of Christianity? We might group it with similar faiths into a broader category—for example, with Buddhism and Islam as a "founded religion." The lives of the founders of Buddhism and Islam, Gautama Buddha and the Prophet Muhammad, represent unique experiences and have become nuclei of inner meaning for their followers. Yet the lives of the Buddha and Muhammad follow a very similar pattern, or outer meaning—each embodies a certain charisma coupled with a developed sense of mission. In his *Die Formgeschichte des Evangelium*, Martin Dibelius compares Buddhist and Christian miracle stories and finds striking similarities. He suggests the theory of the "law of biographic analogy" that holds that "at bottom is to be found a fixed idea of the life of a holy man. . . . His future calling is announced even in his youth, and in the same way his end throws its shadows in advance. Divine powers are always ready to help him in stress and to proclaim his merits."[33]

This biographical analogy is related to the believer's perception of the origin of a founded religion. For, according to the inner meaning of religion, believers often take it for granted that the founder attracted a group of disciples who, in the words of Wach, were "bound together by a common religious experience whose nature is revealed and interpreted by the founders."[34] These disciples generally enjoyed two roles: (1) they were companions of the religious founder, and (2) they were interpreters or apostles to other adherents, especially to those who had no direct contact with the founder. The disciples usually develop into a broader brotherhood that becomes a religious or an ecclesiastical organization.

Those concerned with the social realities of founded religions' outer meanings as adjuncts to their concern with the inner meanings, however, often see the developmental process of religious groups in reverse. For example, the formation of religious groups precedes the acceptance of "founding myths," especially myths about the founders. E. J. Thomas cogently argues that Buddhism began "not with a body of doctrine, but with the formation of a society bound by certain rules," so that "to begin by analyzing the doctrine without first examining the community and the circumstances in which it originated would be likely to lead to quite arbitrary results."[35] We should be equally open to the alternative historical processes concerning the origin and development of the Christian community and the founded religion around which it grew.

Founded religions generally agree that their coherence depends upon three major foci. These include original teachings of the religion, the tradition of the religious community, and the immediate religious experience of individual members. Those primarily concerned with inner meaning tend to stress one of these foci over the others. For example, among Christians, there are, on the one hand, those who propound the supremacy of the Bible and use it as a yardstick for evaluating both the tradition of the community and immediate individual religious experiences. Biblical fundamentalism comprises the extreme right wing of this orientation.

On the other hand, there are those who see the Bible as part of a larger, more encompassing tradition that has created the Bible by accepting it into the tradition's canon; tradition is more fundamental, more basic than scripture. These people believe that only tradition can authenticate or reject members' immediate religious experiences. Critics of this position point out that clergy or professional religionists, both Roman Catholic and Protestant, often fall into such an erroneous traditionalism.

Finally, there are those—and there seems to be an increasing number today—who subordinate both the Bible and tradition to immediate religious experience. Many young people feel that they cannot accept Christian doctrines on the basis of tradition alone, nor can they accept certain traditions merely on the grounds of biblical precedence. Doctrine and tradition are meaningful to modern men and women only when they can be attested by immediate experience and restated in relevant language. D. D. Williams formulates the question behind the contemporary theological renaissance in the Christian world thus: "What is there in the Christian faith which *gives us such an understanding of ourselves* that we must assert our loyalty to the Holy God above all the splendid and yet corruptible values of our civilization?"[36]

Unlike those who, from a sense of the inner meaning, stress any one of these three foci, others, out of a primary concern for the outer meaning, tend to balance them equally, refusing to accept one as more important.

Historically, the Feast of Pentecost is regarded as the birthday of the Christian church. According to the Book of Acts, Jesus' religious career ended tragically at Calvary with his followers abandoning his teachings, leaving only a handful of discouraged believers wondering what it had all meant. The church was born by the miraculous initiation of the Holy Spirit: "Suddenly a sound came from heaven like the rush of a mighty wind" and there appeared "tongues as of fire" that rested on the people, and "they were all filled with the Holy Spirit and began to speak in other tongues" (Acts 2:3-4).

People concerned with the outer meaning of Christianity face the difficult task of deciphering the inner meaning of the

Book of Acts. Something very important happened at Pentecost, something comparable to the Exodus, but Hebrew and Christian biblical writers failed to find adequate language for the nature of their experiences. Here the tension between religious events and historical events is repeated in the intricate relationship between the inner and outer meanings of religions. It might be helpful to attempt to uncover the inner meaning of the Book of Acts.

First, the Book of Acts states that the Christian church is not simply a new society of like-minded people attracted by the teachings of Jesus of Nazareth. Rather, convinced of the continuity between the Hebrew and Christian communities, Acts portrays the Christian church as the "restoration of the Kingdom of Israel." The author further assumes that the Hebrew notion of *qahal* (Greek: *ecclesia*) denotes both the assembly of the people (I Kings 8:14, 12:3) and the worshiping community. He carefully notes that the twelve disciples were gathered and commissioned as representatives of the congregation of Yahweh. As Gerardus van der Leeuw interprets: "The twelve were disciples, but above all they were people, the true Israel, while the events of the Pentecost brought to the disciples, as the assembly of the people, the gift of the Holy Spirit."[37] The Christian community is intended as a fusion of the pneumatic and the given bonds of fellowship.

Pentecost further reveals the paradoxical connection between covenant and community. The Book of Acts accepts the historical Hebrew understanding of the two aspects of God: his role as the transcendental lord of history and his immanental presence in the human Hebrew community. As J. Muilenburg puts it: "God is LORD of the community yet is in some sense a member of the community also. He participates actively in its life, maintains his relationship to it, and assumes the responsibility of one who is in covenant with his people."[38]

Yet Peter declares Jesus to be the fulfillment of the new universalistic covenant prophesied by Joel: "I will pour out my spirit on all flesh. . . . And I will give portents in the heavens and on the earth" (Joel 2:28, 30). However, Peter also preaches: "Let all the house of Israel . . . know assuredly that God has made him both Lord and Christ, this man whom you crucified" (Acts 2:36). Acts emphasizes that the Christian community, the logical and uninterrupted extension of the Hebrew religious community, is the people of God in a spiritual sense and the Body of Christ in a historical sense. This implies a new fusion of covenant and community.

According to the paradoxical Christian understanding of the unity of humankind, the new covenant is, on the one hand, open to people of diverse backgrounds—those beyond the Jewish, Hellenistic, and Mediterranean worlds—and on the other hand it agrees with Paul's assertion that "if you are Christ's, then you are Abraham's offspring, heirs according to promise" (Gal. 3:29). Pentecost signifies the reversal of the legend of the Tower of Babel that scattered and divided people by language, race, culture, and nation. The human race is given the opportunity to be reunited as one people through the intervention of God, who is both the Lord of history and an immanent presence in the total human community.

Since Christianity began as a pneumatic group within Judaism, the earliest Christian scriptures were the Hebrew scriptures or its Greek translation, the Septuagint. As the Christian community gradually consolidated, it collected various writings for official reading, including Paul's letters to the Galatians, the Romans, and the Corinthians; letters of deutero-Pauline tradition such as 2 Thessalonians; the Gospels; and the Johannine letters. These texts, which comprised the New Testament, and the Hebrew scriptures, which comprised the Old Testament, were soon regarded as Christian texts, essential for salvation. After A.D. 450, the two Testaments became the canon, a term reflecting their special status and their role in Christian salvation.

We cannot trace here the historical development of the Christian community, but our assessment of the early phase of the Christian church can be succinctly summarized.

1. The Christian community, open to the idea of humanity having been created without discrimination by the same divine author, but related to the Hebrew religious community, chose only those teachings of Jesus and those writings of Paul that

agreed with their unique orientation; they rejected the Gospel of Thomas and other writings that took a variant position.

The synoptic Gospels differ in detail concerning the life of Jesus, but agree on the Hebraic focus of his life and education. He was circumcised and presented to the Lord in the temple of Jerusalem. His parents and companions were all Jews, and there is no indication that he wished to institute a religion outside that of his forefathers. He worshiped regularly in the synagogues. His religious outlook was based on the historical premises of the Hebrew religious community: God's promise, the Jews' response to God, the covenantal relationship, and the Promised Land or Kingdom of God.

Jesus' mission was not to restore the political independence of the Davidic kingdom but the covenantal community. While he was aware of having been "sent only to the lost sheep of the house of Israel" (Matt. 15:24), he understood the meaning of the covenantal community in the eschatological and not in the traditional biological or genetic sense. He viewed the Hebrew community's history from the time of Abraham as a spiral development of the hidden drama of salvation. The Gospel accounts of Jesus' life follow the pattern of both Abraham and Jacob's lives as well as the themes of the Exodus and the Babylonian captivity. They begin with God's promise of the Annunciation followed by heavenly assurance at his baptism. His faith is tested in the wilderness, and he is commissioned to serve as God's servant and witness to all men; he goes to the synagogue in Nazareth to commence his public ministry (Luke 4:18-19).

How did Jesus understand the meaning of the end of his life? The parable of the prodigal son gives us a clue when Jesus is said to be "resurrected" as the Son of God, much as in the Hebrew Bible when Jacob crossed the river and became Israel: both found the fulfillment of life, or the Promised Land. This picture of Jesus as the new Israel is portrayed in the Gospels, especially in Mark. Jesus is not a triumphant king; he is the suffering servant throughout his life.

The Gospel of Mark skillfully weaves together two interpretations of Jesus' life. The first is that of the disciples, according to whom Jesus was the agent for God's mighty work: ". . . your sins are forgiven" because "the Son of man has authority on earth to forgive sins" (Mark 2:5, 10). In the vision of the Transfiguration, the disciples catch a glimpse of God's plan, according to which a new covenant, greater than the prophecy of Elijah and the Torah of Moses, was to be forthcoming through Jesus.

The second view is that of Jesus as the suffering servant. As his death approaches, he is tormented: "My soul is very sorrowful. . . ." But then, much as Jacob decides to cross the river, Jesus dares to go forward: "The hour has come . . . Rise, let us be going." On the cross, however, he cries, "My God, why hast thou forsaken me?" (Mark 15:34). These two themes—Jesus as the suffering servant/the new Israel, and Jesus through whom the hidden work of God's salvation is revealed—are united at the scene of the cross through the words of the centurion: "Truly this man was the Son of God" (Mark 15:39). The early Christian community's view of Jesus follows the historical Hebrew motif: God's promise is given to Jesus; Jesus' faith is tested; God and Jesus enter the Father-Son relationship; after Jesus suffers and is crucified, he is resurrected. From the disciples' point of view, God's promise is received through Jesus: their faith is tested; they are given the new covenant; and they receive the Holy Spirit.

2. The members of the early Christian community in Palestine—largely uneducated, poor, and without influence—were probably traditional Jews, ardent monotheists with a profound respect for the Jewish law (Torah). They were impressed with Jesus' teaching that the Torah's meaning goes beyond the observance of traditional religious rites and regulations to provide a framework in which *every* human being, not only the descendants of Abraham, could have immediate and direct contact with God. "You shall love the Lord your God. . . . You shall love your neighbor as yourself. *On these two commandments depend all the law and the prophets*" (Matt. 22:35-40; Mark 12:28-31, emphasis mine). "The sabbath was made for man, not man for the sabbath" (Mark 2:27). According to this principle, the Samaritan—a foreigner—who had compassion for a victim of robbery and assault

is a more genuine neighbor than the priest who fulfills the precepts of the Torah but ignores the beaten man (compare Luke 10:25-37).

The disciple Peter was a spokesman for this shift in religious authority from the traditional law to the dictates of the individual's soul. Peter thought that Jesus embodied the culmination of God's promises as revealed to the Jewish people as representatives of all humankind, not that Jesus meant to start a new religion (Acts 2:30-31). Peter's dialogue with God while in a trance at Joppa exemplifies the tormented mind of the early Christian community. "Lord, I have never eaten anything that is common and unclean." The voice then answered: "What God has cleansed, you must not call common" (Acts 10:14-15). Peter spoke for many Palestinians who were emotionally attached to the external requirements of the law while intellectually committed to the meaning of the law as explicated in the teachings of Jesus.

3. The shifts in religious authority from the law to one's soul, and in religious orientation from the Jewish particular to the broader universal within the early Christian community, were intensified by the Apostle Paul, a man conscious of being both a Hellenistic Jew and a Roman citizen. According to his letter to the Philippians (3:5), he was a Greek Jew, "circumcised on the eighth day, of the people of Israel, of the tribe of Benjamin, a Hebrew born of Hebrews; as to the law, a Pharisee." It is difficult to correlate contradictory data about his life. The Book of Acts states that Paul was raised in Jerusalem at the feet of Gamaliel, and that he was in Jerusalem as a witness to the execution of Stephen; but his letter to the Galatians insists that even after his conversion he was "still not known by sight to the churches of Christ in Judea" (Acts 1:21). We also are not certain whether Acts' account of Paul's dramatic encounter with Christ on the road to Damascus is historical fact or legend. By his own admission, Paul never had personal contact with Jesus or with his disciples prior to his conversion. According to Gal. 1:11-12, he says: ". . . I did not receive [the gospel] from man, nor was I taught it, but it came through a revelation of Jesus Christ."

Paul was a controversial figure in the early Christian community. He preached mainly to the Hellenistic Jews of the Diaspora and to the Gentiles, trying to present Jesus as the actualization of the good news that God had promised to the Hebrew community. He argued that ". . . through this man forgiveness of sins is proclaimed to you, and by him everyone that believes is freed from everything from which you could not be freed by the law of Moses" (Acts 13:32, 38-39). He believed that the word of God concerning salvation should be spoken first to the Jews (Acts 13:46). But since many rejected the idea of eternal life, he wrote, "We turn to the Gentiles. For so the Lord has commanded us, saying, 'I have set you to be a light for the Gentiles, that you may bring salvation to the uttermost parts of the earth' " (Acts 13:46-47).

Scholars agree that not many Jews of the Diaspora accepted Paul's teaching; Gentiles more than Hellenistic Jews were attracted by the "universalistic" motif of the Christian gospel. For his part, Paul was proud of his Jewish background, but he made every effort to "universalize" the "particular" Jewish tradition by looking at the Jewish experience from a broader perspective— one more in keeping with the trend of Hellenistic Judaism.

Paul's view of Christ differentiates him from other Hellenistic Jewish monotheists. Christ was central to his understanding of God-humanity-eschaton. Paul accepted Adam as the first member of the human race, and he believed that Adam's descendants, the entire human race, are united in sharing Adam's sin, that of rebelling against his creator. According to Paul, the fact that our image of Adam is essentially Jewish, the historical witness of the Hebrew community points to the universal dimension of Adam. Paul further believed that all human effort—religious, philosophical, etc.—to attain human fulfillment fails without the divine intervention exercised in the life, crucifixion, and resurrection of Jesus.

By his semimystical understanding, Paul affirmed the cosmic significance of redemption through Jesus' crucifixion. He preached that through the sacrament of Jesus' baptism all men share in the Resurrection. Finally, he projected that this redemption initiated by God in the event of Jesus as the Christ will only reach completion at the eschaton, when all people, both living and dead, will be united in the Kingdom of God.

4. Early Christianity inherited such symbols and institutions as the temple, the lamb, and the priesthood from the Hebrew tradition. Also characteristic of the first-generation members of the Christian community, including both those who accepted and those who rejected circumcision, was a belief in the imminent Second Coming of Christ (Greek: *parousia*, "presence" or "arrival"). As they realized that the *parousia* was not imminent, that it had perhaps been partially fulfilled in the Pentecost, they had to adjust to the realities of first-century life. The work of Peter, Luke, John, and Paul greatly influenced the process of adjustment; but even more important was the spiritual dimension of Christianity, the Zoroastrian-Jewish-Hellenistic-Roman culture complex.

Such terms as "savior," "gospel," "epiphany," and "the promised era of peace" that became the hallmarks of the early Christian community had been common in the Roman Empire. Frederick C. Grant cites the famous edict of around 9 B.C. regarding Caesar Augustus. We quote the entire text:

> Whereas the Providence which has guided our whole existence and which has shown such care and liability, has brought our life to the peak of perfection in giving to us Augustus Caesar, whom it (Providence) filled with virtue (*arete*) for the welfare of mankind, and who, being sent to us and to our descendants as a savior (*soter*), has put an end to war and has set all things in order; and whereas having become visible (*phaneis*, i.e., now that a God has become visible), Caesar has fulfilled the hopes of all earlier times . . . not only in surpassing all the benefactors (*euergetai*) who preceded him but also in leaving to his successors no hope of surpassing him; and whereas, finally, that the birthday of the God (viz., Caesar Augustus) has been for the whole world the beginning of the gospel (*euangelion*) concerning him, (therefore, let all reckon a new era beginning from the date of his birth, and let his birthday mark the beginning of the new year.)[39]

Cartlidge and Dungan remind us that the Greco-Roman world accepted various types of savior gods: "offsprings of divine-human unions, who had performed outstanding feats of benefaction (*euergesia*)"; those kings and other leaders who are "temporary manifestations or appearances (*epiphaneia*) of the eternal gods"; and "manifestations or appearances of divine beings through dreams, visions, and sometimes incognito, as mere human beings."[40] There were Christians sympathetic to these different views of savior gods and to the influence of mystery cults and other religious groups. In time, through both communal custom and the influence of these myriad traditions, the Christian community formalized the rites of baptism and the Eucharist; instituted orders of prophets, bishops, and deacons; and endorsed the practice of fasting.

5. Despite its commitment to proselytism and a fervent belief in monotheism, the early Christian community appears to have had a realistic understanding of itself as one of many religions in the Roman world. Consciously or unconsciously, it exhibited a clear sense of its own inner meaning in *monotheism* and of its own outer meaning in *monolatry*—the worship of one deity as the Lord of the universe while recognizing the rights of other religious groups to venerate their own deities. The Apostle Paul, a monotheist *par excellence* with no use for idols, could write:

> . . . although there may be so-called gods in heaven or on earth— as indeed there are many "gods" and many "lords"—*yet for us there is one God*, the Father, from whom are all things and for whom we exist, and one Lord, Jesus Christ, through whom are all things and through whom we exist (1 Cor. 8:5-6; emphasis mine).

The Christian community gradually began to attract the intellegentsia of the Mediterranean world. Unlike the ignorant Galilean fishermen, such converts were well educated, especially in Greek rhetoric and philosophy. Many contributed a great deal to the new faith by refining its beliefs and defending it against criticism from non-Christian philosophers and scholars. Later called "apologists," these scholars did not hesitate to find truth in Greek philosophy and to appropriate Greek philosophical notions in support of Christian truth claims. Some went so far as to claim that Moses and the prophets had influenced Greek philosophy, basing their claims largely on the concept of *logos* (word or principle of order), so important to the Hellenistic-Jewish philosopher, Philo Judaeus of Alexandria. According to Philo:

> In the first instance *logos* is the Divine Reason that embraces the archetypal complex of *eide* that will serve as the model of creation. . . . Next, this *logos* that is God's mind is externalized in the

form of the *kosmos noetos*, the universe apprehensible only to the intelligence. . . . It is transcendent . . . and it is God, although not *the* God . . . but rather the "elder Son of God." . . . With the creation of the visible world (*kosmos aisthetos*) the *logos* begins to play an immanental role as the "seal" of creation. . . . Philo differs from the Stoics in denying that this immanent *logos* is God. . . .[41]

The apologists used the notion of the divine *logos* to understand what came to be known as "natural revelation" in the philosophies of Greece, Egypt, Persia, and India and as *Heilsgeschichte* (the history of salvation) in the Hebrew community, a revelation that finds its fulfillment in the *logos* Incarnate. As Benz observes:

> In relating the truth of the religious and philosophical systems of the heathen world directly to the divine Logos as the teacher, *logos paidadōgos*, Clement [of Alexandria; ca. 150–215] finally removed the basic difference between the character of revelation in the Old Testament and in the history of religions outside Judaism. In his view, the history of salvation, soteriology, was not separated from the general history of mankind; Heilsgeschichte was not a disconnected improvisation inserted into universal history but, rather, included and covered the whole human development.[42]

Clement and Origen provided a universalistic rationale for the outer meaning of Christianity in hopes that the inner meaning would be seen within the total context of its outer meaning. Such an orientation required a thorough training in Greek philosophy and the Christian *habitus* (a cognitive disposition of the soul and a receptivity to divine revelation), both taken for granted by the early Christian fathers. Unfortunately, training in Greek philosophy for Western theologians rapidly declined with the death of Augustine of Hippo (350–430).

6. With Constantine's edict of toleration in 313, the Christian community was transformed from a religion of the minority into the religion of the majority, soon (in A.D. 381) to become the religion of the empire. Constantine's edict brought God and the temporal ruler into a new relationship: whereas the New Testament made a distinction between Caesar and God, the new Roman Christianity insisted that loyalty to Caesar was implicated in loyalty to God. Accordingly, Constantine assumed the dual role of pious servant to God and temporal ruler over both empire

and church. Constantine modeled himself on the examples of Alexander and Augustus, allowing the Eleusinian initiators to call him "most pious." He was convinced that God granted him military victories, the empire, and the Christian religion. An ecumenical council was called to discuss the theories surrounding the nature of the Son, the second element of the Holy Trinity, to be presided over by the unbaptized emperor, Constantine.

The edict of toleration wrought a radical change in the relationship between the inner and outer meanings of Christianity. Until Christianity became the religion of the empire, Christians had to fashion an outer meaning for public acceptance, although they were clear on the inner meaning shared among themselves. Even Justin Martyr (around 100–165), one of the most versatile apologists, stated that "Christians did not claim anything about their Savior beyond what the Greeks had said about theirs."[43]

In sharp contrast, Augustine, who was equally well versed in Greek and Latin rhetoric, Platonism, and Manicheism, and who held a universalistic religious orientation, saw things differently. As Peter Brown explains it:

> The Catholicism of Augustine . . . reflects the attitude of a group confident of its powers to absorb the world without losing its identity. . . . It is a group no longer committed to defend itself against society; but rather poised, ready to fulfill what it considered its historic mission, to dominate, to absorb, to lead a whole Empire. *Ask Me, and I shall give the uttermost parts of the earth as Thy possession.*[44]

Thus Augustine behaved as though the outer meaning of Christianity was the logical and coherent extension of its inner meaning. He felt that Christianity is based on the objective promises of God through Jewish and other histories, and that divine grace is given through the objective efficacy of the church's sacraments. It was this shift, rightly or wrongly in orientation, that provided the theoretical basis for the Catholic Christian domination of the Latin world up to the Reformation.

CHAPTER

3

Visions
from East,
West,
and Islam

In the first two chapters we have seen how early world civilizations approached the question of the unity of humankind. We have looked at Mesopotamia, with its Greek and Roman offshoots, Egypt, India, and China; and have touched upon important religious and cultural traditions, including Zoroastrianism, Buddhism, Judaism, and Christianity. In each case, "universalistic" visions were nurtured through "particularistic" human experiences. People often took for granted the eventual actualization of the unity of humankind, based on the exchange of trade goods and ideas between Asia and Europe.

The global topography of civilization was greatly affected in the seventh century A.D. by the emergence of Islam in the Middle East at the traditional point of confluence of Africa, Europe, and Asia. Islam was simultaneously a religious and a political community and a unique civilization. It is said that in contrast to Jesus, who chose the path of failure, Muhammad chose the path of success. Be that as it may, within ten years after Muhammad's death, the Muslim empire absorbed Syria, Iraq, and Egypt, and in less than a century, Islam conquered the Christian belt of North Africa and reached the Iberian peninsula. In the eighth century, Muslim forces crossed the Pyrenees into

France. Muslim traders were active in China and Indonesia, and Muslim invaders conquered the Sind region and the Panjāb on the Indian peninsula. Despite its widespread influence, the Islamic civilization forged a huge gulf between Europe and Asia. The subsequent centuries of separation strengthened the respective natural tendencies of West and East, that of "unity in variety," characteristic of Western civilization, and of "juxtaposition and identity," characteristic of Eastern life.[1]

Before beginning our discussion of the Islamic vision of the unity of humankind, we will explore the various types of religio-cultural/socio-political synthesis evident before the emergence of Islam. Civilized man sought to integrate all aspects of his life into a coherent whole in an attempt to find meaning in a temporal society guided by religious inspiration.

Joachim Wach once observed that genuine religious experience generally finds three types of expression: the theoretical, through symbol, concept, doctrine, and dogma; the practical, through cults and worship; and the sociological, through fellowship and cult association. From another perspective, one might say that religion, being integrally related to socio-political structures and institutions, is bound to shape and nurture culture, the domain of values, ideologies, the arts, and the imagination— "the fabric of meaning in terms of which human beings interpret experience and guide their action."[2] A series of parallel developments of such religio-cultural/socio-political syntheses occurred in both the West and the East between the third and the fifteenth centuries, among which Islam is the most prominent example. However, before we approach Islam we want to consider certain other examples.

WESTERN CHRISTENDOM

We have seen that Christianity began as an eschatological community with a transcendental orientation. Beginning as one of the minority religions within the Roman Empire, Christianity went on to become the state religion of the empire and in so doing adopted a temporal rather than an eschatological focus.

The infusion of new blood into Roman life, with the fall of Rome to the barbarians in the fifth century, gave all of Europe new energy. Christianity met the challenge by expanding over the continent to convert the barbarians. To be sure, it was not an eschatological, biblical message that appealed to these people. As Peter Brown reminds us, it was as a religion of holy shrines, pilgrimages, and relics that Christianity absorbed the non-Christian peoples of Europe. Yet, Christianity did not degenerate into a superficial cult. Between the fourth and the sixth centuries, it gave the pagan barbarians a new map of the supernatural world.[3] However, while Christianity had lost its eschatological outlook, it increasingly stressed its transcendental aspect, even though it was thoroughly this-worldly as an ecclesiastical institution, adopting the symbolism and structures of imperial Rome.

The early Christian church produced several bishops of Rome with exceptional administrative abilities, including Leo the Great, Gregory the Great, and Boniface. As bishops of Rome, each claimed to be the head of all Western Christendom, invoking the Petrine doctrine: all bishops of Rome are successors to Peter, allegedly the first bishop of Rome and designated by Christ as chief of the church. These "popes," as bishops were commonly called, claimed both temporal and spiritual authority. They were faithfully aided by the various monastic orders that proliferated in the fifth and sixth centuries.

Papal ambition, especially for temporal power, occasioned continuous conflicts with monarchs—Clovis, Pippin, and Charles Martel in particular. At times weak emperors were dominated by powerful popes; on other occasions insecure popes were subjected to the rule of forceful kings. With the rise of Charlemagne, king of the Franks (768–814), as emperor in the West (reign 800–814), a basic Western Christian paradigm was established. After travelling to Rome to crush a conspiracy against Pope Leo, Charlemagne was rewarded with a gold crown and the papal salute as emperor and Augustus. A strong monarch, Charlemagne managed to control the church and utilize it to consolidate the empire.

Charlemagne's reign completed the Germanization of the Roman Empire. He died in 814, after a forty-seven-year reign often compared to that of Alexander the Great. There is no indication that he shared Alexander's interest in the unity of humankind, although he represented the best imperial system of Roman government. He called regular meetings of the general assembly of nobles and clergy and established the privy council. It was his hope that the various peoples in his vast empire would benefit from the imperial system's sensible fiscal policy, adequate defense, protection under the law, and the education of both clergy and laity. These programs crumbled with the decline of the empire after his death, and his own line, the Carolingian dynasty, ended in 987.

The German *Reich* was established with the election of Otto I in 936. Otto was an excellent military strategist and an able organizer. He suppressed rebellious vassals and ended the Hungarian invasion of Germany. Like Charlemagne, he utilized the bishops to consolidate his realm. Determined to bring order to a divided Italy, he had himself crowned king and Holy Roman Emperor (reign 962–973) in 962. He functioned in the manner of a Caesaro-papist monarch, deposing Pope John XII in favor of Leo VIII, and upon Leo's death chose John XIII to succeed him. Subsequent emperors were unable to govern Germany, Italy, and the papacy simultaneously. Eventually each power went its separate way. In 1024, the German crown was taken over by the Franconian monarchs. Among these, Henry III (reign 1039–1056) established himself as a forceful ruling power and soon overwhelmed the papacy in order to exercise control over papal appointments.

BYZANTINE CHRISTIANITY

In comparison with the unstable Western Roman Empire, shaken by the sack of Rome in 410 and totally destroyed in 476, the Eastern empire continued to enjoy the Greco-Roman civic traditions under the monarchical system of Caesaro-papism. Here, one absolute monarch claimed both temporal and spiritual authority. Many people in the Eastern empire felt that they were part of a near-perfect synthesis of religion (inasmuch as Christianity represented divine truth), culture (the advanced Greco-Roman tradition), and the best social and political order (Caesaropapism). Their healthy economy was augmented by growing industry and trade, both by sea and overland; their empire was well governed under Anastasius (reign 491–518), Justin I (reign 518–527), and his learned nephew, Justinian I (reign 527–565), who consolidated the Byzantine empire during his nearly forty-year reign. He promulgated the famous Code of Justinian, completed the new Church of the Holy Wisdom, or the Hagia Sophia, extended his influence to various parts of the Mediterranean world, and made peace with the Sāsānian king, Khosrow, thus ending the Persian monopoly in trade. Justinian's reign witnessed the rise of a popular Christian culture epitomized by the spread of hymns, music, and art among the laity. However, his power and persuasiveness could not reconcile the Monophysites, who believed that the Incarnate Christ had a single divine nature, and the orthodox theologians, who believed that Christ had both divine and human natures.

After Justinian's death, the Eastern empire fell into decline for nearly half a century. In 610, Heraclius (around 575–641), the son of the Roman governor stationed in Africa and reputed to be of Armenian ancestry, forcefully took over the crown and quickly reorganized the government and the army to cope effectively with the constant barbarian invasions. He allowed the Bulgars, the Slavs, and the Serbs to settle in the Balkans after they embraced Christianity; and he defeated the Persians after a series of bloody battles. However, he lost Syria, Palestine, Egypt, and part of Mesopotamia to Islam.

Many issues caused persistent tensions and conflicts between the Eastern and Western Roman empires. A major issue was the Iconoclastic Controversy. Icons—pictures of Christ, the Virgin Mary, or the various saints—were venerated widely among Byzantine Christians. For centuries Christ had been represented by the lamb, but after the seventh century, he and the saints began to be portrayed in human form. This change was not a great issue in Rome itself, where the bishops, or popes, many of whom were Greeks or Syrians, had no strong objections to the practice of icon veneration. The Eastern emperor, Justinian II (reign 685–711), first to use the image of Christ on his coinage, caused little concern in Rome with his act.

Leo III (reign 717–741), however, founder of the Syrian, or the Isaurian, dynasty, instituted a policy of iconoclasm, reflecting, many historians believe, his childhood exposure in Syria to the Islamic attitude toward human representation of the Prophet; the policy was resented by his icon-venerating Byzantine followers. Gregory II (pope from 715 to 731) condemned Leo's policy, launching the Iconoclastic Controversy. Gregory's successor, the Syrian-born Gregory III (pope from 731 to 741), took an equally strong stand against Leo. When Leo refused to give a financial contribution to Rome from southern Italy, a principality of the Byzantine empire, Rome sought aid from the Franks, thus initiating the Germanization of Rome. In time, Charlemagne, king of the Franks, was crowned emperor.

In the Byzantine empire, the icon was restored the year after the enthronement of the child-emperor, Michael III (reign 842–867). Michael's elevation of the layman Photius to the patriarchate within six days was condemned by Nicholas I of Rome (pope from 858 to 867), who excommunicated the patriarch in 863; four years later, Pope Nicholas was excommunicated himself by the Council of Constantinople.

The immediate issues between Rome and Constantinople were ecclesiastical in nature, but underneath them lay a fundamental tension between the German-Latin and the Greek-Byzantine cultural traditions and different perceptions of the papacy: the Western empire understood the pope as the successor of Peter and the Vicar of Christ; the Eastern empire supported the Caesaro-papist style of the Byzantine emperor as absolute monarch and God's vice-regent.

Michael III was assassinated by Basil I (reign 867–886), the founder of the Macedonian dynasty. The Byzantine empire was well governed by the Macedonian kings until the death of Basil II in 1025. The Byzantine empire, which was expanding its influence in Greece and Eastern Europe, inevitably came into conflict with the rising Holy Roman Empire, especially after the coronation of Otto I as emperor in 962. The aggregation of such issues as the Iconoclastic Controversy, the marriage of priests, liturgical practice—for instance, the use of leavened bread at the Eucharist—and theological orthodoxy, especially whether the Holy Spirit proceeds only from the Father (the Byzantine view) or from both the Father and the Son (the Roman view), added to the already existing tensions between Eastern and Western Christendom. Tensions were especially evident in the Council of Constantinople (867) and flared up again in the eleventh century when the papacy tried to enforce Latin customs on the Greeks in southern Italy—the efforts resulted in the patriarch of Constantinople closing the Latin churches in that city, which led in turn to a papal bull excommunicating the Byzantine church. Thus occurred the Great Schism of 1054 between Eastern and Western Christendom, a mutual excommunication that was not rescinded until 1965. The source of the tension lay in the inability of both to agree on the kind of Christian religio-cultural/socio-political synthesis and to recognize the challenge of Islam.

THE SĀSĀNIAN SYNTHESIS

The Greco-Roman world neglected Persia in its preoccupation with devising its own religio-cultural/socio-political synthesis. When the Seleucids, who succeeded Alexander, preoccupied themselves with Syria, the Iranian Parthians arose to rule Persia from around 250 B.C. to around A.D. 230. The Parthians venerated Mithra, an ancient Indo-Iranian deity, who was respected in the traditional Persian religion of Zoroastrianism. Despite an earlier antiritualistic flavor, the religion of Zoroaster had become formalized and also absorbed many features of Indo-Iranian pagan religion. The Parthians, however, were a religiously tolerant people, and under their rule a large number of Jews in Babylon enjoyed legal protection for their religion.

The Parthian dynasty was overthrown in the third century by Ardashir I, who claimed to be the descendant of the half-mythical figure, Sāsān. He called his dynasty the Sāsānian, or neo-Persian, line of the King of Kings, which ruled Persia until it fell to Islam in 651. Ardashir I's dynasty fostered a very tight Sāsānian religio-cultural/socio-political synthesis that comprised an exotic mixture of Zoroastrianism, Babylonian astrology, Mesopotamian demonology, and Hellenistic rationalism with a despotic nationalism. As G. Gnoli points out, during the Sāsānian period

> . . . Zoroastrianism acquired new connotations: it became a religion in the service of the ruling classes, the warrior aristocracy and the clergy, as well as the crown. It became a hierarchically organized state religion, an epic and nationalistic tradition increasingly identified with the Iranian nation. From a universal religion, which had shown its best throughout the Parthian period, Zoroastrianism was transformed into a national religion. . . . [Yet,] if it did succeed in stifling Manichean universalism in Iran during the third century (as it also later suppressed the Mazdakite movement), it was nonetheless able to mount effective opposition against the spread of Christianity, the Nestorian church in particular, and, later, of Islam.[4]

The Sāsānian dynasty and its extraordinarily nationalistic state religion, Zoroastrianism, were haunted by serious religious issues. The initial trouble was with Manicheism, a dualistic religious movement promulgated by Mani (around 216–274) that believed the world to be a fusion both of spirit and matter and of good and evil. Mani was probably related to the Parthian royal family. He considered himself the final prophet in a line beginning with Adam and including Buddha, Zoroaster, and Jesus. Persecuted by the orthodox Zoroastrians upon his return from India, Mani was received favorably by King Shāpūr I (died 272), the son of the Sāsānian dynasty's founder, who wanted to broaden Zoroastrianism by incorporating certain Indian and Greek features. Regarded by some as a Christian heresy, Manicheism was actually an independent religion preaching a universal message that would, in principle, replace all existing religions, including Christianity. Intensely missionary-oriented, Mani gathered many followers in Central Asia, China, Europe, and North Africa; at one time Augustine was an adherent. Eventually, the Muslim persecutions of the tenth century drove the headquarters of Manicheism from Persia to Samakarland.

From the perspective of the unity of humankind, Manicheism marked an important page in the history of the human race. Mani believed that it was possible to unite people of diverse backgrounds with a syncretic method that combined the faiths of different religions. Manicheism was basically a form of gnosticism, offering salvation through special knowledge, or *gnosis*. Similar to other gnostic systems, it taught that the world is full of evil and misery but that there is a spark of light in every person; therein lay the possibility of salvation. Mani advocated the perfectibility of human beings through *gnosis*, fasting, almsgiving, and purity of thought, word, and deed. Enjoining a rigorous asceticism, he preached the importance of love, both of the godhead and of every human being, each of whom bears the divine element. Under his beliefs, this world would hopefully become one huge, unwalled monastery.

In its relations with Rome, Sāsānian Persia represented a major and constant headache. In 260, Sāsānian forces captured the Roman emperor, Valerian, interned him for life and used Roman prisoners for the construction of houses and bridges. Rome and Persia's tensions took on a more religious character during the long reign (309–379) of the Sāsānid king, Shāpūr II. As Pareti succinctly puts it,

> Up till now [the Persians] had been tolerant of the Christians, who in escaping the Roman persecutions were entering their dominions in great number. But in Constantine's day to be a Christian became synonymous with being a Roman, and furthermore his rival Tiridates of Armenia himself became a Christian.[5]

The emperor Julian (reign 361–363), a nephew of Constantine the Great and an avowed antagonist to Christianity, attempted the last great Roman offensive against Persia before his death at the age of thirty-one, although sporadic warfare continued between Rome and Persia after his death. Meanwhile, Shāpūr II continued to persecute Christians in Persia—members of the Ancient Church of the East—because of their religious ties to Constantinople. In the fifth century, many Persian Christians became deeply involved in a schism caused by the Nestorian Controversy. Nestorius, the Syrian-born patriarch of

Constantinople, held that Jesus Christ had two distinct natures, one divine and one human. Many Persian Christians accepted this teaching and as a result were eventually cut off from the rest of the patriarchate of Antioch.

The Sāsānian dynasty was also faced with a third religious problem with the emergence of Mazdakism, a dualistic religion that became prominent in the late fifth century. Some scholars believe that Mazdakism was a movement to reform Manicheism from within, although knowledge of this movement is largely based on hostile records. As far as we can discern, Mazdakism had a strong utopian thrust, working on behalf of the masses against the vested interest of the Zoroastrian priesthood and the landowners. The followers of this movement believed in the virtue of self-restraint and the renunciation of this-worldly pleasures; they practiced a kind of communism, sharing both their possessions and women. Orthodox Zoroastrians naturally resented the movement. King Kavadh I (reign 499–531) was for a time deeply involved in Mazdakism but later suppressed it.

Wearied by religious conflict and constant warfare, Sāsānid Persia experienced a quiet period during the long reign (531–579) of Khosrow I, who possessed the rare combination of interests in reform, culture, the arts, and effective government. Many people credit him with establishing a new socio-political order based on priests, warriors, a bureaucracy, and the common people. He is reputed to have been involved with the codification of the Zoroastrian sacred books, the *Avesta*, and the creation of the Avestan alphabet. He concluded a peace treaty with Emperor Justinian I of the Byzantine empire in 532. His son was not a distinguished king, and his grandson, Khosrow II (reign 590–628), arrogant and bigoted by reputation, was not an effective ruler either, although he witnessed a great expansion of the Sāsānian empire. In 618 his forces conquered Palestine, taking what was believed to be Christ's cross.[6] In 622, the Byzantine emperor, Heraclius (reign 610–641), a noted military strategist and a devout Christian, undertook a crusade, after first consolidating Anatolia in preparation for the invasion of Persia. Upon successfully resisting the Persian attack on Constantinople in 626, he finally moved into Persia the following year.

Persia's history under the Sāsānian dynasty came to an end in 651. A presage of the end might have been seen in the devastating defeat of the Persian forces at the hands of the Arabs at Dhu-Qar in 611.

ISLAMIC CIVILIZATION

We now turn to Islam, the founded religion *par excellence*. According to Islam's inner meaning, Islam is Allah's eternal religion and it was Allah, or God, who chose Muhammad to be his messenger. The Muslim sacred scripture, the *Qur'ān* (lit. "recitation"), is said to have been revealed to Muhammad orally by the Archangel Gabriel; its heavenly prototype is believed to be preserved in the presence of God. We are told that the name "Muslim" ("one who surrenders") came from Abraham. In accordance with the outer meaning of Islam as a historical phenomenon, we trace the origins of the Islamic community back to Arabia in the early seventh century.

The life of Islam's founder, Muhammad, fits Dibelius' concept of a "law of biographical analogy" for holy men mentioned earlier. The facts of Muhammad's life are simple. Born around A.D. 571 into a poor Arabian clan, the tribe of Quraysh, he was orphaned early and raised by an uncle. He married a wealthy widow named Khadījah who bore him several daughters.[7] He is said to have had an intense religious experience around 610 that compelled him to begin preaching the Word of God in the valley of Mecca (Mekkah), urging his fellow Arabs to acknowledge Allah as the only sovereign deity and to submit to the pattern of life prescribed by him. Khadījah and a small number of converts supported Muhammad's preachings, but he was not popular in Mecca. By chance, he met several people from Medina (Madinah or Yathrib); these people were impressed by him and invited him to become their leader. After careful negotiations with the elders of Medina, Muhammad and his new followers left Mecca for Medina in A.D. 622. This event, called the *hijrah*, marks the beginning of the Islamic calendar.[8]

Prior to Muhammad's *hijrah*, the elders of Medina promised him that "we will not worship any but one God. We will not

steal. Neither will we commit adultery. Nor kill our children.
We will not slander in any wise. Nor do we disobey the Prophet
in anything that is right."[9] The primacy of religious authority
over land and tribal authorities was accepted as the basis of
Muhammad's new "city-state" in Medina. M. Mahdi explains
that according to Islam, the best image of human life on earth
was life in a city-state:

> Life [in Medina], the opinions and actions of its citizens, and es-
> pecially of those citizens who were close to Muhammad, became
> the tradition and the Law that was to be considered the ideal way
> of life in Islam. After the death of Muhammad, Medina remained
> the politico-religious seat of an expanding city-empire. Later, the
> outlying regions of this empire revolted against the mother-city
> and established a "worldly" seat in Damascus. . . . Only with the
> rise of Baghdad as the seat of a new "oriental" theocracy, which
> was in many ways as foreign to the way of life of Medina as the
> Umayyad Empire of Damascus had been, was *the city* eclipsed as
> the effective center of Islam.[10]

Opinions vary concerning pre-Islamic Arabia, although
most scholars agree on two main points. First, neither a great
civilization nor a state existed in that region. Second, both Judaism—then a dynamic proselytizing religion—and Christianity
were active on the Arabian peninsula. There is no evidence to
connect Muhammad with those religious traditions directly, but
we can safely speculate that he was familiar with Jewish and
Christian monotheistic lore. Just as the early Christian community was eager to claim the continuity of its religion with the
Jewish tradition, so was Muhammad anxious to connect his religion to Christianity and Judaism, claiming that the Ka'ba (a
divine sanctuary believed to be the navel of the earth) in Mecca
had been consecrated by Abraham and his son, Ishmael. Thus
"he gave greater depth to Arab historical consciousness, he prolonged the memories of his people back to the day of Creation,
and he gave them a spiritually significant tradition of holy history
to supplement their ill-kept records of events of local importance."[11]

Muhammad's efforts to preserve some continuity between
Islam and the Judeao-Christian tradition brought accusations

that he was a false prophet or a heretic in the Judeao-Christian sense, or that Islam had failed to understand Judaism or Christianity properly. Many accepted the Christian premise that Jesus Christ stood for the fulfillment of the Hebrew Law and Prophets but rejected Muhammad's claim to be the seal of the long line of prophets, including Jesus. Since they could not object to the Islamic premise on purely logical grounds, many Christians interpreted the appearance of Islam eschatologically, as the fulfillment of the latter days of the promise of the coming of the false prophet as predicted in the Johannine apocalypse (Rev. 19: 20). The noted Eastern Christian theologian, John of Damascus (675–749), who had been a tax official in the court of the Muslim caliph before becoming a cleric, was convinced that Islam was a Christian heresy. According to him,

> . . . in the days of the emperor Heraclius a false prophet (*pseudoprophetes*) arose among the Arabs. His name was Maméd. He became acquainted with the Old and New Testaments and later . . . "established his own sect. . . ." Later he claimed that a scripture had been sent down to him from heaven.[12]

Similarly, Theophanes Confessor (died 817), the Byzantine historian, wrote:

> In this year (Anno Mundi 6122 = A.D. 632) Mohammed (Mouámed) the ruler and false prophet of the Saracens, died. . . . At the beginning of his public appearance (*parousia*) the misguided Hebrews thought that he was the Messiah (*Christos*) who(se coming) they expected. So some of their chief men joined him, accepted his religion and forsook that of Moses who had seen God (*theoptes*, God-seeing). . . .[13]

Despite numerous attempts to evaluate Muhammad or Islam according to the yardsticks of other religions and cultures, we are inclined to agree with Hamilton Gibb that "Islam is an autonomous expression of religious thought and experience, which must be viewed in and through itself and its own principles and standards."[14]

There are commonalities among Judaism, Christianity, and Islam. All are monotheistic. All accept the premise that the history of humankind begins with Creation and ends at the Judgment Day, when God's will and truth will be fully revealed.

Among them, Islam probably presents the most coherent, this-worldly synthesis of a religio-cultural/socio-political order that integrates all aspects of individual life and society and all aspects of this world and the next.

Von Grunebaum states the three cardinal principles of the Islamic synthesis. First, by interpreting life in this world as preparation for life in the next, Islam taught that "the aims of heathen ambition, such as wealth, power, fame, remain acceptable aspirations only inasmuch as they are integrated in the organizational structure of the new life." Second, by making the individual responsible for his other-worldly destiny, "it made every moment of the believer's life supremely relevant" and forwarded the process of legal and moral individuation. Third, "by accentuating the indispensability of the community [the *umma*] to the fulfillment of some of the basic obligations of the individual Muslim, Islam stressed the necessity of political organization." [15]

The norm for life within Islamic society resides in the *sharia* (law), the God-given ideal and path based on the divine words (the *Qur'ān*), tradition (the *hadith*), analogical deduction according to a set of rules developed by legal experts (*fiqh*), and the consensus (*ijmā*) of the *umma*, or community. Every action is presumably known to God and can be referred to the *sharia*. Eventually, the five pillars of the faith were developed: (1) confession of faith ("There is no god but Allah; Muhammad is the messenger of Allah"); (2) ritual prayers, to be offered five times daily while facing toward Mecca (*ṣalāt*); (3) fasting; (4) almsgiving; and (5) pilgrimage. The *sharia* further reduced the believer's acts of faith into five categories: (1) obligatory; (2) recommended but not obligatory; (3) indifferent; (4) disapproved but not forbidden; (5) forbidden. All Islamic legal systems agree that the *sharia* represents "the whole corpus of regulations by which the Muslim and hence his community operates in order that the proper earthly life [can] be led." [16]

During Muhammad's lifetime, the Islamic community, the city-state of Medina, was a simple theocracy where the Lord exercised political power through Muhammad, his apostle and

deputy who acted as the administrative head of the temporal/
spiritual community. Upon Muhammad's death, the community
chose a solely temporal caliph (or *khalifa*) with no spiritual authority.[17] As third caliph, the Council named Uthman, a member
of the Umayyad clan and a son-in-law of Muhammad, choosing
him over Alī, another son-in-law of the Prophet. Upon Uthman's
assassination, Alī became the fourth caliph over the protests of
many, including Aishah, a widow of the Prophet. Uthman's
nephew, the powerful Mu'awiya, defied Alī's authority and proclaimed himself caliph, and until Alī's death in 661, caliph Alī
ruled from Medina and caliph Mu'awiya ruled from Damascus.
To make matters more complex, Mu'awiya's attempt to keep the
caliphate in the Umayyad family was challenged by Alī's son,
Husain, who was eventually murdered by Umayyad forces.
However, the followers of Husain, and Alī before him, continued
to acknowledge only Alī's descendants as legitmiate *imams*, or
heads of Islam. This group of believers were known as *Shi'a*
("separate party," or the followers of Alī) and are the ancestors
of the contemporary Shi'ites in Persia. The Umayyad caliphate
remained in power until 750; the new Abbāsid dynasty eventually moved the caliphate to Baghdad in 760. The splendor of
Baghdad under the Abbāsid caliphate was reputed to be second
only to the magnificence of Constantinople.

For one hundred years following Muhammad's death in 632,
the Islamic community enjoyed phenomenal expansion. During
the final ten years of Muhammad's life, he exerted his influence
widely on the Arabian peninsula. Soon Syria, which had been
part of the Byzantine empire, fell to the Islamic community.
Jerusalem followed in 638. The Islamic forces then invaded
Egypt, defeated Sāsānian Persia and pacified North Africa. In
711, aided by oppressed Jews, they defeated the Visigoth kingdom on the Iberian peninsula. The Islamic attempt to subdue
France was blocked by Charles Martel in 732 at the Battle of
Tours, but their successful efforts in Spain—or *Al-andalus*, as it
was called by the Muslims—turned Spain into the most highly
civilized region in Europe. In 750, 'Abd al-Rahman I, an Umayyad
who escaped the Abbāsid assassins, became the emir, or prince,
of the Spanish Muslims. This group acknowledged the nominal

authority of the Abbāsid caliphate until in 912, the emergence of a Fatimid caliph in North Africa encouraged 'Abd alRahman III (912–961) to proclaim himself caliph of Spain. Thus, the seeds of internal disunity begin being sown within the Islamic community.

Muhammad originally envisaged a simple theocratic city-state in Medina—a Muslim community (*umma muslima*) founded on the principles of God's holiness and justice, creating a political community coextensive with religious faith. Eventually forced to acknowledge other religious persuasions, Islam divided the entire world into regions under its control (the *dār al-Islām*) and regions not yet converted to Islam (the *dār al-Ḥarb*). Theoretically, there was no compromise between these two regions; in actuality, there were some ambiguities, such as regions of peace, or those with which the Islamic community had made peace pacts, or the respect accorded to the People of the Book, a term originally given to Jews and Christians but occasionally accorded to others who had sacred books, such as the Zoroastrians, the Hindus, and the Buddhists. The People of the Book were, of course, urged to embrace Islam, but they were left alone as long as they paid the poll tax (*jizyah*). The underlying rationale for this divided world was the view that the Islamic religio-cultural/socio-political synthesis was destined to dominate the world.

The Islamic community followed the path of earlier faiths in its development. Specifically, just as the early Christian community lost its eschatological orientation to become the this-worldly state religion of the Roman Empire under Theodosius (reign 379–396), the Islamic community lost its city-state orientation to become an empire under the caliphates. The various caliphates followed different paradigms in their approaches toward compromise with the existing world. As Mahdi points out, the Umayyad

> attempted to establish a secular state on natural foundations, to separate worldly rule from the sacred way of life, and to force the latter into a personal piety which was not allowed to interfere in the conduct of the affairs of state, but must submit to the demands of worldly power. Here Christian doctrine and Byzantine practice seem to have been the model. The second [i.e., the Abbāsid] attempted to absorb into itself the sacred way of life by outwardly

championing it and posing as its defender and protector. Here the Sassanid "oriental theocracy" seems to have been the model. A third attempt, made by the Fatimides of Egypt, seems to have been again modelled after the Sassanid example, together with a mixture of Platonic politics and Neo-Platonic theology which characterized the Isma'ili sect to which the Fatimides belonged.[18]

The Muslim empire interpreted the office of the caliphate as comparable to the office of the Christian pope, and, as von Grunebaum observes, "some Muslims reciprocated by calling the pope 'Caliph of the Franks.' . . ."[19] although in reality the caliph was the administrative, not the religious, head of the Islamic community.

Another characteristic of the Islamic empire was the increasing activity and influence of both non-Arab and non-Muslims—Nestorian Christians, Jews, Hindus, Persians—responsible for the functioning of the caliphate. Originally, Muslims were not noted for culture and education, but they were eager to learn from neighboring peoples and were superb translators of Greek, Latin, Persian, and Sanskrit. In both Sicily and Spain, Jewish intellectuals served as cultural intermediaries between Muslims and Christians, and Aristotle became as much a favorite of Muslims as of Christians. Persia also contributed much to Islamic culture. Under Abbāsid rule, a mercantile class engaged in extensive foreign trade emerged. Although the Arabic language continued to be used in the Baghdad caliphate, "gradually Persian titles, Persian wines and wives, Persian mistresses, Persian songs, as well as Persian ideas and thoughts, won the day."[20] Spanish Muslims contributed a great deal to European culture during the ninth and tenth centuries. The famous library of al-Hakim was reputed to be the most extensive in the world at this time, and the city of Toledo became a major center of learning, attracting many Jewish, Christian, and Muslim students.

The Islamic empire was far different than the theocratic city-state of the early Islamic community in Medina. It developed the *corpus Islamicum*, a multiracial, multinational cosmopolitan synthesis that provided the best common denominator for the peoples of Asia, North Africa, and Europe. Hendrik Kraemer observes,

. . . historically speaking, it did not create a culture but it inherited the Oriental-Hellenistic culture of which Byzantium was the embodiment as building material for creating, within the space of four centuries, Islam as a religious-cultural-social [synthesis]. Or, to put it differently: the civilization which grew up in Asia and North Africa around the Mediterranean as a result of Alexander the Great's meteoric career, entered through Islam into a new metamorphosis. . . .[21]

Greek influence also encouraged the growth of the rationalistic Mu'tazilite school of theology in the ninth century. This school, by effectively interpreting the Islamic faith to non-Arab intellectuals, provoked criticism from orthodox scholastics (Mutakallimun), or the "people of the Tradition (hadith)," as exemplified by the noted al-Asharī (died 942). The impact of the ancient Greek approach to human knowledge was evident in the development of falsafah, the system of comprehensive knowledge that included both humanistic and natural scientific learning. Broader than a philosophical system per se, the falsafah attracted natural scientists, practicing physicians, and philosophers. The tradition included such notable Muslim thinkers as al-Kindī (died 873), often called the first faylasūf; al-Fārābī (died 950) and Avicenna (ibn Sīnā, died 1037), both faylasūf metaphysicians; and Averroes (ibn Rushid, died 1198), the Islamic Aristotelian par excellence. The famous Jewish philosopher-physician Maimonides (Moses Ben Maimon, 1135–1204), physician to the court of Saladin, was a devotee of falsafah; he wrote his Guide of the Perplexed in Arabic.

Neo-Platonism had a profound influence on Sufism, the Islamic cult of mysticism based on a monotheistic concept of God and the universe.[22] Unlike the mystical traditions preoccupied with ecstatic experiences, Sufism encouraged faith in a broad spiritual path that sought truth and meaningfulness in every aspect of life. It began as a nonecclesiastical spiritual movement, but soon developed priestly orders and a mission-oriented liturgy that engendered public statements often irritating to traditionalists. For example, Sufi al-Ḥallāj (855–922) was flogged, mutilated, and burned for his public utterance that "I am Truth" (without doubt because Truth is one name of God). The jurist and *faylasūf*-Sufi, al-Ghazālī (1058–1111), eventually synthesized Sufism, scholastic theology, authoritative instruction, and *falsafah*.

THE MIDDLE AGES, EAST AND WEST

Looking back to the Middle Ages we are tempted to see the Islamic community and Greek and Latin Christendom engaged in constant battle—pointing to the Crusades as proof. Each of these communities was convinced of its spiritual superiority and of being the bearer of the Truth. Each took pride in its religio-cultural/socio-political synthesis as the best framework for human life. Even though these three communities were divided further by linguistic, ethnic, military, and commercial patterns, they shared many things in common. They were fraternal enemies boxed into a common world of fate. For instance, contrary to our current understanding of philosophy as a hopelessly divided, culture-biased discipline, medieval Latin, Byzantine, and Islamic thinkers understood it as a common path for intellectual inquiry. Kraemer observes that for them

> . . . philosophy and theology were [also] always indissolubly combined into one religious philosophy, which dominated thought and life. It is, therefore, more accurate to say that philosophy meant an eclectic mystical religious philosophy, i.e., Aristotelianism and Platonism interpreted in a Neo-Platonic spirit.[23]

This may account for the fact that, the bloody Crusades notwithstanding, Europe, and especially Latin Christendom, learned much religious philosophy from the *corpus Islamicum*.

In contrast to the romantic portrayals of much art and literature, the Middle Ages was a turbulent era. Feudalism imposed sharply divided social classes upon all of Europe until the development of new towns resulted in the shaping of social, political, and economic structures. Kings and popes continued to compete for power over the practices of simony and lay investiture and to control education in England, France, and Germany. Dissension split the Latin West and the Byzantine East in 1054.[24]

There is much truth in von Grunebaum's observation that "the Christian world devoted much more attention to Islam than it received. Hatred, fear, admiration and the attraction of the unknown seem to have coexisted in Christendom throughout the Middle Ages. . . ."[25] The Latin West was keenly aware that despite Charlemagne's efforts to promote education, the West was culturally inferior to both the Islamic community and Greek Christendom. Gradually, the cultural standard of Europe responded to the civilizing activities of the monastic orders, especially such "reform"-conscious orders as the Burgundian monastery of Cluny (founded in 910). Pressure from kings and churches eventually resulted in the establishment of "outer schools," at various monasteries and cathedrals, for the education of secular clergy and laity, in addition to "inner schools" for training monastics. Through these "outer schools" much theological, philosophical, and secular knowledge was introduced into Europe from the Islamic schools on the Iberian peninsula and in Provence and Sicily.

Europe had to learn from the Islamic community that life is a totality of religious, philosophical, and secular domains, and must be approached as such. This spirit first emerged in the Islamic world with the publication of a series of treatises entitled *Mujarrabāt* (Experimenta). According to von Grunebaum, the earliest contributor to this series was Abū l-Alā Zuhr (died 1077 or 78) of Cordova, Spain, father of the famous physician, Avenzoar (Ibn Zuhr, died 1161–62). Von Grunebaum writes:

> . . . he was followed by the Christian Ibn at-Tilmīd of Baghdad (died 1164/65) and the Egyptian Jews, Ibn al-Mudawwar (died 1184/ 85), Ibn an-Nāqid (died 1188/89), and Abū l-Ma ālī, who was perhaps Maimonides' brother-in-law (died 1222). . . . their importance as signs of a reorientation of the investigating mind is very considerable.[26]

The impact of the world of Islam is invigorated intellectual seriousness among European monastics. Significantly, the first translation of the *Qur'ān* was attempted by Peter of Cluny in 1141, and the first school of Oriental Studies was established in Toledo, Spain, by the Dominicans, or the Order of Preachers. The Islamic community was also instrumental in introducing to the Latin West the classics of antiquity, which had been translated earlier into Arabic by Syrian Christians, along with the thoughts of such thinkers as al-Fārābī, ibn Sīnā (Avicenna), Averroes (Ibn Rushid), and the Jewish philosopher, Maimonides. The Arabic translations of the three last books of Plotinus, erroneously attributed to Aristotle, were known as the *Theology of Aristotle*. As Kraemer comments,

> The psychology of Plotinus about the "material *nous*" . . . part of the individual soul, and the "active *nous*" . . . which was eternal, as it was considered an emanation of the First Cause, enabled the philosophers . . . and the theologians . . . to have their common ground in rational metaphysics. . . . Before the 12th century scholasticism was chiefly Augustinian-Platonist. As to philosophical sources it was confined to the Logic of Aristotle. . . . As to Plato, it knew him through Cicero and *Timaeus*, and as to Neo-Platonism, Pseudo-Dionysius was their man.[27]

Given this picture, one can readily understand the influence of the fuller works of both Aristotle and the Muslim thinkers on the Scholastics. Averroes, who insisted on the primacy of knowledge over faith, was especially influential.[28] His ideas and those of Maimonides affected such Christian Aristotelians as Thomas Aquinas (died 1274) and Albertus Magnus (died 1280). The Scholastics greatly contributed to the development of the university in medieval Europe.[29]

Interestingly, the Latin and Greek Christian communities and their Islamic counterparts all encountered political instability at about the same time. During the tenth century, the Islamic community, which was theoretically one entity, had three rival caliphs, one in Baghdad, one in Cairo, and one in Cordova, a situation indicative of internal turmoil and discontent.[30] During the eleventh century, the Latin West was torn by rivalry among three competing popes: Benedict IX (1033–1045), Sylvester III (1044–1045) and Gregory VI (1045–1046). This same century, Greek Christendom was divided into three rival factions, each putting forward its choice for emperor. There were some far-reaching and constructive developments during this time. The charter of Constantine IX in 1045 called for a new university for training educated bureaucrats. But as a whole the Byzantine empire was threatened by invasion from the Pecheneg Turks, the Seljūq Turks, and the Normans.[31] The decline of Europe became obvious shortly after the schism of the Eastern and Western churches in 1054.

The Crusades and the Corpus Christianum. The Crusades, in which religious and secular hopes, fears, and aspirations of the Latin, the Byzantine, and the Islamic communities are intricately interwoven, defies simple explanation. The Crusades were basically a series of campaigns undertaken by West European Christian princes from 1096 to 1291 under the pretext of recovering the Holy Land from Muslim rule. The Crusades accomplished very little militarily. The campaigns accomplished more in terms of cultural fertilization and establishing commercial relations. Moreover, as Hichem Djait points out, Europe learned political dialectic through the Crusades and contact with Islam. As he explains it,

> Islam was at once a military voice threatening Europe and an economic sphere sharing its dynamism, just as later it would be an ideological enemy and a philosophical model. In a word, Europe's emergence into history took place . . . through the mediation of Islam. . . .[32]

The Crusades indirectly facilitated the development of the medieval synthesis of a religio-cultural/socio-political order usually referred to as the *corpus Christianum*. This was not a frozen, closed, static system, however, for Europe was constantly changing, as seen in Anglo-Saxon England after the Norman conquest. Moreover, the *corpus Christianum* did not mean that the papacy dominated the whole of Europe, as is commonly thought. There were many able and strong-willed rulers, including Henry III (died 1056); Henry IV (died 1106); Frederick I, called Barbarossa, "The Redbeard" (died 1190);[33] and Henry VI (died 1197), all of whom resented the temporal power of the popes. Through such rulers medieval England produced the modern English system of common law and the Magna Carta (1215). As a result, from the thirteenth century on, the English Parliament exerted tremendous influence over the government. During this same time France was developing three traditional bodies of political assembly: the King's Council, the Chamber of Accounts, and the judicial body of the Parliament.

On the other side, some resourceful and ambitious popes who sought both religious and secular power emerged during the Middle Ages. Gregory VII (Pope Hildebrand 1073–1085), convinced of the infallibility of the church, used physical force to implement his demands. Urban II (pope 1088–1099) inaugurated the First Crusade by calling the Council of Clermont in 1095.[34] After the fall of Edessa (the capital of the first Crusader state) in 1144, Eugenius III (pope 1145–1153) and his mentor, Bernard of Clairvaux, launched the unsuccessful Second Crusade. Shortly thereafter, the fall of Jerusalem to the sultan, Saladin (died 1193), prompted Gregory VIII (pope in 1187) to call for the Third Crusade, which he entrusted to Frederick Barbarossa. Upon Frederick's unexpected death, England's Richard I, or Richard the Lion-Hearted, negotiated a peace treaty with Saladin.

The most powerful pope was Innocent III (pope 1198–1216), under whom the papacy reached its zenith. He officially sponsored two Crusades: the Fourth, which established the short-lived Latin empire and patriarchate in Constantinople, and the Albigensian, which stamped out (with much bloodshed) certain views in southern France that he considered heretical. During his pontificate, Francis of Assisi (died 1226) founded his order of friars, and in 1215 the fourth Lateran Council strengthened the church with the creation of the dogma of transubstantiation— according to which the bread and wine of the Eucharist physically become the body and blood of Christ—and the obligations of private confession and annual communion. In 1212, a combination of piety and crusading fervor produced the Children's Crusade that cost the lives of thousands of innocent children lost or sold into slavery. The Fifth Crusade, ordered by Innocent III before his death but not undertaken until 1219, was a dismal failure and the last crusade officially mandated by the papacy.

The Crusades dramatically revealed the (diametrically opposed) characters of two of the age's most powerful monarchs, Frederick II (died 1250), King of Sicily and Germany and Holy Roman Emperor, and Louis IX, King of France. Brought up in Sicily, Frederick II had associated with Christians, Jews, and

Muslims from childhood. Reputedly an agnostic, he is said to have commented that Moses, Christ, and Muhammad were three great impostors. Excommunicated twice, he nevertheless considered himself a new David and crowned himself King of Jerusalem in 1229 in the Church of the Holy Sepulchre. Although a key figure in the Sixth Crusade, Frederick was reluctant to fight the Muslims. He finally joined as an ally of the sultan, sailing with a fleet manned primarily by Muslim sailors. His truce with the Muslims ended with the recapture of Jerusalem by the Turks, who held the city until World War I.[35]

Louis IX, known as "Saint Louis" (died 1270) was an extremely pious man, obsessed with the desire to wrest the Holy Land from Muslim rule. He took the initiative in the last two Crusades, the Seventh and Eighth, both of which failed. His death marks the end of both the crusading spirit and the militant activity of the Latin West.

The *corpus Christianum* continued to witness constant power struggles between strong-willed monarchs and ambitious popes. Heated conflicts erupted between the absolute monarch of France, Philip IV, called "The Fair" (reign 1285–1314), and Boniface VIII (pope 1294–1303) over taxation of the clergy. In 1302 Boniface issued the famous papal bull, *Unam sanctam* (One Holy), which claimed that submission to the pope in Rome was absolutely necessary for salvation. Philip's supremacy over Boniface marked the beginning of the collapse of papal power, which soon degenerated into the "Babylonian Captivity" of the papacy (1309–1377) under French monarchical power in Avignon and the Great Schism between the French and Italian popes (1378–1418).

The political geography of Europe also changed. Both France and England emerged from the Hundred Years' War with strong national governments. With the dissolution of the Holy Roman Empire, Germany was divided into separate territories governed by secular and ecclesiastical princes; a few cities remained independent entities. By 1512, Spain, where Christian forces had overpowered the Muslims and completely driven out the Jews between 1481 and 1492, experienced a rapid transition from feudalism to absolute monarchy under Ferdinand V of Aragon and

Isabella of Castile. Politically divided Italy was dominated by the papal state and prominent cities, all of which became important centers of civilization. The Scandinavian and central European nations were slowly moving into the European cultural mainstream, thus planting the seeds of the Renaissance.

The Crusades and the Byzantine Community. The Byzantine community maintained a precarious position throughout the Crusades. Historians suspect that it did not expect a positive response to the papacy's call for the Crusades, a call the Byzantine community agreed with in principle. In practice, however, there were a number of serious problems. First, food supplies and military escort personnel for troops fighting in the Byzantine territories created a severe financial drain. Second, the ranks of the Crusaders included mortal enemies, among them the Normans. There was constant tension between the Crusaders and the Byzantine troops, a tension fed by blame heaped upon Byzantine soldiers for lost battles. Third, the Crusaders often ignored the edicts of the Byzantine emperors, whom they viewed with open contempt. The situation became critical with the establishment of the short-lived Latin empire in Constantinople during the Fourth Crusade under the auspices of Pope Innocent III. The Byzantines maintained that it was their land that was being exposed to the invaders—to the Seljūq Turks, the Mongols, the Arab Muslims, and the Ottoman Turks. They clearly remembered that their emperor, Romanus II Diogenes, had been taken prisoner by the invading Seljūq Turks.

After the fall of Constantinople, the Byzantine emperor, Michael VIII (died 1282), feared a recapture of the city so he neglected to protect his eastern front. The Ottoman Turks easily invaded Anatolia in 1302 and crossed into Europe in 1354. In 1402 the Byzantines cheered their defeat at Ankara by the Mongol leader, Tamerlane.

Meanwhile in the West, the Council of Florence imposed a temporary reunification of the Eastern and Western churches in 1439, by enforcing the new dogma of *extra ecclesiam nulla salus*, "no salvation outside the church." This reunion stimulated some enthusiasm for an aborted crusade against the Turks, but the official celebration at Hagia Sophia was received with loud protest in the orthodox world, for the Byzantines objected to rule by the Latins. Yet of the victorious Sultan Mehmed II, the victor in the battle for Constantinople in 1456, we read:

> The Sultan acknowledged the fact that the church had proved to be the most enduring element in the Byzantine world; and he gave the Patriarch of Constantinople an unprecedented measure of temporal authority by making him answerable for all Christians living under Ottoman rule.[36]

In time the mighty and colorful Byzantine world fell to the Ottoman Turks, and the famous—or infamous—Ottoman empire began its reign.

The Islamic community was fractured by three competing caliphs seated in Baghdad, Cairo, and Cordova. The emergence of numerous sultans and emirs, the rise of the Shi'a and the Ismā'īlī, and the spread of Sufi mysticism added to the community's complexity. Yet from the perspective of the unity of humankind, the Islamic community at this point in history provided an attractive option. By this time relatively stable lines also had been drawn between the Christian world and the world of Islam.

The Byzantine, the Latin West, and the Islamic communities were busy developing their own religio-cultural/socio-political syntheses. Under the Islamic Abbāsid caliphate, the Arabic language culture was radically altered through Persian influence. As Marshall Hodgson states,

> During the five centuries after 945, the former society of the caliphate was replaced by a constantly expanding, linguistically and culturally international society ruled by numerous independent governments. This society was not held together by a single political order or a single language or culture. Yet it did remain . . . a single historical whole. In its time, this international Islamicate society was certainly the most widely spread and influential society on the globe.[37]

As both the Latin West and the Byzantine East had subdued and converted the barbarians within their borders, the Islamic community was also forced to deal with nomadic and seminomadic peoples and the disruption of their assimilation into the

Islamic community. For example, the Seljūq Turks, one of the Turkish tribes that migrated from the Central Asian steppes to the Jaxtartes River in the tenth century, converted to Sunni Islam and founded an empire embracing Iran, Mesopotamia, Syria, and Palestine. In 1071, the Seljūq army defeated the Byzantine forces and captured their empire; the subsequent mistreatment of Christian pilgrims in the Holy Land provoked the Crusades. As Sunni Muslims, the Seljūqs waged bloody struggles against the Shi'ite Fatimid dynasty established in Cairo. The Fatimid caliphate was eventually abolished by Sultan Saladin in 1193.[38]

The invasion of the Mongols, who eventually subjugated the Muslims living between the Oxus frontier and the Euphrates, sacking Baghdad in 1258, was more frightening than the Crusades to the Islamic community. The Mongols—and all remaining Crusaders—were expelled from Palestine by the Turkish Mamluks in 1260. Genghis Khan's grandson, Hulagu, then established the Mongol kingdom of Persia and became its first Il-khan, or king. Equally terrifying were the Ottomans, a tribe of the Ghuzz Turks, who had been driven from their original homes in central Asia by the advancing Mongols. They occupied nearly all of Anatolia by the fourteenth century. In 1402 they were defeated at Ankara by the army of the Tartar leader, Tamerlane. Within several decades they recovered sufficient strength to capture Constantinople in 1453 under the leadership of Sultan Mehmed II (died 1481).

With the fall of Granada, Spain, to Christian forces in 1492, the direct participation of the *corpus Islamicum* in European affairs ended abruptly. By this time the Islamic community had expanded into Africa and central, south, southeast, and east Asia—especially China. We will now look at events in Asia—particularly in India and China—over the ten centuries prior to Columbus's discovery of America in 1492 and Vasco da Gama's voyage around the Cape of Good Hope in 1498.

THE HINDU SYNTHESIS

We begin with events in eastern Eurasia, particularly on the Indian subcontinent, during the ten centuries before the coming of the Europeans in the sixteenth century.

During the Gupta era (around A.D. 320–540), and for a few following centuries, India was relatively free from invasion. This period we now know as "Hindu India," based on what scholars call the Brahmanical synthesis of religion-culture-society-political order, crystallized.[39] Beginning in A.D. 1000, Muslim raiders appeared in India, establishing sporadic rule of northern India in the thirteenth century, without touching Hinduistic south India. Eventually, the whole subcontinent came under Muslim rule with the Mughal dynasty (1526–1761). The nature of the Hindu or Brahmanical synthesis of religion-culture-society-political order, not so much for its historical details as its logic, rationale, and organizing principles, is our current concern.

The Hindu synthesis contains two main principles. The first is the way the Hindu synthesis preserved the integrity of existing theories, practices, and customs. It systematized but did not homologize them, in effect rearranging them under Brahmanical control. The second is that the Hindu synthesis embraced the whole cosmic order, and not simply the natural, human, and social orders that concerned the Chinese synthesis. Yet the emphasis was not on the transcendental aspect of the cosmic order but on its wholeness perceived in a this-worldly sense. Betty Heimann points out that in India metaphysics never acquired the meaning of "beyond all physical facts" as it did in later Greek thought and does today in the West. She goes on to say:

> . . . [Metaphysics] has rather always been pure Physics. If then Indian Metaphysics is concerned with problems centering on the conception of God, that is with Theology, Metaphysics may be called "a second Physics," since God is the heavenly counterpart of earthly physical beings. If applied, again, to cosmic primeval Physics or to Ontology, then the meaning becomes "extended Physics," while when it deals with the fate of Man after death, it is a "renewed Physics," simply because India's ideas of life after death, of the Hereafter, are those of another "here," or a new life on earth in reincarnation.[40]

These perspectives determined the Hindu synthesis.

THE VARṆĀŚRAMA-DHARMA SYSTEM

Central to the Hindu synthesis was the *varṇāśrama-dharma* system, that is, duty or law in accordance with *varṇa*, or "class,"[41] and *āśrama*, or "stage of life," referring to the life of the student, householder, hermit, or *sannyāsin* ("renouncer," one who has renounced the world). This system, which had been more flexible earlier, became increasingly rigid during the first century A.D., whereby *varṇa* (class) became "caste," determined by birth (*jāti*). In principle, the three upper *varṇas*—Brahmans, Kṣatriyas, and *Vaiśyas*—were known as the "twice-born" (*dvijas*), while *Śūdras*, especially "impure" *Śūdras*, could not associate with people of the "twice-born" classes, engage in Vedic study, utter Vedic *mantras*, or perform Vedic rituals. In time, numerous caste and sub-caste groups were added to deal with intermarriage, occupational differentiation, and degrees of ritual purity. The combination of *varṇa* and *āśrama* produced a specific set of duties and responsibilities for individuals. The underlying assumption was that by closely observing the *dharma* of a particular life-situation one could fulfill one's obligation to the *sanātana*, or eternal, *dharma* that governs the cosmic order.

The beginning stage of the student (*brahmacārin*) for a male Hindu and the ceremony (*upanāyana*) that marks the occasion are celebrated. He progresses to the stage of the householder through marriage. Women do not go through the stage of the student. Usually upper-class women are married off before puberty. They are expected to partake in the religious merit of their husbands. The Hindu synthesis depends heavily on the stage of the householder, for the householders produce offspring and insure the preservation of society. Only after one fulfills his duty as a householder is he allowed to live as a hermit. The stage of the *sannyāsin* implies the complete severance of all worldly ties, including one's relationship to wife and family. The assumption is that the *sannyāsin* is born again into celibate childhood. The Hindu synthesis based on the *varṇāśrama-dharma* system allowed people of different temperaments, tastes, and persuasions to live together, relating to each other within a unified society. It might appear to be an unbearably rigid system, but Hopkins confirms that it appears to be quite different from the inside:

> Though hereditary caste identity made social mobility impossible within an individual's lifetime, the principles of *karma* and rebirth

not only explained one's present condition but offered hope of future improvement. The means of this improvement was proper performance of *dharma*, which now meant the full range of duties assigned by both *varṇa* and caste. . . . The result was not social equality but social stability based on karmic principles of cosmic justice and progress by stages to the ultimate goal of release.[42]

FOUR ENDS OF LIFE AND SIX ORTHODOX SYSTEMS

The Hindu synthesis did not make everyone constantly conscious of the ultimate goal of release. In Zimmer's observation success, pleasure, and duty were just as important as final release (*mokṣa*), not so much in terms of Hindu religion but in terms of the Hindu synthesis for individuals and the society.[43] Success (*artha*) implies both material profit and political know-how according to the "Treatise on Material Gain" (*Arthaśāstra*) attributed to Kautilya, advisor to the founder of the Mauryan dynasty (the grandfather of King Aśoka). *Artha* underlies two other human goals—pleasure and duty. What is usually translated as pleasure (*kāma*) has a wide range of meanings from love to sensuality to the enjoyment of art and culture. For instance, it is characteristic of the Indian tradition to consider sex as a positive human need, as illustrated by the common sexual manual, the *Kāma Sūtra*. Duty (*dharma*), mentioned earlier in connection with the *varṇāśrama-dharma* system, varies according to the individual's caste and the stage of life. *Dharma* signifies that one has a definite place in the cosmic order and that life is not a series of difficult decisions. One needs to follow the prescribed course of life: "From the very first breath of life, the individual's energies are mastered, trained into channels, and co-ordinated to the general work of the super-individual who is the holy society itself."[44]

In comparison with the so-called "group of three," *artha*, *kāma*, and *dharma*, the goal of release (*mokṣa*) through the discipline of metaphysics belongs to what Zimmer calls the philosophies of eternity. In his words: "*mokṣa* looks beyond the stars, not to the village street."[45] In this respect, there is much that supports Zimmer's practice of listing Jainism, Sāṃkhya and

Yoga, Brahmanism, Buddhism, and Vedānta as different Indian systems[46] that offer alternative paths toward *mokṣa*.[47] The most well-known philosopher of medieval India was Saṃkara (around 788–832), known for his nondualism within the Vedānta tradition. A devotee of Śiva and both a philosopher and a poet, he opposed Buddhism. He affirmed that only Brahman (Absolute Being) is real, and all else is *māyā* (appearance). Betty Heimann reminds us that "*māyā* is *unreality not in the transient world, but unreality in the eternal world*, since the aggregation of single individual forms can have no static existence, but only a continuity of change."[48] On the other hand, Rāmānuja (died 1137), the advocate of a qualified nondualism, understood that Brahman is not intelligence, as Saṃkara held, but is a Supreme Being whose chief attribute is intelligence. The school of Rāmānuja stressed "devotion" (*bhakti*) rather than knowledge as the means of salvation. This devotion to Viṣṇu—the theistic Brahman—is derived from knowledge and represents a more direct path to salvation.[49] The third famous philosopher was Madhva Ācārya (Madhva the Teacher, died 1278), a realist, pluralist, and devotee of Viṣṇu, the Supreme God. The resemblance of Madhva's system to Christianity is striking; Basham suspected the influence of Syrian Christianity. "The sharp distinction between God and the soul, the doctrine of eternal damnation, and the status of Vāyu [the wind-god and the son of Viṣṇu] are obvious points of similarity. . . ."[50]

Bhakti-yoga. The Hindu synthesis reflected the growing eclectic ethos of religious Hinduism, an eclecticism that displayed a strong theistic tradition affirming *bhakti* or devotion as the preferred path to salvation. This was in opposition to both the gnostic path (*jñāna-yoga*), which stressed Upaniṣadic knowledge and the path of action (*karma-yoga*), which emphasized social duty, ritual action, and religious merit. Hindu theism was greatly facilitated by the popularity of the *Bhagavad-Gītā*, which had been added to the *Mahābhārata* before A.D. 200, as well as another famous epic, the *Rāmāyaṇa*. In the *Bhagavad-Gītā*, Krishna, one of the *avatāras* or incarnations of the god Viṣṇu, is asked by Prince Arjuna if he should slay his kinsmen (who happen to be his enemies) in the battle or be killed by them. Krishna, who disguises himself as a charioteer, explicates the meaning of the traditional paths of Upaniṣadic knowledge (*jñāna-yoga*) and duty (*karma-yoga*). Then, revealing his divine identity, he shows devotion (*bhakti*) directed to Krishna as the highest form of *yoga* and the key to the goal of release.

The expansion of theism made many deities household names, for example, Śiva (whose common image is the *liṅga*), Viṣṇu and his *avatāras* such as Rāma Krishna, and various goddesses. Theism also produced many features we commonly associate with Hinduism, such as *pūjā*, the "ritual offering" for worship that replaced the old customs of sacrifice, temples, festivals, holy places, and pilgrimages.

The Gupta dynasty (around 320–540) patronized theistic Hinduism, especially the worship of the god Viṣṇu and the goddess Lakṣmī. The Gupta period is often called the Classical Age of Hindu India. Indian culture reached its zenith during the reign of Candra Gupta II (around 376–415), as attested to by the Chinese pilgrim Fa-hsien, who spent six years in India during his reign. According to Fa-hsien, Buddhism was still flourishing, but theistic Hinduism, very different from the old sacrificial Brahmanism, was capturing the people's hearts. During the fifth and the sixth centuries a central Asia people called the Hūṇas, or White Huns, known for their anti-Buddhist policies, crossed over the Indian border. They lost their energies before attaining any enduring political power in northern India. The main line of the Gupta dynasty disappeared in the mid-sixth century, but the general policies and spirit of the Guptas were carried on by several dynasties; some claimed a connection with the mainline Guptas. One of the most remarkable rulers at that time was Harṣa. During his forty-one-year reign (606–647), he consolidated his huge domain in northern India, partially restoring the legacies of the Guptas. He was greatly admired by the famous Chinese pilgrim Hsüan Tsang (596–664), who visited India during Harṣa's reign. Hsüan Tsang's diary recorded that Buddhism was rapidly declining in India. Harṣa's vast domain disintegrated after his death.

Tantrism. By Harṣa's time the Hindu synthesis began to incorporate Tantrism, another non-Vedic feature, into its system. The peak of Tantrism actually occurred between the ninth and the fourteenth centuries. According to Tantrism, the human being is a microcosm, endowed with divine powers that actualize a series of cosmic realities by means of *sādhana*, a practice designated to achieve one's identification with the deity in the form of an image. Tantrism penetrated Buddhism and made Tantric Buddhism, sometimes known as Vajrayāna or Mantrāyana, the third main branch of Buddhism. This form of Buddhism taught that the final release could be best attained by acquiring magical power. The divinities of Tantric Buddhism were savioresses (*Tārās*) or the spouses of the Buddhas and Bodhisattvas.

Buddhism. The ten centuries before the Europeans' arrival in the sixteenth century were crucial in the history of Indian philosophy and religion. One of the most important developments was the disappearance of Buddhism in India, one of the two main indigenous currents of Indian tradition, "one having its source in the *ātmā*-doctrine of the Upanisads and the other in the *anātmā*-doctrine of Buddha."[51] Buddhism denied *ātmān* (substance) due to the Buddhist "moral view of reality," to use Murti's expression. While the Vedānta advocates the extreme form of the Substance-view and Buddhism the exclusive Modal-view, "the Jaina ostensibly reconciles these two opposed views by according equal reality to substance and its modes. . . . The Jaina shaped its epistemology on this pattern and formulated the logic of the disjunction of the real. . . ."—in effect, the third approach between "the *ātmā* doctrine and the *anātmā* doctrine."[52] The Hindu synthesis depended heavily on the Brahmanic-Hindu philosophical-religious tradition, including the Upaniṣadic and Vedāntic insights, and replaced Buddhism as the main stage of Indian spiritual life. Thus, the three branches of Buddhism found their respective secondary centers outside India—the southern or Hīnayāna (Theravāda) tradition in Ceylon (Sri Lanka), the northern or Mahāyāna tradition in China, and the Tantric Buddhist tradition in Tibet. The Hindu synthesis did not incorporate the Jain tradition into its system. The Jain community—both the sky-clad, or naked, branch and the white cloud branch—had to find a modest niche in the spiritual life of the populace. From time to time, rulers showed interest in the Jain tradition; for example, a famous Jain pontif, Hemacandra, became a powerful minister to King Kumarāpāla (1144–1173). However, the Jain community was a comparatively insignificant spiritual pocket in Indian life.

The Pārsīs. The history of the Pārsīs ("Persians"), a West Indian community of Middle Easterners who were heirs of the Zoroastrian religion is unclear. Many scholars believe that Persia and India had many centuries of contacts. There were Persian communities in and around India, as evidenced by inscriptions in the old Persian language of Pahlavī in South India. It is unclear when the Zoroastrians migrated to India. The Muslim conquest of Iran (around 642) probably was followed by the migration of several waves of Zoroastrians by land and sea. Basham noted that "according to the Pārsīs' own traditions one band of refugees settled first at Diū in Kāthiāwār, and then at Thānā, near Bombay, in the eighth century." [53] The main Pārsī community has remained there ever since. However, the relationship between the Pārsī and Hindu communities has been cool, though polite, since the coming of the Persians to India. This is surprising considering the Aryan background of both the Iranians and the Hindus, and that the two traditions share common religious notions and practices. Apparently, the Buddhist, Jain, and Pārsī traditions had different views concerning the ideal synthesis of religion-culture-society-political order, and were not acceptable to the Hindus. Yet Hopkins is persuaded that prior to Muslim rule the Hindu tradition was probably the most varied and flexible system in the world. [54]

ISLAM IN INDIA

India was destined to a different fate with Islam coming to the subcontinent. Prior to A.D. 1000, Islamic expansion in India followed the pattern of conversion preceding conquest—mainly in coastal areas following the trade routes. Muslim kingdoms were soon established in Afghanistan, from where Muslim forces invaded India from around 1000 onward. The pattern then changed to conquest preceding conversion. Mahmūd of Ghazunī, known as the destroyer of idols, plundered northern India about twenty times between 1000 and 1027. In 1191 there were fresh invasions led by Muhammad Ghuri, destroying the famous Buddhist monastic university at Nālandā in 1197. In 1206 the Delhi Slave Sultanate held power in northern India under successive waves of Muslim invaders. Toward the end of the fourteenth century, two rival sultans competing for power resided in or around Delhi. In 1398 the famous conqueror Timur invaded India, temporarily restraining Muslim rule in northern India. For the most part, Muslim rulers agreed that all non-Muslims in India were to pay the *jizyah* tax (which was originally applied only to the "People of the Book," that is, Jews and Christians). This policy proved to be a good source of revenue but caused much resentment among populace. Initially Muslim power was confined primarily to northern India, but in the thirteenth century independent Muslim kingdoms were established in the Deccan. Finally, most of India was unified by the Mughal dynasty (1526–1761), whereby the Muslim rule of India lasted until the modern period.

Sikhism. The most amazing fact about Muslim India was that a relatively small number of Muslims ruled the non-Muslim Indian majority. Understandably, there were various kinds of Muslim reactions to Hinduism and different Hindu responses to Islam. In principle, as Hutchison once observed, "For Islam, only conversion could be a satisfactory conclusion, and Hindu India . . . remained unconverted, [whereas] for Hinduism, assimilation of the new faith would have been satisfactory, but Islam . . . remained unassimilated."[55] One of the most important results of the encounter between Islam and Hinduism was the emergence of Sikhism, an eclectic faith influenced by the bhakti movement—advocated by the aforementioned Rāmānuja (1017–1137) and Rāmānanda (1360–1470) as well as by Rāmānanda's disciple, Kabīr (around 1440–1518)—and Sufi mysticism instigated by Guru Nānak (1469–1539). Both Kabīr and Nānak taught the brotherhood of Hindu and Muslim, the fatherhood of the same god, and opposition to idolatry and caste practice. (The next chapter covers the subsequent development of Sikhism.)

BUDDHISM AS A PAN-ASIAN RELIGION

I once characterized the pattern of civilizational and religious topography as that of "juxtaposition and identity," using William S. Haas's phrase, in contradistinction with the Western pattern of "unity in variety."[56] The exception in the East is Buddhism, which migrated from India to establish itself as a pan-Asian religion. Instead of following its development historically, we will describe the expansion of its three main branches.

(1) Southern Buddhism, variously known as Hīnayāna (Small Vehicle) or Theravāda, mainly followed the ocean route and established its synthesis of religion-culture-society-political order in the South and Southeast Asian countries. Theravāda, which made Ceylon its secondary center, incorporated native chthonic elements and some features of Hinduism into its tradition. As a religious system, Southern Buddhism is grounded in the Pali canon (Tripiṭaka)—the three baskets (collections) of Discipline, Discourses, and Doctrinal Elaborations. Theoretically it is a monastic-centered religion with a focus on the spiritual pursuit of monastics seeking release, while the laity partakes of the spiritual merits of the monastics by supporting them. Besides monastics, kings and other royal figures who support the Buddhist synthesis of religion-culture-society-political order are venerated by southern Buddhists. Many kings in Ceylon and the Southeast Asian kingdoms were inspired by the images of Metteyya (Maitreya in Sanskrit), the future Buddha, and of Cakkavatti (Cakravārtin in Sanskrit), the ideal universal monarch who is expected to come at the end of world history. They emulated the example of Aśoka, the Buddhist king *par excellence* in third century B.C. India. Practically, and from the perspective of the Buddhist synthesis, Southern Buddhism is not only a "monastic system," but is simultaneously an "ideological system" and a "ritual system."[57] Southern Buddhism produced interlocking systems of what Spiro calls "nibbanic Buddhism," a normative system that aims at release from the Wheel (of saṃsāra),

"kammatic Buddhism," a nonnormative soteriological system that aims at improving one's position on the Wheel, and "apotropaic Buddhism," a nonsoteriological system that seeks magical protection.[58]

(2) Northern Buddhism, also known as Mahāyāna (Great Vehicle), followed the historical silk route to Central Asia and China. There it encountered Greek and Persian cultures, arts, and religions—Zoroastrianism and Manicheism, Brahmanism, indigenous Chinese systems, and Christianity. Initially Mahāyāna imitated Indian Buddhism, but it soon discovered that it could make a contribution to the Chinese form of a cooperative synthesis of religion-culture-society-political order. In fact, Mahāyāna Buddhism, which made China its secondary center, began to expand into China's neighbors, for example, Vietnam, Korea, and Japan. Unlike its southern counterpart, which dominated the structure of religious-cultural-social-political synthesis, Mahāyāna Buddhism played a humbler role of becoming a supplement to—but not a replacement for—other traditions, such as Confucianism and Taoism in China, and Shinto and Confucianism in Japan.

(3) The third branch of Buddhism, Tantric Buddhism, also known as Vajrayāna (Vehicle of the Thunderbolt) or Mantrayāna (Vehicle of the Sacred Word), is a form of esoteric religion. Its secondary center is Tibet, from which it spread to Mongolia. Tantric Buddhism developed a synthesis of religion-culture-society-political order that resembles "theocracy" in the West. At one time different traditions of Tantric Buddhism were known in Southeast Asia, China, and Japan; but with the exception of certain schools in Japan, most lost their identities.

Thus, Buddhism, which lost ground in India where it originated, became the most influential religion in Asia. It was instrumental in bringing about at least three different kinds of syntheses of religion-culture-society-political order.

LAYERS OF CHINESE SYNTHESES

Rapidly growing China came in contact with many other peoples, cultures, and religions. Buddhism, according to a legend, was

welcomed to the Han court by Emperor Ming (reign A.D. 58–
75). In the history of China, the long Han dynasty stood for one
of the grand syntheses of religion-culture-society-political order.
So classical Confucianism, for example, came to be homologized
with Taoism, the Yin-Yang system, Legalism, divination, nu-
merology, and popular superstition to the extent that the Confucian purist Herrllee Creel questions whether it can still properly
be called Confucianism.[59]

As a vision of the unity of humankind, the comprehensive
Han synthesis was infinitely more satisfying than classical Confucianism, which had been primarily a system of positive rules
and injunctions pertaining to the social order. In sharp contrast
to classical Confucianism, the Han synthesis, which incorporated
the Yin-Yang, Taoist, Legalist and other traditions, astrology,
magic, divination, etc., postulated cosmic and natural orders,
trying to find inseparable connections between terrestrial and
celestial events. Li, which had been taught by classical Confucian
masters to be the principle of human, ethical order, was now
transformed into the universal principle of cosmic order that
governs the entire human race—crossing racial, cultural, religious, and political lines. The Han synthesis influenced peoples
far beyond the Chinese border. Its comprehensive structure was
succinctly stated by George Sansom:

- One original principle at the root of existence
- Two poles, negative and positive, male and female
- Three manifestations, Heaven, Earth and Man
- Four motions—in space the four cardinal points, in time
  the four seasons
- Five elements—wood, fire, earth, metal, water, which con-
  trol the rhythm of life
- Six kinships—ruler and subject, father and child, husband
  and wife
- And so forth on a diagrammatic basis which assumes that
  the course of nature and the course of human events are
  interrelated.[60]

The foundation of the Han synthesis, which achieved a
coherent outlook on cosmic, natural, social, and human orders,

was a moral principle that was social in character. The principle emphasized virtues, duties, obligations, and conformity. The Han synthesis contributed much to the organization of society, but the impact of its *li*, based on Sansom's study of Japanese minds and hearts, "has not been so great as the impact of such Buddhist notions as karma and rebirth. . . ."[61] Moreover, by the time Buddhism came to China, it was no longer a simple, regional religion of Indian ascetics. In addition, Buddhism arrived in China while the Han Chinese synthesis was still being worked out. In this situation, Buddhism had much to contribute to China, for example, Greco-Buddhist art, new architecture, attractive music, sophisticated philosophies, and elegant ceremonials. By A.D. 166 Buddhism had penetrated the imperial court of Emperor Huan. The Han synthesis, which underlay the *Pax Sinica*, was greatly disrupted in A.D. 166 by the power struggle among old aristocratic families, eunuchs, the *nouveaux riches* and intelligentsia, as well as by the Yellow Turban rebellion in 184.

The deepening social and political crisis created a renewed interest in Taoist classics, especially the writings of Chuang-tzu and Lao-tzu, which stressed the virtue of "naturalness" (*tzu-jan*). The period between the end of the Han dynasty in 220 and the reunification of China by the Sui dynasty (581–618), succeeded by the T'ang (618–907), was a turbulent era in China, governed by many competing dynasties. In this unsettling environment Neo-Taoists expounded Taoist and sometimes Buddhaized-Taoist ideas in their famous dialogues (*ch'ing-t'an*). The cultural gulf, which Buddhism embodied within itself, between Indian and Chinese, was greatly eased by the Taoist thinkers, terminology, and communities. (For example, Buddhism owed much to the Taoist tradition in developing the so-called *ko-i* process of matching Indian ideas and plausible Chinese meanings.)

The fall of Lo-yang, the capital of Western Chin (which accomplished a precarious and short-lived unity of China following the rivalry of the three kingdoms, that is, Tsao-Wei, Shu, and Wu), sacked by Hsiungnu horsemen in 311, was as devastating as the sack of Rome by the Goths in 411.[62] The end of the Chin in 316 marked the division of China into two geographical divisions. North China, where Chinese civilization had historically grown up, fell into the hands of the Turko-Mongolian "barbarians" for 150 years. The traditional mainline Chinese civilization, the heir to the Han synthesis, moved to the Yangtze River basin in South China with Nanking (often called the Byzantium of East Asia) as its capital. What took place was the Sinicization of former provincial *territories* in the South and the Sinicization of former barbarian *peoples* in the North. This process provided new creative impulse both to the southern and northern cultures. Buddhism played very different roles in the religious development of the South and North.

Southern China.   In southern China the native aristocrats tended to be conservative traditionalists, nostalgic for the Confucian-centered Han synthesis. They resented the newcomers from the North, especially the effete Neo-Taoist enthusiasts. They welcomed Buddhism, not as the replacement of, but as a supplement to, the synthesis of the religion-culture-society-political order that had taken the Confucian-Taoist dialectic for granted. They were greatly impressed by the figure of Vimalakīrti, who quickly became a paradigmatic model for lay Chinese Buddhists. As Arthur Wright observes: "He was not a naked ascetic but a rich and powerful aristocrat, a brilliant talker, a respected householder and father, a man who denied himself no luxury or pleasure yet possessed so pure and disciplined a personality that he changed all whom he met for the better."[63] One of the most famous Buddhist monks in southern China was Chih Tun (314–366) who, according to Kenneth Ch'en, best represented the "conjunction of Prajñā and Neo-Taoist thought." For example, he gave a new metaphysical meaning, derived from Prajñā philosophy, to the Chinese term, *li*, the natural order of the universe or reason. Thus, Chih Tun

> interpreted it [*li*] as the transcendental absolute principle. . . . In the writings of the Buddhists from the fourth to the tenth centuries, *li* as the absolute was regularly opposed by *shih*, mundane events or facts of empirical experience. Later on, the Neo-Confucians took over this pair, keeping *li* in the sense of the absolute truth, but opposing it with *ch'i*, vital energy or matter.[64]

Another Buddhist cleric who depended heavily on Taoistic insights was Hui-yüan (334–416). Deeply interested in Buddhism as a religion of salvation, he was one of the earliest advocates of the Pure Land sect, which believed in salvation through faith in Amitābha. Hui-yüan's distinction in social status between the monks and lay devotees is well known. He wrote an apologetic treatise "about the śramaṇa not paying homage to the ruler," but was persuaded that lay devotees were expected to respect secular authority.[65] He had a group of unusually talented lay followers.[66] Hui-yüan lived in the South, but he was in close contact with Buddhist activities in the North, especially with the translation efforts of Kumārajīva. Another important Buddhist figure in South China was Chu Tao-sheng (365–434), who pursued the differences in the two paths toward salvation—"gradualism" (*chen*), reminiscent of the Confucian temper, and "sudden (*tun*) enlightenment," similar to some Taoist formulae.[67] This distinction was later carried over to the Ch'an (Zen) tradition.

For the most part, Buddhism in South China, being a supplement to the new synthesis that was still evolving, aspired to a modest place in society, having its own groups and praying for the welfare of the realm. Buddhism conferred extravagant titles, for example, *Chiu-shih p'u-sa* (Savior Bodhisattva) or *P'u-sa t'ien-tzu* (Bodhisattva Son of Heaven), on rulers, such as Emperor Wu of the Liang (reign 502–549), who supported the cause of Buddhism as "patrons."

Northern China.   The Buddhization of North China and the Sinicization of former "barbarian" peoples were, in one sense, parallel movements. The combination of the two resulted in the gradual Sinicization of Buddhism. The new northerners, the non-Han peoples originally from the other side of the Great Wall, had a sort of Freudian—love and hate—relationship to things Chinese. They were eager to become naturalized culturally without losing their original identities altogether. They were somewhat suspicious of the Confucian tradition, which had been the backbone of the Han synthesis. Buddhism was an attractive alternative, especially since the Buddhist *dharma* was universalistic, emphasizing common human existence rather than the racial, national, and cultural backgrounds of peoples. Besides, North China was directly accessible to the silk road through which Buddhist missionaries, scriptures, art, architecture, music, and culture came to China.

The pioneer Buddhist missionaries to North China came from the Indo-Scythian empire of the Kuchans, like the famous Fo-t'utend who came to China around 310. In North China, too, Buddhism initially was welcomed by Neo-Taoists. Wright says upper-class Chinese, who had remained in the North,

> followed the pattern of their counterparts in the South; a substratum of solid Confucian training at home, unsatisfying experiments with neo-Taoism, and then conversion to a faith which seemed to explain the ills of a stricken society and to offer hope for the future. It is from this class that the great thinkers and teachers of northern Buddhism in this period were recruited.[68]

A proper understanding of Buddhism was achieved by Tao-an (314–385). He denounced the Buddhist-Taoist syncretism and urged people to interpret Buddhism in its own logic. In order to improve the quality of the available Chinese texts of Buddhist scriptures, Tao-an persuaded the authorities to invite Kumārajīva (350–409), a linguistic genius, to settle in the capital to work on new translations of scriptures. Thanks to the efforts of missionaries and Chinese monks, many scriptures of various schools and persuasions were translated into Chinese.

Along with scriptures came the images of many Buddhas and Bodihisattvas, enriching the Buddhist pantheon in China. Among them were the popular savior deities, reflecting the Mahāyāna orientation that became the mainstream of Buddhism in China—Maitreya (Mi-lo-fo), Avalokiteśvara (Kuan-yin), Amitābha (A-mi-t'o), etc. In northern Chinese kingdoms, Northern Wei (387–534) became a great promoter of Buddhism. This was one of the Altaic tribes also known as the T'o-pa. Although the earlier Wei kings were anti-Buddhist, the kings after 453 became ardent supporters of Buddhism. In 453, the construction of the Buddhist rock shrines, which were earlier suppressed by anti-Buddhist kings, resumed in the cliffs of Yünkang. During the fifth century the Wei kings systematically destroyed their rivals and dominated northern China. Their policies, specifically their reforms of law and the civil service, were quite advanced. From the time of King Hung (reign 471–479) the Wei abandoned their Turkish dialect and spoke only Chinese.[69] It was reported that in 477 the Buddhist community in the North reached 6,478 temples and 77,258 monks and nuns, whereas "the statistics for south China . . . show 2,015 temples with a clergy of 32,500."[70] In 494, Lo-yang became the capital of Wei, and from 508 to 515 the Weis "had dug out and fitted as Buddhist rock shrines the black lime-stone cliff wall of the Lung-men pass, some eight miles south of Lo-yang."[71] To the end, the Wei kings contributed to the embellishment of the Lung-men sanctuaries, which also show the predominance of the statues of Śākyamuni and Maitreya built by the Wei kings. The popularity later changed in favor of Amitābha and Avalokiteśvara, whose images were built during the T'ang dynasty (around 650–710).[72]

I agree with Arthur Wright's observation about the general characteristics of Buddhism in northern China. Northern kings were closer to the Caesaro-papist monarchs of the Byzantine empire. As such, northern Buddhism had to come to terms with "autocracy," whereas in the South, Buddhism had to struggle with "aristocracy."[73]

THE SUI-T'ANG SYNTHESIS—THE MULTIVALUE SYSTEM

The unification of China was achieved by the Sui dynasty (561–618), and the united China continued to be governed by the T'ang dynasty (618–907), which followed the Sui. The brillance of T'ang China was such that the Sui kings often tend to be eclipsed, but actually the Sui dynasty had prepared much of the solid foundation of T'ang China. Even though many books on art and Buddhism leave the impression that the united China between the seventh and ninth centuries was inspired primarily by Buddhism, the basic structure of the Sui-T'ang synthesis heavily depended on a multivalue system that held in balance Confucianism, Buddhism, and Taoism as well as a synthesis of the northern and southern legal traditions. Wen-ti (reign 584–604), the founder of the Sui dynasty, who behaved more like a Caesaro-papist than many of the Byzantine monarchs, unified China with a self-conscious ideology of the multivalue system, domesticating Confucianism and Buddhism, and Taoism to a lesser degree. He used them as the arms of the emperor, whose claim to a semidivine prerogative was sanctioned and authenticated by various religious symbols.[74] Prefiguring the T'ang system, Wen-ti established an efficient government based on three departments with six ministries. He revived the civil service system and streamlined the local governments. He bequeathed to his son, Yang-ti (reign 605–617), an empire unrivaled in prosperity since the Han dynasty (202 B.C.–A.D. 220). Yang-ti repaired and extended the Great Wall and improved the nationwide grand canal system, thus facilitating the nation's administrative, defense, and economic life.

The T'ang dynasty (618–907) greatly improved the government structure that it had inherited from the Sui, solidified the military system, and developed the Chinese version of *oecumene* in its vast empire that stretched from the China Sea to the Tarim basin. Under T'ang rule China was one of the most advanced nations in the world. Its culture was unusually cosmopolitan, with students, merchants, and religious people going between China and Europe, Persia, India, Indonesia, Korea, and Japan via overland and sea routes. The ruling house of the T'ang was made up of the descendants of Lao-tzu, but the government allowed all domestic and foreign religious traditions, including Islam, Judaism, Nestorian Christianity, Zoroastrianism, Manicheism, and Hinduism. The most visible was Buddhism.

T'ang China was greatly influenced by Tantric Buddhism, called *Chen-yen* or "True Word Sect" in Chinese. It was transmitted by Śubhakarasiṃha (died 735), Vajrabodhi (died 723), and Amoghavajra or Pu-k'ung (705–774). The latter was an instructor to the three successive T'ang monarchs and translator of more than one hundred Buddhist texts. Chen-yen Buddhism, which prospered in Japan, was destined to disappear as a distinct school in China, but its rites for ancestors became essential features of popular religion and were later copied by Taoist esoteric groups. During the T'ang period two other Buddhist schools—Ch'an (Zen) and Pure Land—became well established. A combination of these two schools became the main tradition of Chinese Buddhism. T'ang Buddhism also produced the famous traveller Hsüan-tsang (602–664), who wrote an account of his visit to central Asia and India. His translation of the Buddhist texts that he brought back greatly enriched the Chinese understanding of Buddhism. Empress Wu (died 705), one of the most famous (or infamous) Buddhist rulers of the T'ang era, known for her ability, piety, and cruelity was convinced that she was the incarnation of Maitreya.[75] Yet she did some positive things for Buddhism, such as dedicating the rock Buddha statue of Lung-men and assisting the overseas travel and translation work of I-tsing (635–713). He was author of *A Record of the Buddhist Religion as Practised in India and the Malay Archipelago*.[76] But Wu's arbitrary measures and cruelty also caused much anti-Buddhist sentiment.

The Sui-T'ang synthesis of religion-culture-society-political order, based on the multivalue system, declined because of the T'ang dynasty's disruption, caused by the rebellion (753–763) of An Lu-Shan. He was one of the generals, half Sogdian and half Turk, who controlled the northeastern frontier. The government, greatly weakened by the rebellion, withdrew troops from its outlying provinces. This encouraged the rise to power of various peoples, such as the Tibetans and the Uighurs. Government policies, which had taken the importance of northern China for granted, were slow to adjust to social and economic changes, for example, the steady growth of the Yangtze Valley, and the central government could no longer ignore the power of eunuchs. Partly as a reaction to the pro-Buddhist measures, there was a suppression of Buddhism in 842 and 845, plotted by the Confucian and Taoist elements. This brought about the destruction of temples, a reduction in the number of priests and nuns, and confiscation of temple properties. The government managed to subdue several minor rebellions during the 860s and 870s, but China was destined to be divided into many regional powers: the five dynasties in the North and the ten kingdoms mostly in the South, that ruled China from 907 till 959.

NEO-CONFUCIAN SYNTHESIS: PHASE 1

The next great synthesis of religion-culture-society-political order, referred to as "neo-Confucianism" in the West, took a long time in formation, roughly from the Sung (960–1279) to the Ming (1368–1644) dynasties. Between them was the Mongol Yüan dynasty (1276–1368), which had its own agenda and did not contribute to the neo-Confucian synthesis. Scholars differentiate the Reason School of the Sung Period from the Mind School of the Ming Period as two different theoretical bases for the synthesis. There is also the Empirical School of the Manchu Ch'ing Period (1644–1911), the third theoretical pillar of the neo-Confucian synthesis.

The Sung period can be divided into two distinct sub-periods—Northern Sung (960–1126) and Southern Sung (1127–1179). During this time the northernmost part of China (Manchuria, Inner Mongolia, etc.) was ruled by the Liao dynasty (904–1125) of the Khitan tribe. Its rule collapsed with the attack of the Jurchen Chin dynasty (1115–1234), a Tungusic people in Manchuria. Meanwhile the territory around modern Ningsia was ruled by the kingdom of Hsi Hsia (around 990–1227) of the Tibetan-related Tanguts people. Having the non-Han people in the North caused the Chinese to be self-conscious about their cultural identity during the Sung period. And, following the T'ang dynasty, which supported Buddhism and Taoism, many thinkers during the Sung period tended to think of Confucianism as the pristine essence of the Chinese tradition. Thus, the neo-Confucian synthesis was a complex phenomenon, containing a heavy emphasis on cultural nationalism from the Sung and later Ming eras, which incorporated a lot of Buddhist influence and yet emotionally reacted against Buddhism. The neo-Confucian synthesis was quite able to deal with the secular affairs of government, the economy, and culture, while maintaining semireligious passions and principles.

Li Kou, one of the early Sung theoreticians, was preoccupied by the need for the enlightened rule and the enrichment of the country—not in terms of levying excessive taxes but by strengthening the government and removing unnecessary expenditures. His proposal touched on various practical affairs, such as land reform, military strategy, and the production of metals, silk, and grain. Buddhist and Taoist monks were superfluous consumers from his perspective. He listed such factors as "(1) the monks are clothed and fed by the peasants without doing any work themselves; (2) they are celibate but lead unchaste lives; (3) they avoid corvée labor; . . . (10) lazy people and rascals take refuge with them."[77] He objected to Buddhism because its teachings did not surpass those of Confucianism. "Why then," he asked, "should one tear the cap off one's head and crawl before the barbarians?"[78] Like many other neo-Confucians, Li Kou was convinced of the correctness of the positivist Weltanschaung of the Confucian tradition. To him, Confucian rules of social behavior not only did not contradict human nature but "made possible the free unfolding of [humankind's] natural endowments."[79] Similarly, Chu Hsi (died 1200), the spokesman of the Reason School of the Sung period, maintained that all things are composed of *li* (ordering principles) and *ch'i* (material force). Not only did he hold *li* as the metaphysical principle of government, he presupposed the presence of *li* before the beginning of the world. To Chu Hsi the ultimate standard of the universe is *T'ai Chi* (the Supreme Ultimate): "Everything has an ultimate, which is the ultimate Li. That which unites and embraces the Li of heaven, earth, and all things is the Supreme Ultimate."[80] According to Chu Hsi, we attain enlightenment only by bringing out the Supreme Ultimate that is within us through the extension of knowledge and the attentiveness of mind.

Chu Hsi's selection of the so-called Four Books: the *Analects of Confucius*, the *Book of Mencius*, the *Great Learning*, and the *Doctrine of the Mean* had an impact on the neo-Confucian synthesis. These books were venerated together with the traditional Five Classics of Confucianism: *Book of Odes*, *Book of History*, *Book of Changes*, *Book of Rites*, and *Spring and Autumn Annals*. For the next seven hundred years the Four Books as well as the Five Classics helped shape the minds of Chinese intellectuals. Dun J. Li feels that "whatever advantages it might have, the selection unfortunately compelled students to be unoriginal and conforming and often made them mere echoes of stereotyped ideas."[81]

MONGOL CHINA: AN INTERLUDE

China was ruled for nearly a century by the Yüan dynasty (1276–1368) of the Mongols, the traditional enemy of the Chinese.

During this period, there was no significant movement toward the development of a neo-Confucian synthesis. The Yüan dynasty followed the pattern of the Sui-T'ang synthesis. In sharp contrast to Chinese dynasties, traditionally dependent on scholar-bureaucrats well versed in Confucian classics, the nomad conquerors imposed a military government coexisting with Chinese-type institutions administered through intermediaries. The most powerful was the Central Secretariat that supervised six traditional ministries. Partly because the Mongols did not trust Chinese civilian officials, and partly because the Mongols were very cosmopolitan, they appointed government officials from various nationalities. Thus,

> side by side with Marco Polo, who was a confidential adviser to the great Khan, we find Tibetan monks, Nestorian artisans, Uighur technological experts, Transoxanians, Turco-Iranians, Arabs, and merchants from Central Asia, all of them glib and intelligent as liaison officers, astute as men of business, and devoid of scruple in financial transactions.[82]

We had earlier seen how Mongol forces threatened medieval Muslims and Europeans. Although they were originally adherents of the Mongolian form of shamanism, part of them became Tibetan Buddhists, while others became Muslims. As monarchs, the Yüan rulers were tolerant of all religions in their realm, including Nestorianism and Roman Catholicism. Little is known about the Nestorian monk, Rabban Marcos from Suiyüan, who in 1281 was elevated to the Nestorian patriarchate and was called Mar Yabalaha III of Seleucia-Baghdad. Another Nestorian monk, Rabban Sauma, native of a place near Peking, China, was appointed in 1287 as the Persian ambassador and sent to Europe to form an alliance between the Crusaders and the Mongols against the Mamlūks of Egypt. In Paris he talked with Philip the Fair. According to Grousset:

> In Rome he was received by Pope Nicholas IV, who gave him communion with his own hands on Easter Sunday, 1288, and who discussed with him the organization of a new crusade. It was a strange destiny that led this Mongol subject, born near Peking, to become Persian ambassador to the Pope and the King of France.[83]

During the Yüan period Franciscan missionaries were allowed to enter China and a papal delegate was received by the emperor. Like Sui and T'ang monarchs, the early Mongol rulers were sensitive both to domestic and to international affairs. Under Mongol rule, China was one of the most advanced nations in the world in terms of artistic, cultural, economic, and technological standards. Gunpowder, atlases, and medical books in China were exported to Europe. The regime supported Buddhism because of the rulers' personal adherence, particularly to Tibetan Buddhism. Imperial patronage promoted Buddhist painting, sculpture, and architecture. Among the native Chinese philosophical systems, the Yüan rulers preferred Legalism. But the Yüan dynasty, once greatly admired by Marco Polo, steadily degenerated after the third emperor. The decadence of the regime encouraged strong anti-Mongol sentiment and a series of rebellions toward the latter part of the Yüan period.

NEO-CONFUCIAN SYNTHESIS: PHASE 2

With the establishment of the Ming dynasty (1368–1644) a strong wave of cultural nationalism returned to China. This was partly a reaction to the alien Mongol rule. The founder of the dynasty was previously an aspirant to the Buddhist priesthood and a follower of the Red Turban group, which was dedicated to restoring the native Sung dynasty. It is said that he chose the name, Ming (radiance), under the influence of the Manichean elements in the Red Turban group. One of the most famous Ming rulers was Yung-lo (reign 1403–1424), who usurped the throne from his nephew. Yung-lo wanted to emulate Kublai, the grand Mongol khan, but by reversing Kublai's footsteps in conquering Mongolia and making Peking the main capital of the Ming (formerly Naking was the capital). Yung-lo's majestic imperial vision included sponsoring China's maritime expedition, 1405–1433, conducted by Cheng Ho (died around 1433), a Muslim eunuch from Yunnan who commanded seven successive voyages to Southeast Asia, the Indian Ocean, the Persian Gulf, and various East African ports. Although Yung-lo was a Buddhist, he made the teaching of Chu Hsi (of the Sung period) the state doctrine of the Ming in 1416. He declared Chu Hsi's Four Books and the Confucian Five Classics as texts of equal standing and as the basis for the state civil service examinations. Unfortunately, after Yung-lo's death, the successive emperors were mediocre, a fact that partially accounts for the increased power of the eunuchs. About seventy thousand eunuchs were in service throughout most of the last century in the Ming period.[84]

Ironically, the conservative mood of the post-Yung-lo Ming period made Chu Hsi's thought seem as if it were a water-tight official positivism that dictated the neo-Confucian synthesis of religion-culture-society-political order, allowing very little imagination or speculation. Chu Hsi and other Sung thinkers managed to unify various dimensions of life and society. They tried to place an enormous amount of factors in a close circle of theory, thus trivializing spiritual insights and reflection. Fortunately, Wang Yang-ming (1472–1529), a soldier, judge, government official, and scholar, systematized the so-called Mind School of neo-Confucianism. Rejecting Chu Hsi's view of the *li* (reason) as eternal and independent of human consciousness, Wang equated the *li* with the mind and interpreted the individual mind as a manifestation of the Universal Mind. He was persuaded that in order to reach the essence of reality one should have recourse to intuitive knowledge rather than to discursive language. His Mind School was a necessary correction to the Reason School of Chu Hsi. Both taken together provided the necessary foundation for the second phase of the neo-Confucian synthesis.

The Ming dynasty had checkered relationships with Japan. The principle of a tally trade (*kangō bōeki* in Japanese) was agreed upon between the Ming and the Ashikaga Shōgunate in Japan in 1405. But the decline of the Shōgunate during the sixteenth century resulted in an increase of piracy, conducted by the Japanese joined by Koreans and Chinese, in China's coastal areas. In addition, Toyotomi Hideyoshi, the strongman in Japan (died 1598), conceived the audacious idea of invading China and dispatched his forces twice (1592 and 1597) to Korea to obtain passage. However, Hideyoshi's death ended this venture.

It is a strange fact of history that, unbeknown to Ming China, Vasco da Gama discovered the sea route to India in 1498, and the Portuguese established a settlement in Macao in 1557. With their arrival, Christianity, unknown to China since the end of the Yüan dynasty, returned to China. In 1582, Matteo Ricci (1552–1610), an Italian Jesuit, arrived in Macao. He became a trusted scientific adviser to the Ming Court. His double vocation, religious and scientific, was carried over by the German Jesuit, Adam Schall (died 1666), whose services were sought by the Manchu dynasty after the decline of the Ming dynasty. The enormous success of the Jesuits, both as missionaries and as literati, came to an end when their involvement in the "rites controversy," in which they attempted Christian accommodation of ancestor rites, was condemned by Pope Clement XI in 1704.

The next chapter will discuss what happened in China after the fall of the Ming dynasty in 1644.

JAPANESE SYNTHESES

The Japanese case demonstrates both (1) its indebtedness to Chinese civilization, and (2) the pervasive character of the pattern of juxtaposition of civilizations in Asia. Langdon Warner, on art in eighth-century Japan, writes: "T'ang dynasty of China was hanging like a brilliant brocaded background, against which we must look at Japan and its capital city of Nara to watch the eighth century, while the Japanese were at work *weaving their own brocade on patterns similar but not the same.*"[85] We must be sensitive both to the similarity and the difference between the Chinese and Japanese patterns.

I believe that there have been three main forms of synthesis of religion-culture-society-political order in Japan.

1. The first is the Ritsuryō (Imperial Rescript State), a synthesis of the seventh and eighth centuries based on three principles: a) mutual dependence between the king's way (ōdō), a homology of the native Shinto tradition and the Han Chinese synthesis of Confucianism, Taoism, Yin-Yang system, etc., and Buddha's Way (*Butsudō*); b) the amalgam of Shinto and Buddhist ecclesiastical institutions (*Shin-Butsu shūgō*); and c) the idea that the original substance of Japanese deities of the Shinto tradition

are Buddhas and Bodhisattvas in India (*honji-suijaku*). The Ritsuryō synthesis was never fully realized due to political changes caused by the dictatorship of the Fujiwara family, the rule by retired monarchs (*insei*), and the *de facto* rule by the warrior families (*bakufu* or *shōgunate*).

2. The Tokugawa Synthesis, dictated by the Tokugawa Shōgunate (1603–1867), dismissed the first Ritsuryō principle of mutual dependence between the king's way and the Buddha's way, but kept the second principle of amalgam of Shinto and Buddhist ecclesiastical institutions, as well as the third principle of equating Shinto and Buddhist deities. Instead of the principle of mutual dependence between the king's way and the Buddha's way, the Tokugawa regime appropriated, with a certain amount of reinterpretations, the basic principle of the neo-Confucian synthesis.

3. The Meiji Synthesis (1867–1945) dropped the second Ritsuryō principle of the amalgam of Shinto and Buddhist ecclesiastical institutions but kept the third principle of equating Shinto and Buddhist deities.

In the next chapter, we will discuss the Tokugawa and Meiji syntheses.

CHAPTER
4

Encounters of Peoples, Civilizations, and Religions

History has such fuzzy edges that we cannot be too precise about dates, events, peoples, and places. But we may not be wrong in believing that Columbus's discovery of the new continent in 1492 and Vasco da Gama's discovery of the ocean route to India via South Africa in 1498 marked the beginning of a new phase of world history. The new phase meant at least four things: (1) the cultural topography of the West was changing; (2) Asia, which had developed various autonomous civilizations in juxtaposition, was experiencing internal cultural erosion from India to Japan; (3) because of the availability of alternative channels of contacts between Europe and Asia, the Islamic region, which had been a stumbling block between the West and the East, was losing cultural and commercial importance as an international go-between; and (4) Europeans were beginning feverish activities in terms of migration, trade, colonial expansion, and Christian evangelism in various parts of the non-Western world. Let us first examine the dramatic changes that took place in the West.

DETERIORATION OF THE MEDIEVAL SYNTHESIS AND ITS AFTERMATH

The last chapter briefly discussed the main features of the medieval synthesis of religion-culture-society-political order, which was dominated by religious concerns and ecclesiastical authority even though a stable pattern of ecclesiastical authority did not exist. There seems to be much truth in Bryan Wilson's observation that

> The Church controlled not only the moral fabric of society (perhaps that least of all), but the formal process of political, juridical, commercial, and social intercourse—the institutional operation of society. . . . Society was ordered to effect the glorification of God, to protect the Church, to make plain the afterlife of the righteous and the unrighteous, but all that did not, of course, ensure equal and uniform dedication to God in the hearts of men. Even for that age, "the age of faith" is perhaps a misnomer: we should refer only to the age of religiously-prescribed social order.[1]

Such a religiously prescribed medieval synthesis declined in the face of humanism—advocated initially by the Italian Renaissance in the fourteenth century but that soon spread to other parts of Europe. A multidimensional phenomenon such as the Renaissance (literally "rebirth," referring to the thought, wisdom, literature, and art of antiquity), did not happen like the blast of a sudden trumpet. Arnold Toynbee stated that the earlier infusion of the new blood of the invading Goths and Lombards into Italian veins might have had something to do with it. In his own words: "This elixir of life produced in due course, and after centuries of incubation, the Italian rebirth or Renaissance."[2] But I am inclined to look for more obvious factors—the decline of feudalism, the growing popularity of the vernacular with the increase of national consciousness, the development of towns, trade, industry, the rise of the middle class, etc.—which had prepared for and eventually contributed to the emergence of the new cultural mood of the Renaissance. In so stating, I am stressing the Renaissance simultaneously as the climax and breakdown of the medieval European synthesis.

SCHOLASTICISM, THE UNIVERSITY, AND THE RENAISSANCE

Thanks to the mediation of the Muslims in Spain, Sicily, and Provence, the Latin translations (from the Arabic) of "all the logical works and most of the physical, metaphysical, and ethical works of Aristotle" became available in Europe by 1200, although the Aristotle thus presented was a heavily "orientalized" Aristotle altered by Muslim and Jewish thinkers.[3] The great Christian thinkers of the time, for example, Albertus Magnus (around 1200–1280) and his pupil Thomas Aquinas (1225–1274), were greatly influenced by Muslim and Jewish interpretations of Aristotle. However, the Scholasticism of thirteenth-century Europe, which in a sense prepared the intellectual ground for the Renaissance, tried to come to terms with Aristotle at the very time he was being discarded by Islamic and Jewish thinkers. Usually, Scholasticism is regarded as the embodiment of the (pure) Latin spirit. In fact, prior to 1200 both Islamic thinking and the Greek rhetoric of the Alexandrian tradition (which Augustine and other earlier Christian thinkers had taken for granted as the necessary lining of Christian faith) were influential in Europe. Aquinas, the scholastic *par excellence*, was undoubtedly a brilliant thinker, but "like most of the other scholastic theologians, he had no knowledge of Greek and Hebrew, and was almost equally ignorant of history. . . ."[4]

Scholasticism was influential in developing the university as one of the three great medieval institutions—*Sacerdotium, Imperium*, and *Studium*—in thirteenth-century Europe. Roger Bacon (around 1214–1292), the English Franciscan scholar interested in medicine, astronomy, gunpowder, the calendar, and mathematics, as well as others like him reformulated university curriculum according to the principles of Aristotelian science and the attitude of experiment. Although theology as a theoretical discipline claimed to be the queen of *scientia*, Scholasticism, trying to overcome the conflict between reason and faith, gradually gave way to a spirit of scientific inquiry and humanism. This tendency was particularly evident in Italy where Scholasticism was not as strong as it was in France and other European countries. Italy also had a rich heritage in poetry, literature, architecture, sculpture, and painting. This was exemplified by such notables as Dante (died 1321), Petrarch (died 1374), and Giotto (died 1337). These people lived and breathed in the medieval religious world, but they shifted the center of gravity from heaven to earth, and affirmed the supreme importance of the individual, up to this time not fully appreciated by the Greek or Roman traditions. While adhering to the doctrine of medieval Christendom, Dante presented it from the perspective of the pilgrimage of the human soul seeking meaning and a sense of fulfillment on earth as well as in heaven. For the most part, artists of the Renaissance tradition presented people as they lived in their environment. They did not think that art must have an edifying moral message. In so doing, these Italian artists and men of letters foreshadowed the mood and spirit of the modern period.

REFORMATION, THE NATIONAL CHURCHES, COUNTER-REFORMATION

Reformation. The humanism of the Italian Renaissance nurtured some anti-ecclesiastical elements. When it crossed the Alps to more conservative northern Europe it became a motivating force behind church reform, an important motif for the emerging national churches. There were many Protestant reformations, but the one initiated by Martin Luther (1483–1546) deserves special attention.

The Reformation, like any historically significant event, prefigured itself in early signs and symptoms. Some scholars are persuaded that 1303—when Pope Boniface VIII, who claimed that the papacy had both spiritual and temporal power in his bull *Unam Sanctam*, was humiliated by French mercenaries in Anagni—marked the end of the medieval monarchical papacy. The incident of Anagni exhibited the inner dissolution of the authority structure of medieval Christendom. According to Francis Oakley:

> . . . the subsequent transfer of the papacy from Rome to Avignon . . . the emergence of the nominalist theology, the retreat from the externals of religion reflected in the mysticism of Germany, the Netherlands, and England, the onset of the Great Schism, the rise in the conciliar movement of opposition to the pretensions of Rome, the more radical undermining by Wycliffe and Hus of the whole hierarchical order of the church—all these and more were seen as

a series of interrelated developments leading inexorably to the final onset of the Protestant Reformation.[5]

Within Roman Catholicism opponents of the English Franciscan William of Ockham (died 1349) were convinced that the nominalism he advocated was unacceptable to the mainline theological tradition of medieval Christendom. They often suggested that, inasmuch as Luther was influenced by Ockham, he was rebelling against a Catholicism that was not really Catholic.[6] There may be some truth to such a view, but it seems that the main issue motivating Luther was the age-old problem of the earthly church vs. deity rather than nominalism vs. realism. Moreover, as a member of the Augustinian order, Luther had a high regard for the ecclesiastical hierarchy. Even though he was a medieval churchman in his theological temperament, he was also convinced of the tripartite authority of *Sacerdotium*, *Imperium*, and *Studium*. What Luther learned at the university (*Studium*) about the Bible and about theology—the doctrine of justification by faith alone and its theological implications as set forth by Paul and Augustine—had different kinds of truth claims that were as valid as the *magisterium* of the church (*Sacerdotium*). The occasion that started his Reformation in 1517 was the sale of indulgences needed for the construction of St. Peter's basilica in Rome.

Ironically, Luther's Reformation mainly got off the ground because of political considerations, both on the parts of *Sacerdotium* and *Imperium*. In 1520, Pope Leo, one of the most extravagant Renaissance popes (pope 1513–1521), declared that Luther would be excommunicated unless he returned to the church by the following winter. But Luther burned the papal bull along with the books of Canon Law with the backing of the elector of Saxony and other supporters. Then in 1521, Emperor Charles V (died 1558), heir to the Spanish and Habsburg dynasties and a grandson of the Catholic kings (Isabella of Castile and Ferdinand of Aragon), summoned Luther to the Diet of Worms and condemned him by imperial edict. Since Charles had four main enemies, the Turks, the Protestants, the French (King Francis I), and the papacy (in that order), it was impossible to fight all four simultaneously. He was compelled to compromise with the lesser evil as the occasion demanded. He needed the solid backing of German princes and electors for his effort against French influence and thus did not enforce the Edict of Worms against Luther and the Protestants. Meanwhile, Adrian VI (pope 1522–1523) was drawn into the political activities of Charles V. With Pope Adrian on his side, Charles managed to drive the French forces out of Italy.

Clement VIII, who had been appointed as a cardinal by his cousin and fellow member of the Medici family, Leo X, succeeded Adrian. Like Leo, Clement also depleted the papal treasury by hiring Raphael and Michelangelo. Earlier he had supported Charles V, but shifted his allegiance to the French king, Francis I. Charles then invaded Rome and took the pope prisoner. At this time the English king, Henry VIII, asked for a papal annulment of his marriage to Catherine of Aragon. Since the pope was under the thumb of Charles V, who among other things was king of Spain, Clement declined Henry's request. He was relieved that he did not have to decide on the emperor's extramarital affair, for Charles never made it an official issue. The emperor called the Second Diet of Speyer, reiterating the Edict of Worms against Lutherans. Then the pope officially agreed to crown Charles V as the emperor. This was the last time a pope crowned a Holy Roman emperor.

In 1530, Luther was condemned at the Diet of Augsburg, but Charles made concessions to Protestant princes because support was needed to face the Turks threatening Vienna—hence the truce of Nuremberg in 1532 between the emperor and the German princes. The Emperor began an expedition against the Turks in 1535 and the following year declared war against France who had allied with the Turks. After a short-lived peace with France, the emperor waged another war with them from 1542 until 1544.

The National Churches. A close relationship existed between the Reformation and the rising "national churches" in Europe. In Eastern Christendom the Caesaropapian principle treated *sacerdotium* as though it were a department of *imperium* in that *jus publicum* contained the *jus sacrum;*[7] but in Western Christendom, where popes and monarchs always competed for power, the erosion of the Roman form of *sacerdotium* inevitably nurtured the growth of the territorial churches. The medieval European synthesis of the church and state was based on the assumption that "both in the spiritual and in the temporal realm the social fabric was held together by habit and custom, by reverence and faith, agreement and loyalty, by many of the customs involved in the holding of property in common, and by a mutual helpfulness. . . ."[8] The erosion of the papal church coincided with the decline of the German-Roman empire. Neither the pope nor the emperor could forestall the weakening of the "organic unity" of feudalism and the growth of social differentiation, occurring largely as a result of the popularization of vernacular languages and the increase in cultural contacts, trade, and national consciousness. Actually, Western Christendom was never fully consolidated. The Western European and English princes and monarchs always enjoyed a certain amount of independence. Nevertheless, the modern nation-states did not develop in Europe until after the disintegration of the papal church, the increasing division of labor, and revolutions in thought, communication, commerce, and industry. Not surprisingly, the church viewed the growth of nationalism with suspicion. In the fifteenth century, Machiavelli was considered blasphemous because "he preferred his country to the safety of his soul,"[9] and patriotism was condemned as "a plague and the most certain death of Christian love" by a seventeenth-century Jesuit general.[10] However, the pope and the emperor were as helpless against the rising tide of nationalism as they were against the Reformation.

Two more points concerning the Reformation are worth mentioning. First, the reformers were deeply concerned with reforming and restoring the essential character of the ecclesia as the covenanted community of faith. For example, Luther's view of the church was characterized by Troeltsch as "the Catholic theory of the Church, only purified and renewed. . . . It is a transformation of the idea of a merely universal, all-inclusive Church . . . into the earlier and more primitive conception of a pure Christocentric religion which exalted the idea of grace and faith."[11] Accordingly, Luther understood the church as a "people," "God's people," the "community of believers," and the *"communio sanctorum."* Pauck observes that Luther disliked the term "church." He goes on to say that Luther "preferred to translate the Greek word 'ekklesia' and the Latin word *ecclesia* . . . into the German terms *Gemeinde* (community), *Gemeine* (congregation), *Sammlung* or *Versammlung* (assembly), *Haufe* (crowd, people), *Christenheit* (Christendom, the unity of all Christian people)."[12] Second, in rejecting the papal church's view of the ecclesiastification of the whole social order, the reformers were nevertheless deeply conscious of the fact that the church must manifest itself in the whole social order, which, according to them, was also ordained by God. Thus Luther stated: "The family (*economia*) is the natural order (*ordinatio*), the state or magistrate (*politia*) the protecting order, and the church (*ecclesia*) the spiritual order, and by submission to them the communion of believers can be actualized in this world."[13] Such a view of the church's relationship to the social order took seriously the nation-states that were becoming increasingly important and replacing outmoded feudalism in Europe.

In this connection, Wach observed that after the Reformation, European states had to choose among three alternatives— "(1) remaining loyal to the traditional faith and the established religious community, (2) embracing and establishing one of the Reformed faiths as the official religion of the state, or (3) declining an identification with any of the competing cults."[14] Spain, France (until the French Revolution), and the Italian states chose the first; Saxony, Prussia, and Sweden the second; significantly, the USA alone eventually adopted the third. Incidentally, in every European country, including those that remained within the Roman Catholic orbit, the ruler determined the creed of the subjects. Nevertheless, in both the Catholic and Protestant nations, the medieval form of *sacerdotium* was destined to be radically reinterpreted. For all intents and purposes, the "universal" church became a national church or a state religion. In the main, Europe accepted five types of Christian states, including Eastern Orthodox, Roman Catholic, Reformed, Anglican, and Lutheran.

The national churches did not follow the same or similar principles in regard to the relation of the church and the state. Considerable differences existed among the five major types. For example, the national churches of the Lutheran tradition inherited Luther's idea of two kingdoms or regimes. Some people regard Luther's idea of two regimes as a residue of the medieval papal church's doctrine of the two swords, but Luther objected to the papal church for having assumed powers that properly belonged to secular government. In his view, the state was also God's servant to punish the evil and protect the good. Carlson suggests that Luther's interest was not "man's relation to these two regimes, but God's relation to them." [15] Because of Luther's affirmation about divine grace and the assurance of salvation, his conception of the church was "extremely spiritual and idealistic, making the essence of the church to consist in the Word, the Sacrament, and the office of the ministry, and restricting it to a purely spiritual sphere of influence." [16] In this connection Luther identified the worldly orders and the order of creation. This may account for the fact that most national churches of the Lutheran tradition interpreted the "intimate relation between the political order and human society as a whole as a divine sanction of the national state. . . ." [17]

In briefly focusing on the Calvinist tradition, the difference between the primitive Calvinism of Geneva and its later development should be kept in mind. Nevertheless, it is fair to say that throughout Calvinism's various phases and stages it has been concerned with the restoration of "a holy community, of a Christocracy in which God is glorified in all its activity, both sacred and secular." [18] Theoretically, Calvin made a distinction between the church and the state, each as independent and sovereign in its own sphere. In his view, the church was both the organ of salvation and the means of sanctification. But, because both the church and the state were presumably governed by the will of God and had to work in intimate cooperation, in actual practice, "Calvin thought of the Christian community as a *unit* where the church and the state were *one*." [19] Calvin attempted to establish a theocracy in Geneva with this view. Following his opinion, the Reformed tradition was never satisfied with mere toleration of the church by the state: "The message of the church, on the contrary, has a bearing on all men [and women] and on all aspects of human life, including that of politics."[20] The Reformed tradition made a careful distinction between the "order of creation" and the "order of preservation," and identified the latter with the state. Accordingly, the state was viewed as a law-state: "The Moral dignity and religious justification of the state are dependent on the fact that the coercive power of the state serves the law."[21]

Limited space prohibits discussing many other important features of Calvinism, such as its republican tendency in politics, its capitalistic inclination in economics, or its fascinating relationship to the political, social, and ecclesiastical histories of various countries that came under its sway. The Calvinistic view of the church as "both national and free, a holy community, and an objective institution, a voluntary and a compulsory organization,"[22] presupposed the unity of the *corpus Christianum*, which was disintegrating quickly with the emergence of the autonomous nation-states. This may help explain the friction Calvinism had with various states, not only in Geneva but also in England and the Netherlands.

In comparison to the other churches of the Reformation, the Anglican church enjoyed more natural conditions for a national church because of its geographical insularity. Neill cautions taking the phrase in the Magna Carta, *Ecclesia Anglicana sit libera* too seriously. It simply meant that part of the one church was situated in England. "Yet," says Neill, "the use of such words at all is significant, [because] the development of national feeling, once started, was continuous."[23] The scandalous political factors involved in the English Reformation are well known. However, Streeter states that "being . . . a revolution in method rather than in conclusions, its [theoretical] importance has been overlooked."[24]

In spite of the amount of admiration of some people in England for the continental Reformation, the autocratic Henry VIII initially defended the Papacy against Lutheranism, and the majority of his subjects supported his view. "Henry had the advantage of being himself versed in theology. But he had also the disadvantage of having a disreputable personal axe to grind. It was this that turned him from an ardent supporter of the Papacy to its bitter enemy."[25] Understandably, the question of the national church became *the* issue under Henry's reign. The "Supremacy Act" made the clergy the spiritual servant of the crown, and religious conformity became a matter of patriotic duty. In the latter part of the sixteenth century the Puritans challenged the theory of "royal supremacy." However, the Puritans affirmed the validity of the national church; their objections were simply directed to royal supremacy and Episcopal polity. In this respect, Richard Hooker, who agreed with the Puritans on the kingship of Christ in the church, did not agree with them on their sharp separation between things spiritual and things temporal. Hooker and many other English reformers were very naive in assuming that all the members of the commonwealth held common beliefs. For Hooker, the basis for the religious doctrine of the sovereignty of the state was not a private subjective opinion: "Instead it has its source both religiously and politically in the objective organic, hierarchical principle joining together individuals to each other in the community and themselves to nature in the universe."[26] Hooker identified the visible church and the commonwealth as two different aspects of the same government. Hooker spoke for all the national churches when he wrote: "so far forth as the church is the mystical body of Christ and His invisible spouse, it needeth no external polity. But as the church is a visible society and body politics, laws of polity it cannot want."[27]

This does not imply that after the Reformation era in Europe the division into national churches was complete or undisputed. The Protestant separatists struggled to be emancipated from the framework of the national churches. Attempts were also made to establish a "Christian state" on radically "reformed" principles, for example, the Anabaptist groups in Zwicknau and Münster. But the churches in Europe generally accepted the norm of the national church. The historical distinction between the earthly church and the "church triumphant" was not forgotten, but the visible churches in Europe in the seventeenth and eighteenth centuries were preoccupied with the problems of this world. By accepting the state as an integral part of the order of creation, the national churches in Europe—which were also divided along ecclesiastical lines—acted as though national and ecclesiastical divisions were a natural state of the Christian community on earth. Curiously, they had no passion for the unity of Christendom, for the world outside Europe, or for the unity of all humankind. Ironically, the representatives of this divided Christendom were destined to accompany the colonial expansion of the European nations into the non-Western world in the eighteenth and nineteenth centuries.

Counter-Reformation. The Counter-Reformation attempted to restore the corporate unity of the papal church. Contrary to the popular view that the reformers were usually Protestants, throughout history there were many reformers in the established church. In fact, the Catholic Reformation was going on long before the Protestant Reformation came into existence. The medieval synthesis of religion-culture-society-political order, which began with Emperor Constantine, had reinterpreted the early Christian community's self-understanding of being the eschatological and eucharistizing (that is, having trans-human and social elements) assembly of God by equating the Christian community with the state church and by attempting to accommodate eschatological and transcendental elements into this-worldly perspectives. This outlook was made more explicit by the Renaissance, which shifted the center of gravity from heaven to earth. Following this approach, various reformers, in addition to correcting the abuses of the church, attempted to locate some "earthen vessels," not as vessels for the sacred but as the sacred itself. Monastic reformers located the sacred in the monastery, John Wycliffe and John Huss in the Bible, Luther in the coexistence of *Imperium* and *Sacerdotium* (and *Studium* by implication), reform popes in the papacy, mystics in mystical experience, and the advocates of conciliarism in the councils. Most, including spokesmen of both the Eastern and Western churches, went so far as to agree with the Council of Florence that *extra ecclesiam nulla salus*—"there is no salvation outside the church."[28] Also, like many other religious people, Christian thinkers "looked backward" as well as to scriptures and tradition to find supporting evidence for their current conclusions.

It was a strange coincidence that one of Martin Luther's contemporaries was Paul III (pope, 1534–1549). He was a remarkable person but a bundle of contradictions. He was the last of the Renaissance popes, highly educated, a restorer of the University of Rome, a patron of the Vatican library, another one who commissioned Michelangelo—this time to paint "The Last Judgment" in the Sistine Chapel. He is reputed to have sired four children and appointed two teenage grandchildren as cardinals. Paul III was also the first pope of the Counter-Reformation (a movement to counteract Protestantism, heresies, and paganism). He encouraged Emperor Charles V to suppress the German Protestants, influenced the French King Francis I to annihilate the Huguenots, and excommunicated Henry VIII. He also confirmed the Society of Jesus (the Jesuits).

When Paul persuaded Cardinal Giovanni del Monte to assemble the Council of Trent (1545), he was hoping to bring Protestants back into his fold. Rejecting the conciliar structure earlier councils agreed upon, Trent allowed cardinals, bishops, and the heads of religious orders to discuss only scripture, tradition, and discipline, but not matters pertaining to church reform. The Protestants refused to attend the council. The council's decisions concerning the sacrificial nature of the Eucharist, the celibacy of the clergy, and the doctrine of purgatory were destined to bind the Roman Catholic church for years. Meanwhile, true to the principles of the Counter-Reformation, Emperor Charles V declared the Schmalkaldic War against the German Protestants in 1546 and triumphed. The German Protestants then allied with Henry II (even though he was an extremely anti-Protestant king of France, reign 1547–1559) against the emperor, forcing the Peace of Passau upon him in 1552. This prepared the way for the religious Peace of Augsburg (1555), which recognized the legal existence of Lutheranism. This acknowledgment of the division of the Western church into two parts gave equal rights to Protestants and Roman Catholics. The religious and political developments greatly distressed Charles V. He was also dis-heartened by the fact that his widowed son, Philip II, had married Mary I of England, the daughter of Henry VIII and his Spanish wife, Catherine of Aragon. Despite such marital maneuvers, the English parliament refused to crown him. The accumulation of political, religious, and personal burdens persuaded Charles V to abdicate the throne in 1556. This act caused Ignatius of Loyola, another spokesman of the Counter-Reformation, to utter: "The emperor gave a rare example to his successors . . . in so doing, he proved himself to be a true Christian prince."[29]

INTERNAL EROSION OF EASTERN CIVILIZATIONS

One of the most intriguing enigmas of history is how the tran-sitional period of the West—the time of ascendancy of the Eur-opeans in the premodern or modern period following the decline of the medieval synthesis—coincided with the general internal erosion of traditional civilizations in the eastern part of the Eur-asian continent. (Remnants of these parallel trends persisted until as late as World War II.) We want to analyze a few cases as examples of general trends in Asia, showing how the Hindu and neo-Confucian syntheses lost currency and how the new situations under the Mughal (1526–1761) and the Manchu (Ch'ing) (1644–1912) dynasties were perceived as anti-Hindu (Mugals as Muslims) by Hindu traditionalists and as anti-Chinese (the Manchus as non-Han) by Chinese traditionalists. In reality, the Mughals attempted to integrate their Muslim elements and the Hindu heritage just as the Ch'ing leaders attempted to blend the Machu and mainline features of Chinese tradition. But these attempts were perceived as a rupture from the past by the tra-ditionalists. We will also look very briefly at how the Japanese Tokugawa regime (1603–1867) tried to develop a new synthesis by utilizing the principles of the Chinese neo-Confucian tradi-tion.

From Hindu Synthesis to Muslim India. The transition from Hindu to Muslim India was not abrupt. From the thirteenth to the sixteenth century much of northern India was already ruled by a series of Muslim dynasties, while in the south a fierce rivalry between Hindus and Muslims continued until the seventeenth century. The famous Muslim southern kingdom was ruled by the Bahmanid dynasty (around 1347–1527), which had consolidated much of the Deccan. Then most of India came under the Muslim Mughal empire (1526–1761), founded by Babur (died 1530), a Chagatai Turk and a descendant both of Timur and Genghis Khan. It is said that his earlier attempts to restore his ancestral realm in central Asia was unsuccessful. This is why he turned his attention to India. The Mughals were not strict Muslims, and the first two Mughal rulers did not enforce Muslim law in India where the majority of inhabitants were non-Muslims.

The most famous Mughal emperor was Akbar (reign 1556–1606). His capacity for leadership was widely recognized. During his fifty-year reign he brought more of India under his sway through conquest and alliance than had ever been ruled by one man. He could neither read nor write, but he surrounded himself with persons of talent and quality, carefully balancing between Hindus, Muslims, Afghans, Turks, Iranis, and Turanis (people from the Oxus basin). He abolished the Hindu pilgrim tax, thus helping the Hindu religious revival. He convinced different communities that he was their personal lord by appointing their members. He married a Hindu Rājput princess and allowed her to carry on her Hindu worship in his palace. He allowed the building of Hindu temples and celebrated Pārsī festivals. Gradually he moved away from Islam into a personal mysticism and an eclectic religion. Convinced that the unity of humankind could be attained by the unity of religions and common worship, he built the Hall of Worship for the purpose of worship and discussion.

> These discussions, over which Akbar presided, were attended by Sunni ulamā, Sufi shaikhs, Hindu pundits, Parsees, Zoroastrians, Jains, and Catholic priests from Portuguese Goa. The mere fact of such discussions . . . is the measure of the bias against orthodoxy at court. Akbar's personal religious searchings were followed by . . . the enunciation of the "Divine Faith" (Dīn-i-Ilāhī), Akbar's own

eclectic faith of 1582, and by a series of conciliatory gestures toward the Hindus.[30]

Akbar attempted to end such practices as *sati* (cremation of the widow), excessive dowries, slavery, and the loss of inheritance due to conversion from one faith to the other.

In the issue of the unity of humankind Akbar displayed both positive and negative examples. He was very different in personality and approach than Alexander, but he was just as serious as Alexander in creating an *oecumene* for the human race. He did not, however, as Alexander evidently did, claim to be the "savior and benefactor of the human race." Akbar was more religiously focused than Alexander; he held that the problem of the unity of humankind should begin and end with the religious quest. He was amazingly well informed on religious matters. For example, he was interested both in worship and discussion. He felt that anyone who did not practice his or her religion may be philosophically subtle and yet not understand the meaning and reality of religion. Nevertheless, his eclectic religion of "Divine Faith" was an arbitrarily concocted system. The main tenets of his faith—universalistic monotheism with a tinge of pantheism—lacked particularity in terms of time and space. It was destined to decline after Akbar's death because it lacked any stable social principle that would enable it to become one of the numerous communal groups following the logic and grammar of the Indian heritage.

Akbar did not accomplish religiously what he wanted to implement, but many creative things happened in India under the Mughal dynasty, in spite of the fact that many Hindus did not become Muslims. Many Hindu scholars lament the fact that most of India was under Muslim rule for so long. However, Indian Muslims tried to accommodate a great deal of Hindu values, customs, and Sanskrit literature. As Marshall Hodgson states:

> Except in point of religion, Muslims and Hindus shared the same arts and learning. Especially in northern India, many Hindus read Persian (and some Muslims read Hindi); the cultivated painting and, to a degree, architecture of Muslims and Hindus, their music,

and, in many polished circles their manners also came to be essentially one. . . .[31]

The atmosphere was not so amicable in the more Hinduized sections, especially in the south and coastal regions. When the Portuguese arrived in the Indian Sea toward the end of the fifteenth century, with vivid memories of fighting against the Muslims in the Iberian peninsula, they found the rulers of the Hindu Vijayanagar kingdom in south India passionately against the Muslim rulers in north India. Thus, as K. M. Panikkar states: "To both Portugal and Vijayanagar, Islam was the enemy, a factor of considerable importance . . . in the establishment of Portuguese authority in Goa."[32]

From the Neo-Confucian Synthesis to Manchu-Chinese Dyarchy.   The long history of China witnessed a steady movement from simplicity to complexity, from diversity to unity, and from discordance to consistency in its multilayered syntheses of the religion-culture-society-political order. The neo-Confucian synthesis that the Ming dynasty (1368–1644) inherited from the Sung dynasty (960–1279) embraced such universalistic factors as cosmic, human, and social orders, and yet it was rooted in the particularity of the cultural nationalism of China. This synthesis was securely grounded in two foci: the family and the national community, thought to be intimately related to each other. In a sense, the state was regarded as a projection of the family and commanded both the respect and the loyalties of the people. A characteristic of the Chinese tradition was that throughout imperial rule, from the third century B.C. to the twentieth century, the state was regarded as a combination of an enlarged family system and a centralized bureaucratic structure supported by the civil service system and the dual principles of *li* (ceremonials) and *hsing* (penalties). At the top of the family was the father, and at the top of the state was the emperor (the Son of Heaven), who was given the heavenly mandate to rule with the help of gentry-bureaucrats. The Yung-lo emperor (reign 1403–1424) of the Ming dynasty wanted to symbolize graphically the neo-Confucian synthesis in his northern capital of Peking by building the "imperial city" (*Huang-ch'eng*) and within it the "Forbidden Purple City" (*Tzu-chin-ch'eng*) with their ensemble of buildings, porticoes, terraces, gardens and stretches of water—a plan that was all the more remarkable since its aesthetic aspect has to harmonize with very strict astronomical and geomantic considerations. Outside the Imperial City, and southeast of the Chinese City, Yung-lo built the Altar of Heaven (*T'ien-chen-t'an*), a circular temple resting on three marble terraces. . . .[33]

The Yung-lo emperor also dispatched the eunuch-admiral, Cheng Ho, on seven maritime expeditions and incorporated as tributaries some of the Southeast Asian nations into the Chinese sphere of interest.

After the death of the Hsüan-tsung emperor in 1435, the Ming dynasty managed to survive difficult years thanks to its dedicated bureaucrats who ably supported mediocre monarchs. Following Vasco da Gama's voyage to India, Alfonso de Albuquerque occupied Goa in 1510. In 1511 his forces destroyed the Chinese outpost in Malacca and then reached Macao in 1565. Yet the Chia-ching emperor (reign 1522–1567) totally neglected his monarchical duties in favor of Taoist practices. As a result, the Ming regime was further weakened by Japanese piracy on the coast and Mongolian invasions in the North.

In 1582 the Italian Jesuit Matteo Ricci (known as Li Ma-tou in China; died 1610) arrived in Macao and began his careers in religion and science in China. He must have seemed a welcome improvement over many of the Portuguese adventurer-traders who had preceded him, known for their inhumane behavior and misplaced piety: "They were professional adventurerers, and they did not care whether they robbed or traded, as long as there were profits to be realized. Their consciences would not bother them. . . . As one Portuguese trader . . . put it, 'Why should I be afraid of going to hell, as long as I have faith? The Almighty's mercy is unlimited.' "[34]

The Ming court was relieved by the death of Japan's strongman, Toyotomi Hideyoshi (died 1598), who had dispatched his forces twice to Korea for the purpose of invading China. Early in the seventeenth century, the Dutch traders arrived in China, much to the annoyance of the Roman Catholic Portuguese who wanted to monopolize China trade. Recognizing the situation in China's mainland, the Dutch established their colony in Formosa (which was eventually taken over by the Ming loyalist, Cheng Ch'eng-kung). In 1644, the last Ming monarch committed suicide when Peking was overrun by rebel forces.

The Manchu (Ch'ing) dynasty (1644–1912), that succeeded the Ming was probably the most "Sinized" of all the non-Han dynasties that have governed China. The Manchu regime's intention was to retain the neo-Confucian synthesis intact, but in reality the regime viewed this synthesis as only one wing of its dyarchy, the other side being the Manchu tradition. This dyarchy emasculated the meaning of the neo-Confucian synthesis, which was meant to be a comprehensive and unified system unto itself. Nevertheless, the Manchu monarchs were amazingly adept in this complicated role. Thus, during the Ch'ing period and the Ming period China did not look any different. They honored the traditional family system and the Confucian-oriented civil service system. The Ch'ing emperor claimed himself the Son of Heaven in the traditional sense and offered sacrifices to Heaven. Even the state cult of Confucius was promoted by the Manchu regime. The situation was very different internally. In their private chambers the Ch'ing monarchs worshiped their own Manchu deities. Side by side with the neo-Confucian synthesis, the Manchus introduced the "banner system," a structure of administrative units, each of which was assigned a different colored (for example, yellow, white, blue, or red) banner for the supervision of military and civilian populations. Each of the six government departments had both Chinese and Manchu ministers. They claimed that the Manchu tribal nobility stood side by side with the Chinese nobility; actually, they stood above the ruling Chinese gentry. This complicated dyarchical machine worked very well under certain despotic monarchs. In 1750—during the reign of the Ch'ien-lung emperor (reign 1736–1796)—there was no question that China was the strongest and wealthiest nation on earth.

The Manchu dyarchy greatly disfigured, if not altered, the neo-Confucian synthesis of religion-culture-society-political order. For example, in traditional China, since the government was not too rigid, there was room for social change and individual initiative, dependent more upon moral persuasion than legal enforcement. But Manchu despots assumed that morality should be enforced by law and punishment. "The happy and prosperous state, as pictured by the Manchus," says Paul Eckel, "was one built on filial respect and blind obedience of the people. This training must begin with the children and be carried into every department of home and state."[35]

Although China was not colonized in the usual sense of the term during the Manchu (Ch'ing) period, various powers from Europe (and North America and Japan later on) encroached on China, often exploiting the anti-Manchu feelings on the part of the Chinese populace.

NOTES ON THE TOKUGAWA SYNTHESIS[36]

Much was happening in the rest of Asia—the Himalayan border areas, Tibet and Mongolia, Southeast Asia, and Korea. But we will now look at the Tokugawa feudal regime (1603–1867) that attempted a new synthesis in Japan.

We mentioned earlier that the Japanese imperial regime attempted to establish the first great synthesis of religion-culture-society-political order in the seventh and eighth centuries. Such a synthesis was never fully achieved. It began to undergo many changes by various factors. However, for centuries no one questioned the validity of the principles of this synthesis.

Two strongmen, Oda Nobunaga (died 1582) and Toyotomi Hideyoshi (died 1598), annihilated the first principle and also destroyed several powerful Buddhist institutions. In 1603, Tokugawa Iyeyasu (died 1616) established the feudal regime bearing his family name. He envisaged the establishment of the second great synthesis. He, like Oda and Toyotomi before him, had no use for the principle of mutual dependence between the king's way and the Buddha's way. But he kept the second and the third principles of the first synthesis: the institutional amalgam of Shinto and Buddhism as well as the theory that equated Japanese deities with Indian Buddhist deities. In lieu of the first principle, the Tokugawa synthesis appropriated some of the features of China's neo-Confucian synthesis in order to legitimatize the Tokugawa regime. In doing so, the Tokugawa regime—unlike the ancient Japanese imperial regime that advocated the heavenly model *àla* Shinto for the Japanese nation—followed the Chinese principle that affirmed that the order of heaven is inherent in the conditions of human existence, that is, the social and political orders. One of the undercurrents in Japan during the Tokugawa period was the tension between the Chinese and the historical Japanese models of society, as exemplified by the Shinto revival and the rise of the National Learning.

During the fifteenth and sixteenth centuries one of Japan's most troublesome problems was its contact with European powers. The chance arrival of shipwrecked Portuguese in Japan in 1543 was followed by the arrival of Francis Xavier and other Jesuits in 1549. Japan's subsequent development was greatly conditioned by the introduction of gun powder, brought by the Portuguese traders, and Roman Catholicism, propagated by the missionaries. The Tokugawa regime was determined to terminate Catholicism in Japan and closed Japan's door to foreign contact in 1639.

The examples of India, China, and Japan testify to the fact that the fifteenth, sixteenth, and seventeenth centuries exhibited an internal erosion of traditional Asian civilizations. The tragedy of the fifteenth through eighteenth centuries has been that rulers in Asia, no doubt capable people in many ways, have failed to comprehend that "culture is a product of the human spirit, and that particular sort of product which is never finally produced; that is, culture is nothing but the *life* of human beings, and for culture to be alive means that actual human beings live in it."[37]

DISUNITY OF THE ISLAMIC COMMUNITY

The period of the European ascendancy also coincided with one of the low periods of the Islamic world. Some believe that Europe took advantage of the disunity within the Islamic community, others feel that European ascendancy resulted in the low posture of the Islamic region. There is evidence that might support both views since these trends were closely interrelated.

In a way, Islam never recovered from the Mongolian sack of Baghdad in 1259 that ended the myth of the unity of the Islamic community under the caliphate. (However, toward the end of the thirteenth century, the Mongols in Iran were converted to Islam.) Following the end of the caliphate in Baghdad, various Islamic states, such as the Mamlūks in North Africa, the Ottomans in Anatolia, and the Islamized Mongol Il-khāns in Iraq and Iran, regardless of their titles, yielded effective control of midwest Asia. Meanwhile, stimulated in part by the Crusades, such Italian cities as Venice and Genoa busily engaged in shipbuilding, subcontracting for transportation and trade in the Mediterranean world. The Italians' adventurous spirit in those days might be illustrated by the example of Marco Polo (died 1324), a Venetian traveler who became the confidant of the Mongol emperor of China, Kublai Khan (died 1294). Both Venice and Genoa became deeply interested in spice trade with India and Indonesia. In the main, Venetians played ball with Cairo, which had access to the Red Sea, and tried to monopolize the spice trade in Europe, while Genoa unsuccessfully flirted with the rulers of Iran, who controlled the Persian Gulf, to compete with Venice. Geographically, Genoa was well situated and closely connected with other European cities. For example, in 1317 a Genoan nobleman, Manoel Pessanha, became the hereditary admiral of the Portuguese fleet that included many Genoans among its officers.[38]

The world of Islam experienced two great tragedies during the fourteenth and early fifteenth centuries. The first was the Black Death (1347–1348) that drastically reduced the population everywhere. The second was the whirlwind devastation of Timur Lang (or Tamerlane; died 1405), a Turkish Muslim who had Mongol connections through a maternal line. He is also a contradictory figure. He was a devout Muslim but also had a real thirst for personal achievement and a desire for bloodshed. "Though he overthrew the Mongol ruler," says Hodgson, "Timur was devoted to the Mongol idea. He set up a Mongol of another line as titular ruler, under whom he was supposedly merely a general, an amir, or (later) sultan. . . ."[39] His policy of Mongol-style total terror weakened the political fabric of the world of Islam from India to the Middle East.

Meanwhile, the glorious history of Islam in the Iberian peninsula was coming to an end. As though to prophesy the coming of a new day, Prince Henry the Navigator (died 1460), a passionate anti-Muslim and son of King John I of Portugal (died 1433), was exploring ocean routes around Africa with the hope of finding a new way to the East. In 1454, Dom Henry received the right to all discoveries up to India from Pope Nicholas V. The following year this grant was confirmed by another papal bull of Calixtus III. In 1492, the Muslim state in Spain was overwhelmed by Christian forces who gave the Spanish Muslims the ultimatum of baptism or exile. Also in 1492, Genoan navigator Christopher Columbus (died 1506), with the support of King Ferdinand of Aragon and Queen Isabella of Castile, set sail for the new continent. In 1494, Portugal and Spain signed a treaty, fixing "a line 370 leagues west of Cape Verde Island as the demarcation of their respective zones. This was confirmed by Pope Alexander VI and thus became the final line of division between the discovery of the two Iberian States."[40] In 1497 Vasco da Gama (died 1525) of Portugal, assisted by experienced mariners trained by Henry the Navigator, left the Iberian shore. He safely arrived at the Indian Ocean in 1498, signifying to the world that the supremacy of the Muslim middlemen in Indian trade had come to an end. The disunity of the Islamic community was further demonstrated when the Ottoman forces that had conquered Egypt took the last titular Abbāsid Caliph to Constantinople in 1517.

NOTE ON JEWRY

We are told that

> between 85 and 90 percent of world Jewry lived in the Muslim world in the period from the eighth through the tenth century. As that world became increasingly anarchic in the twelfth century . . . Jewish migration to Christian lands increased. By the mid-seventeenth century, there were approximately three-quarters of a million

Jews in the world, half of whom lived in the Muslim realm and half in Christian Europe (primarily Poland and Lithuania).[41]

By the end of the Middle Ages there developed two distinct types of rabbinic civilization among European Jews: the Ashkenazic (Franco-German) and the Sephardic (Andalusian-Spanish) branches, each with its own self-contained society and way of life. In Muslim Spain, the Jewish elites were highly revered by Muslim authorities, but they shared the tragic fate of the Muslims in being expelled from Spain in 1492 and from Portugal in 1497. (Actually, the Jewish exodus from Spain had begun in 1391 due to waves of discrimination and violent pogroms.) Many of the refugees chose to settle in Algeria, Morocco, and other parts of North Africa. It was from North Africa that many moved again to various parts of the Ottoman empire. The Jewish migration to Palestine increased after 1516 when Palestine was conquered by the Ottomans.

Equally heartbreaking was the experience of the "Marranos," or the Jews forcefully converted to Roman Catholicism. They were not exiled as the unconverted Jews were, but the Marranos discovered that baptism did not end discrimination and ostracism. For example, although a number of Jews became Catholic in Spain and Portugal during the fifteenth century, their beliefs and behaviors were severely scrutinized by the Castilian Inquisition of 1478. In fact, both the Spanish and the Portuguese "New Christians"—including some former Muslims occasionally referred to as Marranos—were discriminated against on account of "purity of blood" statutes that identified their Jewish, or Muslim, ancestries. The Portuguese Inquisition established in 1536 was as harsh as its Spanish counterpart. Moreover, with Portuguese and Spanish colonial expansion abroad, inquisitions were conducted in Goa, Lima, and Mexico during the sixteenth century. The conversion of Jews to Islam, by coercion or otherwise, also took place in the Islamic world. They were referred to as "New Muslims."[42] On the whole, Jews found safe refuge in the Ottoman empire after 1492.

The Jews initially had difficulties in the New World, but they eventually became better established. It is believed that Columbus's crew included some Jews or Marranos. The first Jewish community was established in Brazil when Dutch rule started in 1630. In North America, the Sephardic Jews established their first synagogue in New Amsterdam as early as 1692. Then, following the Dutch defeat in Brazil at the hands of the Portuguese in 1694, a group of Jews came to New Amsterdam. Other Sephardic Jews settled in Newport, Rhode Island, followed by some Northern European Jews settling on the Atlantic seacoast. But North American Jews experienced prosperity only as late as the nineteenth century.

EUROPEAN COLONIAL EXPANSION
(1500–1600)

The term *colonialism* has various meanings. In theory it refers to the establishment of a *colony*, which according to Webster is a company of people transplanted from their mother country to another land but remaining loyal to their original state. In this sense colonialism is as old as the history of the human race. In ancient times, the Phoenicians "colonized" the Mediterranean seaboard, and the Greeks established their colonies in North Africa and the Middle East. In the East, somewhere between 1500 and 1200 B.C., Aryan tribes started colonizing northwest India. They eventually became not only the dominant group in the Indian peninsula but also colonized various parts of Southeast Asia. The colonization policy of imperial Rome resulted in the establishment of a multiracial and multilingual empire around the Mediterranean Sea at the turn of the common era. In the thirteenth and fourteenth centuries, some of the city-states in the Italian peninsula established their colonies on the Spanish coast and the Greek islands. Even the Crusaders' brief settlements in and around the Holy Land could be considered European colonies. But usually the term *colonialism* refers to premodern and modern European colonial expansion to the non-Western world. The first phase roughly covers the period from the sixteenth to mid-eighteenth centuries. Looking back, it becomes evident that Phase 1 of European colonialism had two types of results. First, such regions as North and South America (as well as Australia later on) were completely colonized by Europeans and remained European, culturally and religiously, even though peoples in those regions were destined to become politically independent. Second, there were regions like many parts of Asia and Africa that were subjugated politically and economically to European nations but were not converted culturally or religiously to European orientations. In both cases, colonial expansion, aiming at conquest or settlement and economic exploitation, was made possible by a combination of colonial (often monarchical) support and an advanced technology.

Portugal was the first European nation to establish an overseas colonial empire. It initially explored parts of Africa, not only for the sake of economic gains but to fight the Muslims on "their own soil," to search for a legendary "Christian ally, Prester John," and to find "a way to the rich spice trade of the Indies."[43] Prince Henry (1394–1460) is usually credited for the initial colonial success of the Portuguese; however, there is no record that he travelled beyond Tangier. Henry, being the governor of the Order of Christ (founded in 1319 by Denis, sixth king of Portugal, to increase the power and wealth of the monarchy), utilized the Order's vast resources to attract and train navigators for overseas expeditions. Following the Treaty of Tordesillas (1494), dividing the non-Western world into Spanish and Portuguese territories, Portugal exploited Africa, India, East Asia, and Brazil. The Portuguese idea of colonialism was based on the monopoly of trade, with well-fortified Portuguese settlements strategically placed (usually in coastal cities) to facilitate such a policy. Notwithstanding the fame of Vasco da Gama, who discovered the ocean route to India in 1498, the Portuguese never fully dominated the Indian Ocean. The failure of the Portuguese to take Aden, for instance, left the Red Sea open as a route for Muslim and other European powers.

In 1505, Francisco de Alameida was appointed as viceroy of India, and the Portuguese victory over Muslim naval forces off Diu in 1509 solidified Portuguese control of sea trade in Asia. In 1510, Alfonso de Albuquerque occupied Goa, which would remain the center of Portuguese trade in Asia for nearly a century.

Meanwhile, Portugal established a series of settlements on the African and Persian coasts, in Ceylon and Malacca, as well as in Ningpo and Macao in China. Brazil gave Portugal many headaches but produced little profit.

In contrast to Portugal, which pushed along Africa, India, and headed eastward, Spain took the westward course to the West Indies and on to the Americas. Both the Jews and the Muslims made important contributions to Spain, the only multiracial and multireligious region in Western Europe during the medieval period. Partly inspired by Islam's example, the this-worldly religion *par excellence*, Spanish Catholicism became a strong this-worldly religion. To compete ostensibly with the Islamic community, it became characterized by its extreme and uncompromising piety, authoritarian dogmatism, and crude exercise of power—exemplified by its royal absolutism, barbarous inquisition, and inhumane treatment of Jews and Muslims. After 1479, Ferdinand II of Aragon and Isabella of Castile jointly ruled as "Catholic monarchs" in both kingdoms of Aragon and Castile, two countries that were very different in tradition and orientation. The Catholic monarchs exhausted their financial and military resources to regain the Iberian peninsula for Catholicism. They recognized potential conflicts in their colonial affairs with Portugal and obtained a series of papal bulls from Alexander VI (the Spanish pope) and concluded the 1494 treaty with Portugal. We are told that in 1504, "the Spanish sovereign created the House of Trade [ostensibly] . . . to make the trade monopolistic and thus pour the maximum amount of bullion into the royal treasury. This policy, seemingly successful at first, fell short later because Spain failed to provide necessary manufactured goods for its colonies. . . ."[44]

Spanish colonialism could not be divorced from its many domestic problems. In 1516, Ferdinand died, and his grandson, Charles, who could not even speak Spanish, ascended the Spanish throne. Initially the Spaniards did not welcome their new foreign-born ruler, but they eventually accepted Charles grudgingly. The new king was devoted to Catholicism and ardently anti-Muslim and anti-Protestant. Spain suffered financially due to a series of wars in which Charles indulged against the Turks, German Protestants, France, and even the papacy. Much to their regret, the Spaniards were at first unaware of the potentials in the New World. For example, they occupied the larger West Indian islands by 1512 but completely neglected the smaller ones. In 1519, Cortés entered Mexico, rich in gold and silver, from Cuba. Silver mining soon became an important industry in the New World and benefitted Spain immensely. In 1524, Emperor Charles V established the Council of Indies as a lawmaking organ with the hope of gaining material support from the New World for his military campaigns in Europe. However, the Council was not very effective. Nevertheless, Spain expanded its suzerainty from the 1530s to the 1560s into the regions that would become Peru, Argentina, Ecuador, Colombia, and Florida. Spain's vice-regal system in the New World began in 1535 with the appointment of Antonio de Mendoza as the viceroy of Mexico (New Spain), followed by the appointments of viceroys in Peru and other strategic spots. In time, the New World under the viceregal system evolved a rather rigid class or caste system, consisting (in descending order) of Spaniards from Spain, American-born Spaniards, the *mestizo* children of white and Indian parentage, and the offspring of Indian and black slave marriages.

When the exhausted Emperor Charles abdicated in 1556, his son Philip II (reign 1556–1598) took over all his father's domains except Germany. His own Castilian upbringing and his emotionally rigid Catholicism made Spain, with the help of such figures as St. Teresa and St. Ignatius Loyola, "the intellectual, as well as the financial and military, spearhead of the Counter-Reformation."[45] In 1565, Philip, now known as the "most Catholic of kings," established the Spanish settlement in what came to be known as the Philippines (which had been discovered by Magellan in 1521). Spanish interests in Asia, with Manila as their base and supported by Mexico-Philippine commercial traffic, were destined to encounter Portuguese interests in Japan, as eloquently portrayed in the popular novel, *Shōgun*. In 1580 the Spanish king, Philip, took advantage of the vacancy of the Portuguese throne, to which he had some blood claim, and seized it after a clever intrigue. Philip, realizing the suspicion and resentment of the Portuguese, considered the Portuguese-Spanish union personal and not political. He endeavored to respect Portuguese autonomy both at home as well as in colonial matters. Nevertheless, the union provided new fuel for an old Spanish-Portuguese feud that became even more apparent under the reign of Philip's son and grandson. Eventually, this hostility resulted in Portugal's independence from the Spanish yoke in the seventeenth century.

Spain's invincible armada was defeated in 1588 by the British navy. In hindsight, this symbolized the decline of Iberian leadership in European colonialism. This vacuum was filled quickly by the Dutch who became a leading maritime and colonial power during the seventeenth century. Their sphere of interest extended from South Africa, Ceylon, Java, Formosa, Japan, to New Netherland in North America, Guiana, and some Brazilian settlements in South America. The Dutch colonial enterprise was directed primarily by the United East India Company, established in 1602, and the West India Company, established in 1621. The powerful nation of France only flirted with overseas colonialism during the sixteenth century because of its preoccupation with inter-European affairs. During the seventeenth century, however, the newly established Western Company (Campagnie d'Occident) in France began to take an active role in overseas enterprise, especially in French Canada where many Frenchmen eventually engaged in lucrative fur trade. Also in the seventeenth century, Cardinal Richelieu and his council Marines explored opportunities prospering with the slave trade in the French West Indies. France did not hang on to other settlements in the New World, with the exception of French Canada, the French West Indies, and Guinea. In 1665, with the death of Philip IV of Spain, Louis XIV (died 1715) of France, as Philip's son-in-law, claimed part of the Spanish Netherlands. In 1700, Charles II of Spain bequeathed all of his dominions to Louis's queen. The continuing war of the Spanish succession ended in 1713 with the ascension of the French prince to the Spanish throne in exchange for valuable French colonies. Although the French monarchy remained intact as a despotic institution, the French economy was nearly ruined. Unfortunately for France, its Company of the East Indies was not successful in Africa and Madagascar. Even though France was in a favorable position in India several times vis-à-vis England, the lack of support from the home government and French investors resulted in the decline of French power, prestige, and influence in India.

Unlike France, England took a keen interest in colonialism and overseas trade in the sixteenth century, establishing the Moscovy Company as early as 1553. In 1660, the East India Company was established. England began to control such cities as Madras and Bombay during the seventeenth century. Following the collapse of the Mughal Muslim dynasty in 1707, England and France were in fierce competition for colonial stakes. By 1763, the year the Treaty of Paris was signed, French influence in India declined sharply, leaving the stage open for the British East India Company. During the seventeenth century England was also active in controlling the West Indies as well as maintaining colonies in North America, for example, Virginia (1607), Plymouth (1620), and Massachusetts Bay (1630). By the French and Indian War (1754–1763), England's American colonies were enjoying prosperity along with a growing population—approximately 1,296,000 whites and 300,000 blacks. In the north, Russia was determined to expand to the Pacific and established a settlement in the port of Okhotsk in 1638 and then continued to expand along the Amur River as well as on the east and west shores of the Caspian Sea.

Roman Catholic Overseas Missions.   The colonial expansion of the Iberian kingdoms during the sixteenth century marked the beginning of the Roman Catholic overseas missionary enterprise. People in the Iberian peninsula, where Muslim Spain was defeated by Christian forces in 1492, were emotionally anti-Islamic. Their commitment to the cause of the Counter-Reformation also made them very anti-Protestant. The Roman Catholic overseas missionary activities were carried out under the patronage (*patronato*) of Portugal and Spain, who agreed to provide missionaries and maintain religious institutions in return for extensive power in ecclesiastical matters at home and in

Rome. In order to keep peace between the two nations, the papacy asked Portugal to be in charge of Africa, Asia, and Brazil, while it depended on Spain to carry on the missionary activities in Central and South America and the Philippines. Both the Portuguese and Spanish colonists carried with them the *Santa Fe*. "In fact," says Sweet, "the early Spanish *conquistadores* considered themselves Christian crusaders and brought over to the New World the ideas which had grown up in the long wars which they had fought against the Moors in Spain, using the same battle cries and evoking the same saints in the New World that had served them in the old."[46] One cannot overemphasize the importance of the role played by the religious orders, for example, the Franciscans, Dominicans, Capuchins, Augustinians, and Jesuits, in converting the non-Christian natives.

The Spanish missionaries in the Americas and the Philippines tried to Christianize entire non-Christian peoples along with their cultures, societies, and religions, while the Portuguese missionaries tried to convert a smaller number of non-Christian individuals (mostly in the coastal cities)—to reorient them to think and believe as the Portuguese did—and expected that through them Christian influence might penetrate the larger non-Christian world. It is understandable, therefore, why they were attracted by a sizable number of Syrian Christians in South India. They were not Roman Catholics, but their beliefs and practices were sufficiently similar to those of the Portuguese to instill confidence in the new colonizers. Both the Portuguese and the Spanish missionaries were inclined to treat the native churches as permanent wards and expected them to remain dependent on the Western churches and colonial governments.

Goa became a center of Portuguese trade and evangelism in the East after it was captured in 1510. From Goa, the Portuguese were to reach Malacca, Macao, and eventually Japan. Accordingly, in 1534, the Bishop of Goa was given jurisdiction extending from the Cape of Good Hope in the west to China in the east. Many Portuguese missionaries took it for granted that the native religions and cultures were to be displaced and supplanted by Roman Catholicism and Portuguese culture. The coming of the Jesuits brought changes and new insights into missionary thinking.

In 1541, Francis Xavier (died 1552), a nobleman from Navarre and one of the original members of the Society of Jesus, arrived in India. As Apostolic Nuncio, Xavier had unusual prestige and power. Because of his Iberian experience, Xavier was emotionally anti-Islamic. Otherwise, he had an intelligent, pragmatic, and consistent approach to his missionary vocation. For example, "Xavier sought, whenever possible, to convert kings and the leaders of society . . . he never hesitated to call upon the powers of the state and complained bitterly and bluntly on several occasions that the secular rulers were not co-operative enough."[47] Xavier's career in Asia is usually divided into three phases—his activities in South India (1540–1544), his work in the Moluccas and in Malacca (1544–1548), and his final years in Japan (1549–1551). His untimely death on an island off Canton deprived him of his work in China. In spite of his brief stay in Asia, Xavier—known as a conquistador of souls—enormously influenced the Roman Catholic missionary enterprise in subsequent centuries.

Under the patronage (*patronato*) system, all missionaries were appointed and supported by, and expected to serve, civil authorities. But in 1575, the Jesuit visitor, Alessandro Valignano, sought to reduce to a minimum such relationships between missionaries and royal agencies.[48] However, Valignano and his fellow Jesuits were willing to utilize various means, including the use of political power, for the cause of missions. Valignano agreed with Francis Xavier that the future of the mission in Asia lay in Japan and China rather than India. He also advocated such policies as "accommodation," that is, being very conciliatory to Far Eastern cultures and religions, and training native clergy. This may account for, at least in part, the conflicts between the Jesuits and other Catholic missionaries, but it might also explain the Jesuit missions' great success in Japan. The Jesuits utilized a series of Buddhist terms such as *Jōdo* (pure land), *sō* (Buddhist monks), and *Buppō* (Buddhist law or teaching) to explain Christianity. Also, the Jesuit-inspired Japanese Catholic groups followed the general pattern of tightly knit medieval Buddhist societies, such as the True Pure Land sect or the Nichiren sect. With a definite form of religious society and sacramental assurance of salvation for souls, the Roman Catholic church in Japan boasted a membership of approximately 150,000 by the end of the sixteenth century. Yet in 1639 the Tokugawa feudal regime eliminated Catholicism and even executed its policy of national seclusion.

As for China, Valignano, an advocate of the new policy of accommodation, felt that the Portuguese Jesuits who had been engaged in missionary work there were "too ethnocentric, conservative, and not well enough trained to innovate this radical new program," and so turned to "the new Italian recruits," notably Matteo Ricci (died 1610), for leadership.[49] Ricci was well trained in Western philosophy and science, especially in mathematics, astronomy, geography, and physics as well as in Chinese culture. During his stay in China, 1582–1610, he worked both as a missionary and a scientist. Toward the end, he became a stipendiary of the Ming Court. Ricci lived in China during a turbulent era. The Ming Court felt the threat of Toyotomi Hideyoshi, the strongman of Japan who dispatched his military forces to Korea in order to invade China. (His death in 1598 ended this threat.) In Europe, the defeat of the Spanish armada (1588) and the death of four successive popes (1590–1591) occupied the imagination and energies of the political and ecclesiastical leaders. Such drama so close to home tended to channel attention and energy away from the Far East to more familiar soil. Meanwhile in China, Valignano and Ricci found

> a cultivated and integrated society which prided itself upon being the supreme civilization of the World and disdained the learning of others. To break through this wall of Chinese isolation and ethnocentricism, it was clear to both Valignano and Ricci, though not to all of their colleagues, that Jesuit influence in China would be directly proportional to their ability to "win friends and influence people" in high political office.[50]

It was also clear to Ricci and other advocates of the "accommodation" policy that Christianity should incorporate some of the native (Confucian) terminologies and rites into its system in China. This stance was the heart of the prolonged dispute, known as the "Rites Controversy." It involved missionaries, native converts, the papacy, and the Chinese court, as to whether or not Chinese converts could participate in certain Chinese rites.

Such participation was eventually declared un-Catholic by Popes Clement XI (1704) and Benedict XIV (1742).

Valignano had no "musicality" for things Indian. It took an Italian Jesuit, Robert de Nobili, originally from a noble Roman family, to hammer out a new missionary policy of "adaptation." Upon his arrival in 1606 at Madura, the center of Tamil culture, he observed that cultured Hindus were alienated by the way Portuguese missionaries presented Christianity. Talented as a linguist (he was the first European Sanskritist in the opinion of Max Müller), de Nobili adopted the manners and customs of a Brahmin ascetic. He abandoned European ways and associations, donned the Hindu dress, and even wore the sacred thread, the symbol of the "twice-born castes." He was able to convert some high caste Hindus. However, his policy of "adaptation" was bitterly attacked by many missionaries in India and critics in Europe.

In 1622 the Vatican established the *Congregatio de Propaganda Fide* to centralize the Roman Catholic missionary enterprise in Rome, to withdraw missionary initiative and control from Portugal and Spain, and to counteract the "errors" of accommodation and adaptation that had emerged in the mission fields. In theory, the central purpose of this measure was to place papal authority over the propagation of the faith in foreign lands and in parts of Europe that had lapsed into Protestantism and other heresies. In practice, the congregation had to depend primarily on French missionaries, thus causing friction between the *patronato* system and the congregation, between Iberian and French missionaries, and between residential bishops and Apostolic Vicars.

The missionary experience of the Roman Catholic church during the sixteenth and seventeenth centuries teaches many important lessons in visions of the unity of humankind. We are aware that the human race is divided along, among other factors, religious lines. And we know that each religious tradition, according to its own "inner" meaning, is convinced of its truth claims with different degrees of exclusiveness. Ironically, when one religion exists as the only or predominant religious system in a state or region for any length of time, like Christianity in Europe or Hinduism in India, that religion seems to operate with only its "inner" meaning and neglects to develop an "outer" meaning that would enable it to be sensitive to the rival claims of other religious traditions. When other factors, such as colonialism, empower the bearers of one religion to influence peoples of other religious backgrounds, very intricate and complex relations develop between peoples and religions. The Roman Catholic church during the sixteenth and seventeenth centuries attempted many different experiments, such as converting whole societies, cultures, and religions, as in the case of the native Americans in the Americas, or aiming at the conversion of individuals, as in Asia. Organizationally, Rome at times depended on the initiative of the political authorities, for example, the *patronato* system. At other times it tried to centralize the whole enterprise, as epitomized by the *Congregatio de Propaganda Fide*. As for missionary approaches, it had a wide range of options, from authoritarian methods to such progressive measures as accommodation and adaptation. The Roman Catholic missionary experience during the sixteenth and seventeenth centuries demonstrates how tempting it is for any religious tradition to be convinced of its own exclusive truth claims, its "inner" meaning, and to superimpose this belief onto others. As a result it completely neglects to develop its own "outer" meaning that would enable it to interact objectively and humanely with other traditions.

Contrary to many peoples' impression, the Protestant churches in Europe did not develop a missionary outlook until the eighteenth century. In his *Table Talk*, Luther lamented the fact that Asia and Africa had no way of knowing the Christian gospel. Calvin, on the other hand, did not believe in any special agency for the conversion of the heathen. He held that "the kingdom of Christ is neither to be advanced nor maintained by the industry of men, but this is the work of God alone."[51] When A. Saravia (died 1613) of Canterbury advocated the evangelization of the world, Theodore Beza of Geneva disputed him by insisting that Christ's missionary commandment did not extend beyond the first century. The theological faculty of Wittenburg thought that the command to go into all the world was only a personal privilege of the apostles, and it had already been fulfilled.[52]

The seed of the Protestant missionary orientation was planted by Pietism, which arose as a reaction against the rationalism and romanticism of the seventeenth and eighteenth centuries. The pioneer of Pietism, P. J. Spener (died 1705), advocated Bible study, the priesthood of all believers, and practical Christianity. Pietism did not prosper in Germany, but it had a strong impact on the Moravian movement. The influence of Pietism was also strongly felt in Denmark, Holland, and England.

In 1622, the University of Leyden established the *Seminarium Indicum*, which trained pastors and missionaries for the service of the Dutch East India Company; but this experiment turned out to be a disastrous failure. In the main, the colonial activities of the "Protestant nations" had no organic relation to the Christian missionary enterprise. For the most part the churches of the Reformation were national or state churches. They were inclined to hold that the spiritual care of the colonial subjects was the responsibility of the temporal rulers, who showed little interest in the missionary endeavor. It was the combined efforts of the continental Pietists and English evangelicals that eventually developed into the strong Protestant missionary spirit of the eighteenth century.

The situation in the New World was unique in that the European colonists far outnumbered the original inhabitants. In addition, some of the early colonists were religious refugees from Europe. They were soon outnumbered by colonists who were motivated by this-worldly objectives, but even then, these colonists brought with them the churches and synagogues that were familiar to them. For example, the Church of England was established in the colonies of Virginia, New York, and Georgia. The Congregational church was strong in the New England colonies. The Church of Scotland was transplanted by Scotch-Irish immigrants, and the Dutch and German Reformed and the Lutheran churches were brought over by Dutch, German, and Scandinavian immigrants. The Baptists gradually gained strength in Rhode Island and the Middle Colonies.

In Canada the picture was quite different. The great landowner in New France became the Roman Catholic church. During the French and Indian War (1756–1763), French colonists were overpowered by the British, and Canada was officially ceded to England in the Peace of Paris (1763). The Protestant population increased after the American Revolution began in 1776—many loyalists migrated to Canada from south of the border. This complex religious map in Canada led to the passing of the Reunion Act of 1841, which ruled that no one religious group was to receive special privilege from the government.

In the eighteenth century, the cumulative effect of the earlier colonial expansion of European nations, together with rapid social and economic changes in Europe, brought about the Industrial Revolution that destroyed the economic basis of the colonial system. In the meantime, the socio-political changes in Europe loosened the European nations' grip on their colonies in the New World. Starting with the United States, independent nation-states, freed from the political yoke of their homeland, emerged in Central and South America. However, the new independent states in the American continents remained European in religious and cultural tradition.

CHAPTER
5
The Search
for a New Synthesis

A brief account of the experiences of various civilizations as presented in previous chapters makes it clear that our contemporary habit of polarizing the world into East and West, or dividing the global society into the First, Second, and Third Worlds, is based on a relatively recent phenomenon in the history of the world, traceable to around the sixteenth century. We should honestly acknowledge and not minimize the depth of the chasm that exists between the West and the non-Western world, based on layers and layers of events and experiences, including colonialism, Christian world mission, racism, dominance of Western science, economy, technology, and the non-Western reactions to them.

Throughout history, side by side with the tragic reality of human divisions, or perhaps because of it, we have also noted the persistent longing of various peoples, religions, and cultures for a glimpse of the vision of unity. Such a longing has not been confined to dreamy-eyed idealists and romantics. There have been a countless number of hard-boiled realists, including political, economic, religious and philosophical leaders and social reformers, who were persuaded of the imperative for human unity and attempted to find sound bases for such an ideal. Humbly, we realize that we are all creatures of habit and products of our own particular experiences, and that we are inclined to impose our own version of human unity on others. From this perspective, it is important for us to reexamine the events of and our experiences in the so-called "modern period," because our own perspectives, derived from modern experiences, often determine our understanding of our historic legacy—we have learned to read history backward—and color our perceptions of the future. In this respect, the Western domination of the entire world during the past four hundred and fifty years, at least until the end of World War II; the phenomenal expansion of the global Christian missionary enterprise; and the passion for independence from things Western on the part of non-Western peoples, nations, cultures, and religions present real challenges to our sensitivities, intellectual honesty, and moral courage. It would be far too easy for both Westerners and non-Westerners to resort to a simpler alternative of assuming that each side alone has claim to the right vision of human unity.

COLONIALISM (1750–1850)

During the latter half of the eighteenth and the first half of the nineteenth centuries England propelled itself as the unrivaled colonial empire. Waves of British immigrants settled in British colonies in Australia, Canada, New Zealand, and South Africa. The great Mughal Islamic dynasty crumbled. India as well as Ceylon and Burma were added to the British overseas empire. The British colonial office also controlled a number of "crown colonies"—Hong Kong and Singapore—that were springing up in various parts of the world. Great Britain engaged in wars against the African natives, the Afghans, and the Boers. In the nineteenth century other European powers began to compete with the British in the colonial race, extending their spheres of interest in the non-Western world. The rising industrial and financial capitalism allied with colonialism, which opened new markets and new opportunities for investment. For example, Africa was almost completely partitioned among British, French, Dutch, Spanish, Belgian, Italian, and German interests. King Leopold II of Belgium and his capitalist associates reaped an enormous fortune in the Congo by means of very cruel, inhumane methods of exploitation.[1] In many respects other nations were just as crude and vicious as Leopold. After the disgraceful Opium War (1840–1842), China was penetrated by British, French, Russian, German, and later Japanese interests. Indo-China was soon taken by the French; the islands of Java, Sumatra, Celebes, parts of Borneo, and New Guinea were taken by the Dutch; the Bismarck Archipelago, the Ladrone Islands, and some islands of Samoa were occupied by the Germans; and the islands of Hawaii, the Philippines, Puerto Rico, Guam, and Wake came under American control. By the end of the nineteenth century, the Western powers had developed a powerful colonial imperialism that combined political and economic control over much of the non-Western world. Strangely, this development coincided with the expansion of foreign missionary work by the Protestant churches.

Apologists of colonialism assert that it had some positive features. But in all the colonial territories "the principles of democracy and nationalism for which they had fought [in Europe] were denied to the peoples"[2] who came under their rule. Also, the European nations, who were eliminating the evils of serfdom in their own countries, had developed a new system of "colonial slavery." Initially, the Spaniards introduced the slave trade to the New World, but with the growth of the European colonies and the increase of demand for slaves, the British, French, Dutch, Danish, and Portuguese slave traders made a huge profit. The horror of the transit of these human cargoes across the ocean aroused the conscience of some ecclesiastical and humanitarian leaders in Europe. But it was not until the middle of the nineteenth century that slave trade was legally abolished by European nations. Slavery as such was not introduced into the European colonies in Asia, but the Asians were often regarded as a means of the same economic ends.

According to many Asian and African writers, two main characteristics of European colonial imperialism were economic exploitation and a feeling of racial superiority on the part of the colonists. Most Europeans felt that their culture, religion, science, technology, and socio-political and economic systems were superior to those of their colonial peoples. This was chiefly because they saw themselves as a superior race. Such a view became widely accepted not only by politicians and businessmen but by educators and religious leaders. Many of the philanthropists and missionaries who went abroad were not free of a feeling of superiority—unconscious if not conscious—in their paternalistic attitudes toward non-Westerners. Such an attitude fits into Drinnon's definition of *racism*, which refers to the "habitual practice by a people of treating, feeling, and viewing physically dissimilar peoples—identified as such by skin color and other shared hereditary characteristics—as less than persons."[3] Many Africans and Asians objected to such an assumption on the part of the colonial masters in their relations with peoples in the colonies. An Indo-Chinese writer poignantly expressed the sentiment of his people toward the French when he wrote:

> In your eyes we are savages, dumb brutes incapable of distinguishing between good and evil. You not only refuse to treat us as equals, but even fear to approach us, as if we were filthy creatures. . . . There is a sadness of feeling and shame which fills our hearts during the evening's contemplation when we review all the humiliations endured during the day.[4]

Christianity came to play an important role in a colonialist synthesis of religion, culture, society, and political order—a synthesis that served to legitimize colonial objectives in non-Western societies. Modern Europeans used a rather simplistic formula:

$$European = Christian = Superior Race$$
$$vs.$$
$$non-Westerner = Pagan = Inferior Race$$

It is important to understand Christianity as a part of this formula. Otherwise, it is difficult to understand how colonial masters treated native populations as though they were things. The "pig-trade," which kidnapped (or "shanghaied," as the practice was called) and illegally shipped Chinese laborers abroad in the mid-nineteenth century, was no less cruel than the earlier slave trade of African natives in the New World. Lord Elgin, who ordered the burning of the Summer Palace in Peking, no doubt acted with the mistaken belief that such a wanton destructive action showed his mighty power in dealing with the pagan Chinese and did not realize the negative impact it would have on future European and Chinese relations.[5] Thus, unfortunately, the East-West relationship, that historically—although it probably had no such nomenclature—meant an encounter of rival groups on the same plane, each with its peculiar beliefs, traditions, and practices. In the modern period this came to be seen by many Europeans as a vertical relationship with the superior European race on top of the inferior non-Western races. This kind of vertical relationship was built into all colonial government structures, as illustrated by the British *raj*. The *raj* attracted many ambitious youths trained at Oxford and Cambridge and provided them with top jobs in the ICS (Indian Civil Service) and IP (Indian Police), the two most important units of the *raj*. There were other, less crucial, technical services—education, agriculture, and forestry—all of which had more Indian personnel. Next to the above types of All-India Services were many Provincial Services that were staffed mostly by Indians with a small number of Britishers. Obviously as a whole the British *raj* employed many more Indians than Britishers. This fact has been mentioned many times by the colonial officials as an indication of the fairness and broadmindedness of the British attitude toward Indians. Indians wish to point out that the most important, decision-making jobs with better pay were monopolized by the Britishers.

Racism, which usually spawns a series of ugly phenomena (superiority complex, ethnocentrism, discrimination, segregation, irrational hatred, genocide, etc.), was institutionalized into the social and cultural systems wherever modern colonialism was established, such as Africa, Australia, Asia, and the New World. For example, even before South Africa enforced apartheid, "white Australia" excluded (until the middle of the present century) all colored immigrants. Even the United States, which presumably always welcomed all freedom-and-opportunity-seeking peoples from other continents, has blatantly practiced discrimination against the native Americans, Blacks, Orientals, and Latinos.[6] The most persistent racial discrimination in American society has existed vis-à-vis black Americans. Many European immigrants came to the New World with a biased view that black people were inferior and that they were to be exploited for white people's benefit. Slavery became the political issue over which the war was fought between the North and the South. Segregation remained an unresolved issue in many parts of the country even after the Civil War. Blacks legally acquired the right of naturalization in 1870, but their participation in normal life has been minimized by what amounts to a color caste system. The fact that racial segregation, not only against the blacks, but also against other groups, has existed so pervasively in the "land of freedom" is a complex issue. Racism was at the heart of America's colonial heritage, and it was further amplified by misguided and/or ill-motivated social, political, economic, religious, and cultural evils. Even today, an amazing number of Americans are inclined to agree with Rudyard Kipling's ethnocentric poem:

> *The Stranger within my Gate*
> He may be true and kind
> But he does not talk my talk—
> I cannot feel his mind.
> I see the face and the eyes and the mouth,
> But not the soul behind.
> The men of my stock
> They may do ill or well
> But they tell the lies I wanted to,
> They are used to the lies I tell;
> And we do not need interpreters
> When we go to buy and sell.[7]

EUROPEAN CIVILIZATION AS RELIGION OF SECULARIZED SALVATION

Racism has been an almost insurmountable stumbling block to the cause of the unity of humankind, but it was only one ingredient (although it was one of the pertinent factors) of the larger phenomenon—the modern European civilization that gradually developed in Europe after the Renaissance. People during the post-Renaissance period rejected the medieval notion that civilization was to be religiously inspired and ecclesiastically controlled. (Actually the Renaissance only confirmed publicly what had been accepted in the West since the time of Constantine—the significance of the phenomenal world as an existential reality rather than as a "fallen state," as it was understood in classical Christian views.) The spirit of the Renaissance may be illustrated by the new canon of historical inquiry—"(1) Reason rather than authorities must be the ultimate tribunal of historical judgement. . . . (2) Probability is the second law of historical judgement. . . . (3) Literature should not be the only source of historical knowledge. Stones may be more reliable than scribes."[8] The humanism of the Renaissance, inspired by antiquity and authenticated by human reason, slowly brought about the new worldview of the age of the Enlightenment of the seventeenth and eighteenth centuries with its own cosmology, which relied heavily on the sciences and mathematics. An increasing number of modern Europeans felt that the state was not to be subservient to ecclesiastical authority as it was during the medieval period, but that the human personality must accept the political community as the necessary framework of civilized life. Thus, similar to the way the ancient Hebrews understood themselves as the chosen people to proclaim the true creed, modern Europeans regarded themselves as the creators and bearers of a new and true civilization. Here is the root of a strange modern European form of racism, derived from the fact that many men and women came to affirm that

> Biology and sociology point to the superiority of the Caucasian or white races over the coloured races of the earth. Superiority in physical and mental constitution, together with superiority in civilization and organization [however,] entail responsibility as well as privilege.[9]

The preoccupation of the Renaissance with human reason left imprints on Christianity—more positively on Protestantism, which had earlier rejected monolithic authorities in matters of faith and doctrine, and more or less negatively on Catholic orthodoxy or the tradition of the Counter-Reformation. According to Randall's observation, religious rationalism had made many inroads into the Dutch Reformed tradition as early as the seventeenth century, for it insisted "more on a rationalistic interpretation of the Scriptures, because these new sects multiplied most rapidly, and because Calvinism itself was the most medieval of all the Protestant systems."[10] However, it was England that became the motherland of the religion of reason, known as Deism. There were also supernatural rationalists, for example, John Tillotson, John Locke, and Samuel Clarke.

What gave new confidence to people during the Renaissance period was scientific thinking, based on the combination of the conviction regarding human reason, the knowledge of Greek scientific works, the influence of Arabic notions regarding experiment, etc. In such an intellectual climate the German cardinal Nicholas of Cusa (died 1464) experimented on a growing plant, Copernicus (died 1543) arrived at his theory of the earth's revolution, Leonardo da Vinci (died 1519) used his device of perspective vis-à-vis human and animal bodies. These men prepared the way for scientific advancement during the age of the scientific giants Galileo (died 1642), Kepler (died 1630), Descartes (died 1650), and Harvey (died 1657) of the seventeenth century. All these giants were persuaded that scientific methods enable men and women to decipher the law of calculable regularity that underlay the operation of the world. For them, one of the most urgent but difficult questions was whether or not there was a connection between the operation of the world and the history of humankind.

Of course there had been many speculations and theories as to the status of human history. One of the most influential views on the subject was Augustine's theory of three ages—(1) before the fall, (2) under the law, and (3) under Christ. According to Augustine, human beings were living in the third age, and the end of history was shortly to come as taught in the New Testament. It is interesting to observe that Joachim of Fiore (died 1202), abbot of a Cistercian monastery, revised the Augustinian scheme and proposed a new view of the three ages and the three orders of society—(1) the Age of the Father, from Adam to John the Baptist; (2) the Age of the Son, from the reign of King Uzziah of Judah (around 750 B.C.) to the mid-thirteenth century; and (3) the Age of the Holy Spirit, from Benedict's establishment of the monastic rule (around A.D. 500) to the golden age of the future. It is to be noted that Joachim's notion of the future—or the age of justice and freedom—was to be fulfilled *within* history, and not *beyond* history as in the case of Augustine's scheme. Joachim's scheme was appropriated by Auguste Comte (died 1857) into his threefold system of (1) the mythico-religious, (2) the philosophical-speculative, and (3) the scientific states of history.[11] Another issue that taxed many thinkers was the relationship between history and nature, exemplified by the discussions in *Scienza Nuova* by Giovanni Battista Vico (died 1744), in *The Origins of Species by Means of Natural Selection* by Charles R. Darwin (died 1882), and in *Zur Kritik der politischen Oekonomie* by Karl Marx (died 1883).

The rationalism of the Enlightenment was followed by romanticism. It is Dawson's observation that rationalism *à la* Voltaire would not have been so influential if not for the contribution of the romantic humanitarianism of Rousseau.[12] Rousseau took seriously the original feelings and passions of mankind. "He wanted to transform social institutions until they conformed to these needs of human nature."[13] Dawson characterizes Rousseau's ideology as the new "moral basis of Western society and the spiritual inspiration of Western culture," replacing orthodox Christianity.[14] In general romanticism shared rationalism's hostility toward religious authority and Deism's conviction about natural religion. Van der Leeuw helps analyze the three stages of romanticism. First, the period of philosophic romanticism regarded specific religious manifestations as symbols of a primordial revelation. Second, the period of romantic philology, while reacting against the speculation of romanticism, remained romantic "in its desire to comprehend religion as the expression of a universal mode of human thinking." The third period of romantic positivism, although preoccupied with the principle of development, still accepted religion as "the voice of humanity."[15]

Modern Europeans who had experienced the Renaissance and Enlightenment regarded themselves as the creators of new cultural values and the bearers of true civilization, which was *de facto* a pseudo-religion of secularized salvation. This view was the underlying ideology of both the Industrial Revolution and the French Revolution and was also the motivating force in the colonial expansion of modern European nations. As far as can be ascertained, modern Europeans did not question the essential unity of humankind.[16] They were persuaded that human unity would be achieved only when all peoples were enlightened by the true civilization that was invented and transmitted by Europeans, who had to propagate it for the edification of all the backward peoples. "This is the philosophy of the white man's burden, as Kipling called it—a strange compound of genuine idealistic responsibility, blindness and hypocrisy, with a strong dose of will-to-power as the basic component."[17]

CHRISTIAN WORLD MISSIONS

A small group of pietists during the seventeenth and eighteenth centuries totally rejected the modern Europeans' view that they were the creators of cultural values and the bearers of a true civilization offering secularized salvation.[18] One of the well-known early pietists was Philip Jakob Spener (died 1705) of Halle. Emerging after the tragedy of the Thirty Years' War (1618–1648) and rejecting the prevailing emphasis of human reason as well as the one-sided, this-worldly orientation that had been stressed by Christianity since the time of Emperor Constantine, Pietists aspired to return to the simple religious experience of the early Christians. Pietists were not sophisticated systematic theologians, but they stumbled into a refined "inner meaning" of their Christianity as the *ecclesiola in ecclesia*, an intimate fellowship of faith within—in their eyes—the watered-down framework that was then called the church. They lamented the fact that many members of the this-worldly church did not know the difference between the Kingdom of God and the Kingdom of the world. To them, the Kingdom of God was nothing but "the sum total of the converted, as those saved from the world . . . [and] as a purely futural, eschatological entity."[19] It was their conviction that those who were converted had the obligation to bring others into conversion, foregoing reliance on political rulers to accomplish this conversion. The pietist approach contrasted with the secularized European view that Western civiliation is a pseudo-religion of secularized salvation that can enlighten non-Westerners without any need for Christian salvation. However, Pietists failed to realize that their "inner meaning" of the Christian religion alone would provide insufficient rationale in the non-Western world, where Christianity would become one of the many religions competing for souls.

Pietism did not gain much influence in Germany, but it gradually began to have an impact elsewhere. King Frederick IV of Denmark asked the University of Halle to send missionaries for the Danish East Indian colonies in 1704. Spener's pupil at Halle, Count von Zinzendorf (died 1760), inspired the Moravians with a zeal for foreign missions. Their first mission was established in 1732 among the slaves of the Danish island of St. Thomas in the West Indies. The Moravian missionary work eventually extended to Jamaica, Antigua, Greenland, Labrador, North America, South Africa, and Dutch Guiana. It should be remembered that during the eighteenth century most state churches in Europe did not concern themselves with foreign missionary work. In addition, European colonial authorities did not welcome Christian missionary work. For example, in the eighteenth century the British East India Company followed the policy that "to hold India in subjugation Christian missionaries must be excluded. It was not only that the arrival of Protestant emissaries of this faith might anger Hindu priests and Muhammedan mullahs, but it would open the eyes of the Hindus to the great facts of the world."[20]

In the meantime, under the influence of the continental Pietists and English evangelicals, a number of private missionary societies came into being. Many of them became semiofficial organs of the European churches, which in turn pressured colonial authorities to open doors for missionary work in the colonies. Thus, colonial governments could not forestall the penetration of missionaries.

The religious society movement of the seventeenth and eighteenth centuries in England had a close spiritual kinship with continental Pietism. Its development led to individual members forming associations within the Church of England rather than separating from the state church. The SPG (the Society for the Propagation of the Gospel in Foreign Parts) and its parent society, the SPCK (the Society for Promoting Christian Knowledge), grew out of the religious society movement in the seventeenth century. The eighteenth century brought the Methodist movement and the formation of the CMS (the Church Missionary Society). The evangelical revival in England, which began with Methodism, also encouraged the formation of the Baptist Missionary Society (1792) and the London Missionary Society (1795). Other lands also manifested deep interest in the missionary endeavor. In fact, "by the end of the Nineteenth century, almost every Christian body, from the Orthodox Church of Russia to the Salvation Army, and almost every country, from the Lutheran Church of Finland . . . to the newest sects in the United States, had its share in the missionary enterprise overseas."[21]

Under the *patronato* system of the sixteenth century, Spanish missionaries aimed at the conversion of whole non-Christian peoples, their societies, religions, and cultures while the Portuguese missionaries focused on the conversion of individuals and used them as the means of evangelizing the non-Christian world. In a sense, the Congregation of the Propaganda of Faith, established in the seventeenth century, combined the two approaches and also avoided such experiments as "adaptation" and "accommodation." The Christian missionary enterprise of the eighteenth and nineteenth centuries, initially inspired by the vision of continental Pietists and English evangelicals, did not intend to convert the non-Christian societies and cultures, nor did it aim solely at the conversion of individuals. These modern missionaries were persuaded that those who had been really "converted"—and were made members of the *ecclesiola in ecclesia*—had the obligation to bring others to the salvation experience. Like their spiritual ancestors, the Pietists, they rejected the notion that Europeans (or any other human group) were creators and bearers of the true civilization that imparted secularized salvation.

The rapprochement between colonialism and Christian world mission is very complex. Briefly stated, there developed a practical compromise on both sides based on necessity and expediency. Colonial authorities gradually realized that they needed the assistance of missionaries. This became dramatically evident in 1833 when Thomas Macauley, the first legal member of the Governor-General's Council in India, advocated the policy of Anglicizing Indians—an enormous task that needed the help of missionary personnel. There was also a growing feeling among colonial officials, since European civilization was becoming an effective substitute for religion, that Christianity should become one of the constituents of Western civilization and should be presented in the non-Christian world.[22]

On the part of many missionaries, there was some feeling that the prestige of colonial authorities was a plus factor for Christianity. In addition, the missionaries were willing to co-operate with colonial authorities in educational and philanthropic, if not religious, activities that in their eyes contributed positively, though not completely, to Christian values and morals. Further, they did not promote the transcendental and eschatological aspects of the Christian message in order to show that Christianity provided guiding principles to human beings, both individually and collectively. Instead of presenting two contradictory paradigms, one for colonialism and one for Christian world mission, the cooperation of colonialism and missionaries enabled the development of one great synthesis of *religion* (this-worldly Christianity)—*culture* (Western culture, supported by Western science, technology, etc.)—*society* (with built-in "racism" that differentiated the ruling white groups and the non-Western peoples that were to be ruled)—*political order* (which authenticated colonial structure). This compromised synthesis enabled the dominant Europeans to live with the strategy of contradictory objectives: for commerce (colonialism) and Christianity simultaneously *à la* David Livingstone.

In retrospect, it becomes very clear that during the eighteenth and nineteenth centuries the combined forces of Western civilization, Christian missionary activities, and colonial expansion brought about social, political, economic, cultural, and religious changes in much of the world.

Although the colonialization of non-Western cultures had a devastating impact on these indigenous cultures, colonialism conversely had an unexpected positive value for Europe and America. The contact with non-Western peoples ushered in an age of "de-provincialization" of the Western religious terrain. Among numerous changes brought about are the unique features of religious development in America.

MIXED FEATURES IN AMERICAN TRADITION

From the time of Columbus many people realized the geographical importance of the New World situated between Europe and Asia. Yet most people who settled in North America took their European orientation for granted to the point that, as Daniel Boorstin has demonstrated, the American revolution had no dogma or cultural self-consciousness of its own.[23] On the other hand, things European, which were inherited, were bound to be reinterpreted by people's experience in the New World. For example, many North American churches reflected the continental Pietist orientation of biblicism, devotionalism, and activism. As early as the eighteenth century, a "Great Awakening" swept through the colonies. Sweet points out the three waves of revivalism in the South: "In its first phase it was largely a Presbyterian movement. . . . In its second phase it was largely a Baptist movement. . . . In its third phase it marked the beginning of Methodism in America."[24] The revivals were intercolonial and cross-confessional in scope, and they left lasting marks on the Protestant churches in America. They may in part account for the American Protestant passion for the Christian world mission.

Side by side with Pietism, the continental Enlightenment, and Deism, the English notion of the "public" also influenced people, especially the educated in the New World. For example, if the pietistic missionaries portrayed China as a land of pagans to be saved, such a spokesman of the Enlightenment as Voltaire praised it as the only country where the pure religion of Nature was preserved: "Worship God and practice justice—this is the sole religion of the Chinese literati. . . . O Thomas Aquinas, Scotus, Bonaventure, Francis, Dominic, Luther, Calvin, canons of Westminster, have you anything better?"[25] Comments regarding exotic traditions were not based on serious inquiries into Eastern religions and cultures, but the tradition of the Enlightenment left distinct marks on American intellectuals, including the framers of the Constitution. Deism, with its conviction of *Religio Naturalis*, was warmly welcomed by some New England intellectuals who had a proclivity for nature mysticism. Many of the creative thinkers and artists, for example, Emerson, Thoreau, Bigelow, Lowell, La Farge, and Henry James, shared their European counterparts' idealization of Eastern cultures and religions. The British notion of "public" also penetrated deeply into American culture and society from education to the government. I agree with Glenn Miller's observation that the term *public* in traditional England referred to the elites who were leaders in church and state.

> The government relied on the public to support its policies and to see that order was maintained in the countryside. Parson and squire worked together for the common good. One purpose of university education was to create patterns of loyalty in this important segment of the society.[26]

The convergence of these contradictory European influences and North American experiences produced an all-out Christian world missionary enterprise; voluntary religious groups, usually referred to as of the "denominational type"; and the principle of religious liberty.

The Role of Americans in the Christian World Mission. Two things should be mentioned about the role of Americans in the Christian world mission. First, American churches became part of the global missionary enterprise shortly after European missionaries and colonial authorities hammered out a pattern of compromise *à la* Livingstone—of commerce (colonialism) and Christianity. Second, unlike European churches that depended on semiautonomous missionary societies, most American churches accepted missionary work as a task of the total church body. Thus, in 1814 the first missionary society was formed as the only national organization of the Baptists. The Baptists were followed by other church groups, including the YMCA (Young Men's Christian Association), the YWCA (Young Women's Christian Association), and the Student Volunteer Movement (which stirred the imagination of American Christian youths with the slogan, "the evangelization of the world").

America entered a new era after the Spanish-American War. As Americans began to exert leadership in global affairs, American Protestants took the initiative in the international missionary conferences in Edinburgh (1910), in Jerusalem (1928), and in Madras (1938). At home, America faced, as Frederick Jackson Turner had prophesied earlier, a transition "from the frontier to the factory."[27] Faced with numerous difficult issues, American churches developed two diametrically opposed solutions, which were expounded in Rauschenbush's *Christianity and Social Crisis* (1907) and a conservative work called the *Fundamentals* (1909). The former was an attempt to find God's redemption in a new industrial society, while the latter combined an individualistic, agrarian mentality and a nontheological biblicism.

Early in the twentieth century, many churches under the impact of Liberalism and the Social Gospel not only criticized society but also attempted to actualize the Kingdom of God on earth. In spite of such optimism, churches showed little interest in political programs. They were concerned with improving the character of individuals by urging them to refrain from alcohol and other evils, but not by changing institutional patterns. That simplistic moral optimism was transformed into patriotism with the outbreak of World War I, whereby churches became propaganda agencies for the nation at war.

The Social Gospel and Liberalism also replaced pietistic moralism in the mission fields. Preoccupied with the educational and philanthropic activities of the Christian missions during the early twentieth century, many liberal missionaries became the spokesmen of the American Way of Life—"a kind of generalized American religion."[28] Their Christian missionary zeal was often equated with the enthusiasm for America's mission to humankind. And, as the Beards pointed out, "America was now fairly out upon the imperial course," because "with the growing economic surplus . . . ran an increasing pressure for foreign markets and investment opportunities."[29] Ironically, many missionaries naively became spokesmen of American interests as well as of Christianity, thus creating an American version of the Livingstonian pattern of mission-and-colonialism.

Following World War I, many American churches rejoiced that God had given the Allies victory, and they continued their works of mercy in cooperation with the Red Cross and other agencies. But the Christian world mission was beginning to lose its appeal among church members. Meanwhile, America was destined to be swept up by the depression, while Europe soon witnessed the rise of Fascism and Nazism. In this situation, the optimism and "do-goodism" of liberalism and the Social Gospel came under sharp attack from two quarters: neoorthodoxy and fundamentalism. By 1938, the year the World Missionary Conference was held in Madras, India, it became evident that the whole world was threatened by Fascism, Nazism, and Japanese militarism. There was the growing realization that not only the Christian world missionary enterprise and Christianity but also the entire world order should be reexamined in light of the revolutionary changes taking place worldwide. The Europeans and Americans, however, were still hopeful that the whole world order might be salvaged by accepting the great Western synthesis of religion (Christianity)—culture (predominantly Western)—society (liberal bourgeois)—political order (dominated by the West).

Voluntary religious groups (denominational type). While in many ways Americans behaved as faithful followers of the European heritage and its orientation to the Christian world mission, it should be pointed out that they also instituted far-reaching changes in the European pattern in their religious groupings at home. (Although we have focused our attention on American Protestants vis-à-vis the Christian world mission, American Roman Catholics also shared the Europocentric orientation.) What developed in the New World was the type of voluntary religious association usually referred to as a *denomination*, a term usually used in connection with Christianity, although a similar structure can be found operating in Jewish, Islamic, and other religious groups. We will restrict ourselves to the Christian groups, which set the tone for all religious groups in American society.

Historically, the Christian community has never achieved uniformity in doctrine, practice, or ecclesiastical structure. The division of the church in Corinth, which the Apostle Paul bitterly criticized (1 Cor. 1:10), was probably a widespread phenomenon among the early Christian community. In time, the Christian community began to make a distinction between two terms that were originally used interchangeably, *heresy* and *schism*. During the Middle Ages there were three main groups within the Christian fold—orthodox Christians who belonged to a hierarchical church, the heretics within the fold who held unorthodox beliefs, and the schismatics who seceded from the historical church.[30] Then came the Protestant Reformations. (The churches of the Reformation considered themselves ecclesiastical bodies, situated between the papal church and the left-wing groups.) Troeltsch's classical definition of the ecclesiastical body—what he called the "church type"—described it as "a universal institution, endowed with absolute authoritative truth and the sacramental miraculous power of grace and redemption, [which] takes up into its own life the secular institutions, groups, and values. . . ."[31] Although both the churches of the Reformation and the Roman church belonged to the "church type," the former stressed the subjective fellowship while the latter the objective meaning of the Incarnation.

In the "sect type," as formulated by Troeltsch, the religious community evolved its social ideal primarily from the gospel and the Law of Christ, rejecting the identification of the ecclesia with any objective institution: "it is conceived as a society whose life is constantly renewed by the deliberate allegiance and personal work of its individual members."[32] The term *sect* had a derogatory connotation earlier, but in later years it has been used in a descriptive sense, referring to a contractual ecclesiastical group in contradistinction to an ecclesiastical structured body.

Unfortunately, Troeltsch's twofold classification leaves many loose ends. (His concept of "mysticism" involved other difficulties.) Howard Becker attempted to refine Troeltsch's typology, using a fourfold classification: ecclesia, sect, denomination, and cult.[33] To summarize, American religious groups tend toward the "denominational type," which is distinguished from the "church type" by the principle of voluntary association and by congregational polity, and from the "sect type" by size and democratic leadership. Historically, both the Baptists and the Congregationalists based their groups on the Calvinistic idea of the covenant. Following this concept, the New England Puritans attempted to inaugurate a form of theocracy. Modern American denominationalism is a blending of Congregationalism and the rationalist concept of the church. According to de Jong's observation the "denomination" is *the* American church form, and democracy has played a decisive role in the formation of modern American denominationalism.[34] American experience, coupled with the impact of Pietism, revivalism, and rationalism, tended to transform both "church-type" and "sect-type" churches, which had been transplanted from Europe, into the "denominational type." The American experience also produced two new phenomena—nondenominationalism and American forms of cult groups.

Nondenominationalism implies the victory of religiosity over theology. "Intellectually speaking, 'religions' are unimportant in American life; but religion is of enormous importance. To conform in the United States, it is important to be a member of *a* church. . . . Which particular church is far less important. . . ."[35] Said President Eisenhower: "I am the most intensely religious man I know. That doesn't mean I adhere to any sect. A democracy cannot exist without a religious base. I believe in democracy."[36] Many Americans agree with John Locke that a church is a voluntary society for men and women joining themselves together of their own accord for the public worship of God. And, as Boorstin observes, religions in America "commend themselves for the services they perform more than for the truths which they affirm."[37] This instrumental emphasis and nonde-nominationalism have produced the so-called "community churches" all over America.

Nondenominationalism de-emphasized the traditions of various church groups. The loosening of ecclesiastical tradition was accentuated by the revival movement, which brought different religious groups close together. Those who came under the sway of revivalism were inclined to hold that emotional satisfaction needed no intellectual criticism or support. Those who rejected revivalism tended to reduce Christianity (or religion) to an ethical intellectual system. Mead observed: "So the Unitarians have commonly thought the Methodists weren't intelligent, and the Methodists have commonly thought that the Unitarians weren't religious—and the tragedy of Christianity in America is that both have always been more than a little right and more than a little wrong."[38]

Ironically, the American experience also produced a unique form of cultic group. A visitor to North America in 1828 was struck by "an almost endless variety of religious factions." In addition to the church groups known in Europe, "there are innumerable others springing out . . . each of which assumed a church government of its own."[39] Clarke notes that of approximately seventy-four million Americans who were affiliated with some religious groups in 1947, more than 90 percent belonged to two dozen bodies. "There are, however, more than four hundred different religious groups in the country. Most of these are very small groups, about half of them having fewer than seven thousand adherents each."[40] He divides these groups into five major types: (1) "Pessimistic or Adventist" groups, the Millerite Movement or Seventh Day Adventists; (2) "Perfectionist or Subjective" groups, Black Methodist groups or National Holiness Movement; (3) "Charismatic or Pentecostal" groups, Assemblies of God or Pentecostal Holiness Church; (4) "Communistic" groups, Oneida Perfectionists or House of David; and (5) "Legalistic or Objective" groups, Mennonites or "Hard-Shell" Baptist groups.[41] Although similar to nondenominationalism, these "cultic groups" also exhibit strong denominational tendencies. Recently the picture has become infinitely more complex with many new groups emerging constantly.

Religious Liberty in America. The principle of "religious liberty" in America, historically such a lofty idea, was hammered out as a necessary evil by less than noble—actually very egoistic—motivations of various religious groups. The notion of religious liberty emerged out of the unique American experience, characterized by the development of the democratic form of government, the denominationalization of various religious groups, and other factors. Religious liberty did not imply that each group gave up its absolute religious claims. But the practical necessity of diverse religious groups cohabiting in the same continent resulted, in hindsight, in what might be characterized as a revolution in religious thinking. Unfortunately, its relevance was ignored by most religious groups in America.

Historically, the religious life of free white persons in the New World included many different orientations, from New England theocracy to Virginia's Episcopalianism. In time, however, all groups, including Roman Catholics and Jews, had to agree on a pragmatic approach to establish a viable social, cultural, political, and religious order in the New World. It took many twists and turns before they agreed on a common course. From the start, the inhabitants of the thirteen colonies were not known for religious tolerance. Their approach to the Native Americans and their religions and cultures exhibited extreme forms of ignorance and bigotry. And, initially even Jews and Roman Catholics had a difficult time among "free white persons."

Records show that Jews in New Amsterdam were originally excluded from the charter of liberties and privileges. Around 1820 there were fewer than fifteen thousand Jews among the ten million Americans. They posed no threat to the common life but were exposed to various kinds of discrimination. With the massive Jewish migration from Central Europe, Russia, Rumania, and Poland in the late nineteenth and early twentieth centuries, the situation improved, but subtle, and not so subtle, discriminations continue. Meanwhile, all Jewish religious groups, Reformed, Conservative, and Orthodox, have been deeply concerned with the danger of secularism. Jews became just as "this-worldly" as Protestants and Catholics did in America, and their "ecclesiastical" structure has also been denominationalized, even though such expressions are not ordinarily used in reference to Jewish groups. Like the Jews, Roman Catholics also had a difficult time being accepted by colonial American society. Internally, American Catholicism, which had grown with immigration and conversion, was beset with ethnic struggles, as for example, between the Germans and the Irish. Catholicism's ambiguous character in North America arises from its unique blending of dogmatic exclusiveness. This was based on a monotheistic doctrine, coupled with a church-type ecclesiastical structure, and a *de facto* denominational ethos that was common to all American religious groups.

In retrospect, it becomes evident that the American colonies, following the British notion of "public," regarded religious institutions and the commonwealth as two different aspects of the corporate life of the same people. Colonists used such terms as religion, Protestantism, and Christianity almost interchangeably to refer to a variety of modes of human experience. Religion in America, including Christianity, Judaism, and other traditions, had to adjust to what Mead calls "separation of 'salvation' from responsibility for the institutional structure of society."[42] In this process, America discovered the lofty principle of "religious freedom" by means of a unique dialectic between sectarianism and "civil" or "public" religion. Religious freedom was qualitatively different from the religious toleration known in some European nations. During the colonial period, each religious group initially aspired to the kind of freedom that would allow each group to press its absolute claims. "But what had become obvious to all by the end of the Revolution was that the only way to insure such freedom for itself was to grant it to others."[43]

Religious liberty or freedom meant that each religious group "is enabled to act as if there were no other [groups] in existence, but in so doing concedes to other [groups], which *do* actually exist as its neighbors and rivals, the right to practice the same kind of isolationism."[44] Nevertheless, before the end of the eighteenth century religious groups in America "learned to dwell together in relative peace—that first they learned to tolerate each other and eventually to think of freedom for all as an inherent or natural right."[45] Few religious people realized it, but religious freedom implied an unusual combination of the "inner" meaning of each religious group, based on its exclusivistic claims, and the "outer" compliance with the civic virtue of religious liberty. Unfortunately, this dual schema, which authenticated religious freedom, was rejected by subsequent religious leaders who were motivated by the simplistic notion that the "inner meaning" of their religions alone was a sufficient guide for their followers' salvation as well as for their civic life. What they failed to realize was that they were destroying the foundation of religious freedom, the cornerstone of the American Constitution.

The World's Parliament of Religions held as a part of the Columbian Exposition (1893) in Chicago needs to be mentioned. Most Americans, even Chicagoans, have forgotten this event, but it was one of the monumental occasions for leaders of diverse religious and cultural traditions to meet as a group for the first time in the Western Hemisphere.[46] The great courage, ingenuity, and foresight of the Christian and Jewish volunteers in America who managed to invite leaders of various non-Western religions to attend the Parliament deserve recognition. Although some leaders, notably the Sultan of Turkey, reacted negatively, articulate leaders from Hindu, Buddhist, Chinese, and Japanese traditions were delighted to come and present comprehensive statements of their respective religions.

What the planners of the Parliament had in mind was similar to the formula of the eighteenth-century American religious leaders, both Christian and Jewish. Despite their differences in theological views, religious moods, and ecclesiastical styles they agreed on the principle of religious liberty or freedom that would guide various religious groups to live together in the common social and political life. Both groups—the architects of the principle of religious liberty and the planners of the Parliament—had no intention of giving up their own groups' truth claims, the "inner meaning." However, both groups knew that the only way to preserve their group's "inner meaning" of religion was to grant the same privilege to other groups. The Christians among them knew what the Apostle Paul said: "For although there may be so-called gods in heaven or on earth—as indeed there are many 'gods' and many 'lords'—yet for us there is one God, the Father . . . and one Lord, Jesus Christ" (1 Cor. 8:5-6). Jewish colleagues also made the similar distinction between what they held as religious truths for themselves and the truths that other groups had every right to hold.

The World's Parliament of Religions guaranteed that no one was asked to surrender any conviction believed to be the truth, nor was anyone asked to participate in any part of the Parliament's program that compromised one's relationship to his or her religion. Thus, the Parliament was able to recognize the supreme validity of each religious tradition's "inner meaning." The Parliament was equally clear that each religion must respect other groups' right to their own "inner meanings." The program stated clearly: "All controversy is prohibited. No attack will be made on any person or organization. Each participant body will affirm its own faith and achievements, but will not pass judgment on any other religious body or system of faith or worship."[47]

In retrospect, it becomes evident that it was a new experience for many of the Parliament's planners to be self-conscious about the distinction between the "inner meaning" and "outer meaning" of religions. Those planners—mostly Christians but also some Jewish members—were children of the nineteenth century during which the West dominated the entire world. It was difficult for them to transcend their own experience when they were confronted by non-Western religions. As Kraemer said later: "It was not only the eye of faith, but also the eye of the Westerner who subconsciously lived in the conviction that he could dispose the destiny of the world, because the absorption of the Eastern by the Western world appeared to come inevitably."[48] Instead of articulating the genuine "outer meaning" that would treat all religions on an equal footing, C. C. Bonney, who originally proposed to have the Parliament, called it a friendly conference—a sort of "royal feast to which the representatives of every faith were asked to bring the richest fruits and rarest flowers of their religion."[49]

CONTEMPORARY REVOLUTION AND TRADITION IN THE NON-WESTERN WORLD

According to Arnold Toynbee's well-known imagery, the drama of history during the past four and a half centuries has had two main actors—the "West" and the "rest of the world." Until this century, the West was the predominant power: "it is the world that has been hit—and hit hard—by the West." However, in our own time there are signs that the tables may be turning. Writing in 1953, Toynbee goes on to say: "The West's alarm and anger at recent acts of Russian and Chinese aggression at the West's expense are evidence that, for us Westerners, it is today still a strange experience to be suffering at the hands of the world what the world has been suffering at Western hands for a number of centuries past."[50]

The traditional ideal of Asia was the integration of all values and the balance and harmony of diverse elements within society. This ideal presupposed the existence of a certain fluidity within an ordered society that was maintained by a strong sense of allegiance to the traditional way of life. In the past, people in Asia had a sense of security in their identification with the land and membership in their communities. In such a situation, customs and mores were authenticated implicitly by religious authority. The fluidity and flexibility of Asia were lost with the stratification of society, the stagnation of cultural values, and the excessive institutionalization of religious systems. Moreover, during the last several centuries, the ruling classes superimposed predominantly "political values" upon all other values, for example, the Mughal dynasty in India, the Manchu rulers in China, and the Tokugawa feudal regime in Japan. These rulers actually meant to support traditional cultures and religions, but they also took it for granted that everything in their societies had to bow before political authority. Furthermore, the rulers wanted to confine religious leaders to what the rulers understood to be the narrow domain of "religion," ignoring the traditional role of religious leaders in transmitting spiritual and cultural values of the past and interpreting the contemporary experiences of the people in light of accumulated wisdom. Instead, the political leaders assumed the traditionally "priestly or religious functions" of interpreting the nature and destiny of the people. As a result, the traditional pattern of Asian cultures was disrupted.

The encounter between the East and the West during the past four hundred and fifty years must be seen in this larger historical context. We do not intend to probe the moral implications of Western colonialism, but want to understand the minds of Eastern peoples as they came in contact with Western civilization. Evidently, peoples of Asia with their confused self-images, with their cultures and societies stagnating from within, could not halt the onslaught of Western civilization. One result of the modern Western impact on the East was the emergence of a small number of Western-educated "new Asian elites" who quickly overshadowed the "old traditional elites" who resented anything new or Western and competed for leadership over the masses. Of course the influence of the West was felt differently in various parts of Asia. In Japan and China, leaders attempted to utilize Western learning and technology without losing their traditional cultural values and patterns. In India and other parts of South and Southeast Asia, Western colonial administrators attempted to "transform" traditional cultures by means of the modern Western synthesis. In both cases, the "new Asian elites" claimed to interpret the peoples' contemporary experiences. They did this through the modern Western synthesis of religion-culture-society-political order, not by means of accumulated traditional Eastern values and wisdom. This often resulted in the separation of literacy from culture, implying that those who preserved traditional cultures would not adjust to new situations.

Despite their newly discovered love for Western civilization and its secularized salvation, the "new Asian elites" were passionate "patriots" and not vanguards of Western colonialism. It cannot be denied that some of them were manipulated by colonial administrators. But for the most part they were determined to reform the disintegrating Asian cultures with the newly imported gospel of salvation, which included liberty, equality, fraternity, science, and democracy. Some of the "new Asian elites" embraced Christianity and later communism. Under the impact of modern Western civilization and by the effort of the "new Asian elites," Asian societies began to have a new appearance. The "old Asian elites" were losing influence in modern Asia, where the old system of education, which was entrusted to religious institutions, was replaced by a new public school system. Even the sacred domain of religion was invaded by critical scholarship imported from the West. People lost their status and were treated as individuals who were expected to fight for their opportunities in a competitive society.

Such radical changes in Asia caused social and economic upheavals as well as mental agonies for the "old elites" and the "masses," who developed mutual sympathy and affection. They did not resent foreign intruders, but they were bewildered, not knowing what to believe and how to act in the new situation. Both the "old elites" and the "masses" were torn between the new wants they acquired in the modern period and a sense of nostalgia for the old order that they continued to idealize. They began to envisage the restoration of past glory at some future time. In this situation, the "modernization of tradition" became inseparable from "traditioning modernity," the combination of which has not been widely understood.

In addition to, or between, the "new" and the "old" elites was a small number of Asian elites of a third type, whom I refer to as "modern religious reformers." They were often criticized, attacked, and ridiculed by both the "new" and the "old" elites. Yet these modern religious reformers were convinced that their inherited religious and cultural traditions had sufficient resiliency to come to terms with the serious issues raised by modernity. They had been influenced by Western education and Western thought, but they were proud of the languages, cultures, and religions of their homelands. They were leaders and practitioners, rather than thinkers and scholars. They also had an astute understanding of the religious, cultural, social, and political situations of Asia without being narrow nationalists. Moreover, they had a global vision. It was fortunate that some of the able, young, modern religious reformers, such as Vivekānanda (died

1933) of India, Dharmapāla (died 1919) of Ceylon (now Sri Lanka), and Shaku Sōyen (died 1919) of Japan, participated in the World's Parliament of Religions. In Chicago they had a platform from which to address the whole world. Even though their homelands were strongly influenced by Western civilization, they had the dream of reversing the tide of history and thought of the possibility of "Easternization of the West."

The era of the two world wars was a turbulent period worldwide. Most Asians, compelled to sit on the sidelines of world history, were interested but frustrated spectators. They sensed that World War I signified the moral bankruptcy of Western civilization. After World War I they watched with keen interest the emergence of two men, Wilson and Lenin, who offered their new gospels to the troubled world. Long before the tension between the USA and the USSR became apparent, these two philosophies became live options in the minds of Asian leaders, as exemplified by the emotional conflict that haunted the life of Sun Yat-sen of China. But neither Wilson nor Lenin presented a solution to the predicament of Asians, who therefore felt compelled to think of their future in terms of political independence. It was for the cause of independence that the "new" and the "old" Asian elites cooperated. Both groups were determined to rectify the political injustices rendered to them under the Western colonial administration. Even the Westernized intellectual Nehru candidly affirmed: "We are citizens of no mean country and we are proud of the land of our birth, of our people, our culture and tradition."[51] A powerful convergence of cultural tradition and revolutionary goals, each supporting and enforcing the other, was established. In this situation, the "old" and the "new" elites utilized "anti-Westernism" effectively to arouse the masses to join the movement for independence.

People in Asia realize that the current dilemma is due to the fact that the success of Western domination of the whole world was such that the Westerners neglected to be critical of the so-called Western synthesis of religion-culture-society-political order. Consequently, in the eyes of many Westerners, the nineteenth century, which might be characterized as a Western-and-Christian era, lasted a little longer than the year 1900. Actually, to the majority of the human race, which lives in the non-Western world, it was not the year 1900 but the year 1945 that marked a line of demarcation between two worlds of experience, as Irving Kristol observed.[52] The real problem of our time is not the emergence of many new quarrelsome nations in Asia and Africa in the post-1945 era, but rather what both caused and resulted from their political independence—the redefinition of peoples' conception of the dignity, value, and freedom of human beings. Conversely, people in Asia and Africa are now destined to experience, as much as Westerners do, the anguish and agony of life in the twentieth century.

Those who know Asia agree that the kaleidoscopic changes that are taking place there today reflect the revolutionary whirlwind that is sweeping all Asian nations, from Afghanistan in the West (where the situation became more complex after the Russian occupation)[53] to Japan in the East. What disturbs many people, especially those with a traditional image of Asia, is the unique intertwining of revolution and tradition. MacMahon Ball called our attention to the intriguing problem of the multidimensional character of contemporary Asian revolution shortly after World War II. According to him, in the first place, it is a revolt "against Western colonialism"; second, it is a revolt "against the gross inequalities of fortune"; third, it implies "a determination that the destinies of the East will be ends in themselves, not means to Western ends."[54] The characteristic ethos of post-war Asia was not concerned with communism. "Their outlook was overshadowed by past conflict with imperial power; for them the greater fear was the entrenchment of colonialism, and not the advance of a new and aggressive expansion [of communism]."[55]

Ironically, some people in the West still confuse Asian revolution with communism. Actually, Asians know little about communism, and Marxism as an ideology does not seem to attract the intelligentsia, except the diehards, as it did before the war. The phenomenon of Asian communism should dispel the popular notion that poverty is the cause of communism. MacMahon Ball is empathetic in stating that "it is not poverty, but the way people come to feel about it, that may create communists." He goes on to say: "The impact of the West has destroyed the old religious and family and village loyalties, and robbed life of its spiritual comfort and purpose. People ask for a new code, a new certainty, a new religion, and some of them find it in communism."[56] Many Asian youth find inspiration in thinking that communism is the most viable guide for social change that ends corruption and inequality among the semifeudalistic regimes that have been kept alive mostly with the financial backing of dreaded Western powers. But, as an Indian observer points out, "communism is not the same as the social revolution which is shaking . . . our complacent world of traditional values. Nor have communists brought it about. What the communists claim to do is to explain the revolution and to have the right to lead it to a successful end."[57]

If it is true that the wind of revolutionary change is blowing all over Asia, it is equally true that tradition exerts tremendous influence on various aspects of life. It should also be pointed out that Asian revolution often transforms modernity into a new tradition. Political independence not only meant the transfer of political sovereignty but also the restructuring of personal, national, and cultural identity—the pride and dignity of the people. Confronted by such a monumental task, various nations in Asia, including India, Pakistan, Southeast Asian nations, China, and Japan, have attempted different ways of harnessing revolutionary and traditional drives for the task of establishing a national and cultural identity for themselves. An increasing number of people in Asia take it for granted that they are destined to export to other parts of the world not only material goods but also their versions of spiritual liberation and political freedom.

THE YOUNGER CHURCHES AND THE
EASTERNIZATION OF THE WORLD

As we observe the current global picture, two important matters require mentioning: the case of the "younger churches" and the "Easternization of the world" (a short-hand expression for the growing influence of the non-Western world on the West), both of which have been often overlooked, exaggerated, or misunderstood. Efforts are made in various quarters to ignore these terms, but I feel that we had better try to understand the nature and implication of these phenomena.

Using the term "younger churches" to refer to Christian churches in traditionally non-Christian Asia and Africa is somewhat ambiguous, since some of the oldest Christian churches are found in these parts of the world. The fact that the European-based churches, in their unfamiliarity with these ancient churches, now call them "younger churches" does not make sense, but we will use this term for lack of any better designation.

William E. Hocking once stated that "a religion is always a truth (embodied in a creed), a ritual, and a code"[58] to which we might add "and a community." According to Hocking, Christianity has been more belligerent than, say, Buddhism, in its approach to other religions. "Professing to supply all the religious needs of mankind, it has called for singleness of allegiance. . . . The march of Christianity has therefore been a demand for Either-Or decisions: the temples and idols of the 'heathen' have had to fall."[59] Previously, we mentioned that the European Christian missionary societies followed the colonial expansion of European nations to Asia and Africa. And in the nineteenth century, American churches joined the global missionary enterprise. In 1915, according to Robinson: "Of the 117 foreign and 19 indigenous missionary societies working in India and Ceylon, 41 are British, 41 American, 12 from the continent of Europe, 8 from Australia, and 3 are international."[60] Similarly, Africa, the Middle East, and Southeast Asia, as well as the Pacific islands and the Far East, became fields of European and American missionary work by the early twentieth century.

During recent centuries in Asia there was a widespread feeling that Eastern cultures and religions were disintegrating from within, and that the Eastern world was threatened by the advance of the West. There were basically three kinds of indigenous reactions of the East in confronting the encroachment of the West. The first was a positive reaction to things Western by small groups of mostly young people in urban areas who wished to be emancipated from their traditional cultural and religious traditions. The second was a negative reaction by a group of

conservative people who rejected anything Western. The third
was the indifferent reaction of a large majority of the masses.
Christianity, especially Protestantism, initially attracted the first
group, who welcomed the new faith together with the ideologies
of Darwin, Huxley, Voltaire, Rousseau, Kant, Hegel, Schopen-
hauer, Nietzsche, Bergson, and Tolstoy.

Early European Protestant missionaries protested against
the compromises and laxity of the established churches in Europe. They believed, in the words of H. Richard Niebuhr: "Whatever may be the customs of the society in which the Christian
lives, and whatever the human achievements it conserves, Christ
is seen as opposed to them, so that he confronts men with the
challenge of an 'either-or' decision."[61] Some of the early Asian
converts to Christianity echoed the "Christ against Culture"
mentality of early missionaries. Those missionaries wanted to
separate the native converts from their "pagan" surroundings
to enable them to grow in the "Christian" way of life. They
resorted to establishing strange structures usually referred to as
"mission compounds" in which missionaries exercised absolute
authority. In them, as Neill graphically pointed out, the missionary usually "determined what should be done, and how it
should be done. The function of the convert was to listen and
obey."[62] The missionary thought of himself or herself as the sole
fount of Christian knowledge, but was almost unconsciously
found to be the sole depository of Western learning. Missionaries
did not deliberately offer themselves as agents of the imperialist
policies of the European nations. Nevertheless, they shared the
prejudices of colonial officials in dealing with the colored races
and accepted the intrinsic superiority of white people. In other
words, even though missionaries left Europe with the gospel of
"Christ against Culture," in the East they behaved as though
they believed in the "Christ of European Culture." They taught
European cultural values as though they were Christian values,
and demanded that their native converts abandon the customs
of their pre-Christian, "heathen" past. Deciding for Christ often
meant that the native converts be "denationalized" and Westernized within the mission compounds, where "loyalty to
Christ" was tested by "loyalty to missionaries."

The tragedy is that these mission compounds had self-perpetuating tendencies, which have not totally disappeared even after the departure of Western missionaries. Nationalist leaders, motivated by the ideal of self-determinism, have been critical about the residue of the "alienness" of Christianity in Asia and Africa, especially since World War I. The continued Western political and economic control of the Middle East, Africa, and much of Asia made nationalist leaders engage in a series of campaigns against Western domination. The rising nationalistic sentiment in the non-Western world, coupled with the Western churches' increased interest in foreign missions, resulted in the frequent use of the term "younger churches" rather than "missionary churches," as well as the discussion of the relation between the younger and the older churches starting with the Jerusalem meeting of the International Missionary Council (IMC) in 1928. It was suggested that "to face the unfinished task of world evangelization" the cooperation of both groups was required.[63] For this task, "self-support" was proposed not only as an important financial principle but also as the correct expression of the genuine church's life, even though the mission-compound mentality and the bureaucratic structure of the Western missionary societies made the transfer of management and leadership from missionaries to indigenous personnel very difficult.

Ironically, many "younger churches" in the non-Western world were encouraged to become carbon copies of the Western churches, which reflected the old order of their society that had made inevitable compromises with vested interests and colonial policies in the past. Also, some Eastern Christians, products of the missionary churches, feel closer to Western churches than to their non-Christian neighbors in the same localities. Only in the Missionary Conference in Madras (1938) was it pointed out that every younger church should bear witness to the gospel with "new tongues," that is, "in a direct, clear and close relationship with the cultural and religious heritage of its own country."[64] The Madras meeting raised many important questions regarding the nature of the younger churches, but this discussion was abruptly terminated by World War II.

During the war, the younger churches, cut off from Western tutelage and support, had to mature quickly. Some of them had to engage in serious soul-searching concerning their religious and cultural identities. These "younger churches" were destined to be greatly misunderstood both by Western Christians and by their non-Christian neighbors.

The younger churches are misunderstood by Western churches because the latter expect the younger churches to be an extension of Western Christendom. They pay lip service to the changing situation in the world, but in actual practice they act as if the world has not changed. Western churches still have a paternalistic attitude toward the younger churches. Asiatic and African church leaders continue to be sent to the West for "higher" training. What is overlooked is that, just as the religious groups in America developed an unknown "denominational type," religious groups in the non-Western world are bound to develop their own new structures. And just as various religious groups, Jewish and Christian, learned the art of living together with the principle of religious liberty in eighteenth century America, it is very natural that the "younger churches" in the non-Western world learn the art of coexistence with Hinduism, Buddhism, Islam, folk religions, and other religious and semireligious traditions. Already, Indian Christians proposed the principle of the "secular state"—something comparable to religious liberty—as the goal of the younger churches. They are persuaded that it is possible to have a secular state in a deeply religious society—"a secular state in which real religious freedom and real respect for the conscience are accepted by all." They further state: "if the secular state is to be a reality . . . Christians must learn to initiate activities and schemes for social welfare and social change which might be adopted by men of good will even if they do not accept the faith which inspires such activities." [65] Although many Western Christians think that the goal of the "younger churches" would be fulfilled by achieving a self-governing, self-supporting, and self-propagating status, they often fail to understand that Asian and African Christians should develop *simultaneously* both the "inner meaning" of Christianity for themselves and the "outer meaning" of Christianity as an integral part of religious plurality in order to live meaningfully and participate in the reality of the non-Western world.

The "younger churches" are also misunderstood by their non-Christian compatriots. Many Asian and African Christians, reflecting the heritage of uninformed missionaries, are ignorant of, and indifferent to, the non-Christian religions and non-Western cultures of their own environment. Also, as Indian Christians admit, many of them are "ineffective spectators" of the contemporary scene, as they have never been trained to concern themselves with contemporary events.[66] A more crucial reason for misunderstanding is the absence of a common frame of reference. During the era of Western colonialism, culture and education meant that which had been imported from abroad to the non-Western world. Western logic, rhetoric, and categories were expected to serve as a common frame of reference, not only between Westerners and non-Westerners but between Christians in the East and their non-Christian neighbors. But the modern Western synthesis of religion-culture-society-political order, which had influenced the whole world during the nineteenth and early twentieth centuries, did not remain intact even before the end of Western colonialism and the erosion of missionary zeal on the part of Western churches. Some of the non-Western intellectuals who appropriated Marxism, rational humanism, and scientism, which are critical of religious traditions in the West, began to ridicule Asian and African Christians who continued to live in a dated Westernized world without being enlightened by modernity. These Eastern critics of the "younger churches" tend to be more tolerant, as much as Western critics of Judaism and Christianity are about the Western counterparts of the "younger churches" of Eastern religions, such as groups of Western devotees of Zen, Yoga, Tibetan Buddhism, Nichiren Shōshū, and other modern Indian, Korean, and Japanese religious groups.

The "Easternization of the world" is a short-hand way of saying that the era of monolithic Western domination of the whole world is over and that the influence of the East is beginning to be felt in the Western world. No one at the World's Parliament of Religions in 1893 ever thought that the time would come for the West to be on the receiving end, either materially or spiritually. Even astute Western thinkers believed that the modern history of the non-Western world was an appendage to the history of Western expansion. It must be admitted that modern development in the East might have been easily misconstrued by those who view the world from an Europocentric perspective. When progressive Eastern youth eagerly adopted certain features of Western civilization during the past century and a half in order to restructure the social, cultural, economic, and political dimensions of their societies (whereby Eastern societies and cultures might be accepted as equals by the West), many Westerners thought of it in terms of "westernization" of the East. The actual intention of the Eastern youths was "modernization," which is qualitatively different from "westernization," despite superficial similarities.

The conservative elements in the East also mistook "modernization" for "westernization." (Unlike Westerners, Eastern conservatives resented what they regarded as the "westernization" of the East.) A large number of young people from the non-Western world studied in European and American universities. This fact was also misunderstood by Westerners as well as by Eastern conservatives. In fact, many people in the West, including missionary-minded people, were convinced that ancient cultural traditions in the non-Western world were doomed to extinction, despite views to the contrary of a small number of scholars. As late as 1928, a spokesman of Western Christendom asserted that Eastern religions and cultures were "going to be smashed anyhow, perhaps not too quickly, but surely, and what is going to do it . . . is modern science, modern commerce, and modern political organization."[67]

The experience of the West with the non-Western world during recent centuries resulted in the deeply ingrained mental habit among Westerners of regarding the world as a vast territory to be exploited and viewing non-Westerners as peoples to be enlightened by true civilization. Meanwhile, it is widely felt that the West could live happily without the non-Western world, peoples, cultures, and religions. Most Western education has been concerned primarily with the Western tradition; people can complete their education without learning anything about non-Western histories, geographies, religions, or cultures.

Evidently, even the globe-conscious educators, who presumably appreciate the values of non-Western traditions, are persuaded that only the Western civilization is really important and sufficient for Westerners. In 1952, writing his Introduction to the *Great Books*, Robert Maynard Hutchins, the former chancellor of the University of Chicago, stated: "A frantic concern to understand Russia or the Orient will lead us nowhere, unless the student brings to these problems skill in analysis, order in valuing, knowledge of history and such social experience as gives him a basis for judging what he finds out about Russia and the Orient." But he went on to say: ". . . at the moment we have all we can do to understand ourselves in order to be prepared for the forthcoming meetings between East and West. . . . The time for that will come when we have understood our own tradition well enough to understand another."[68] Unfortunately, Hutchins is not alone in feeling this way. First, amazing numbers of people agree with his statement that only "when we have understood our own tradition well enough" should we be willing to proceed to understand another, as though it is humanly possible for us to understand our own tradition well enough. Second, there is an implicit notion that such qualities as "skill in analysis, order in valuing, knowledge of history and certain kinds of social experience" can be learned only from the Western tradition, and that the only things to do when you meet others is to be able to cope with them and try to understand them in your "Western" categories. (Ironically, much of the so called interreligious dialogues are conducted similarly.)

Notwithstanding the understandable inertia, indifference, and ignorance, we can detect a new spirit, a new attitude, and a new cultural fashion in our time. Shortly after World War II, a learned Catholic priest-scholar, Henri de Lubac, shocked many people by his observation that Europe was ripe for spiritual colonization by the East. He pointed out that there is no shelf in European bookstores more patronized than the shelf of books on Indian spirituality at all levels, and that this was true in Catholic bookstores as well.[69] This observation was shared by a Dutch Protestant missiologist, Hendrik Kraemer. In his own words:

> There is evident in the fields of pictorial art, of novels, of thinking and of depth-psychology, a kind of premonition. They manifest a spontaneous openness, *a readiness to be invaded*, to become "spiritually colonized" by the Orient. There are open "gates" for Eastern invasion, a *pénétration pacifique*, in the forms of dispositions and needs of mind, of intuitions, which are transparently expressed in the thinking of the Orient. . . . This remarkable fact has not yet been appreciated in its true and profound significance.[70]

Today no observing person can fail to see that the Eastern influence has penetrated into Europe and North America. The appeal of the East in the West is no longer confined to a relatively small number of romantic thinkers or those who are interested in something "far away and long ago."[71] The East has come into the immediate experience of many average Westerners through art, literature, cuisine, movies, karate, jūdō, Aikidō, flower arrangement, transistor radios, TV, computer technology, and automobiles. Perhaps more significant is the popularity of various kinds of Eastern spirituality and different religious traditions in the West. The fact that the Unification church can hire many talented young men and women to work for their lucrative fishing business in Gloucester, Massachusetts; their processing plants in Norfolk, Virginia; their shipyard in Bayou La Batre, Alabama; or their retail fish stores in New York,[72] and at the same time bring together highly respected philosophers, theologians, and scientists—including several recipients of the Nobel Prize—to their conferences testifies to the fact that the Unification church and other Eastern religious groups are penetrating deeply into Western culture and society.

There are different Western reactions to the phenomenon of the "easternization of the world." The simplest reaction is either to deny that there is such a phenomenon or plead ignorance about things non-Western. Second, there are a wide range of ethnocentrisms—from a gentle and passive kind that accepts the legitimacy of non-Westerners to stick to their inherited traditions just as Westerners have been reared to hang on to their own, to an aggressive and militant attitude that asserts that only the Western-Christian tradition is true and the only right thing for non-Westerners to do is to give up their own traditions in favor of the Western option. Many Westerners, including many convinced Christians and Jews who had never been interested in other religions and cultures before, are now looking for easy lessons and quick answers regarding the art, literature, culture, and religion of the non-Western world that attract their children and grandchildren. With the increasing Eastern influence, the spiritual and mental world of the Westerners is beginning to be as bewildering as their non-Western counterpart has been since the beginning of the westernization of the world in the modern period.

GLOBAL SYNTHESIS AND THE UNITY OF HUMANKIND

It is impossible to predict the distant future of our rapidly changing world. It is even hazardous to guess what might happen before the year 2000—assuming, of course, that there will be a year 2000. However, we must try to understand the present-day situation as accurately and as honestly as possible.

Unfortunately, there is no vantage point from which to view crisscrossing contemporary currents and movements that can be interpreted in many ways. All of us have certain prejudgments, presuppositions, and prejudices. We are caught up in their confusing streams. In addition, every individual, and every culture and people, lives not only in the geographical, physical world but also in what might be termed a "world of meaning." Some are quite conscious of the mental and psychic processes involved in ordering the diverse experiences and meanings that comprise the mystery of life to attain their own self-identity. Most of us, however, are not always aware of just how we acquire our particular "worlds of meaning"—bit by bit at home, in playgrounds and schools, and through our association with a wide variety of people and events. For the most part, we inherit not only our language, ideas, and values, but also the small intimate habits of daily life, such as how we prepare our food, put on our clothes, and hush our babies to sleep. Thus, consciously or unconsciously, our own "world of meaning" approximates the worldviews implicit in our cultural and religious traditions, which in turn exert decisive influence in patterning our behavior, beliefs, and goals of life.[73]

Throughout this book we have seen repeatedly in different geographical regions the natural inclination for religions, cultures, and social and political orders to develop seamless syntheses, even though we can theoretically talk about each component separately. Religion(s) and culture(s) have especially close dialectic relationships. According to Paul Tillich, if religion wants to be realized, it has to assume form and become culture, while culture,

> even when it is not religious in intention, is religious in substance, for every cultural act contains an unconditional meaning. Yet when religion becomes culture, it may lose its depth and its sense of relatedness to the unconditional; it may degenerate into an absolute devotion to conditioned cultural realities. On the other hand, culture, even in the act of opposing "religion," may rediscover the unconditional threat and support, and it may bring forth new religious creation.[74]

Our study has revealed how various religions, many which possess an explicit or implicit vision of the unity of humankind, have become components of the grand syntheses of the religion-culture-social-political orders. In so doing they came to pay their absolute devotion without regard to "conditioned" (and provincial) cultural-social-and-political realities that tended to identify the "religious-cultural-social-political synthesis" as new religious realities.

Once the seamless "religious-cultural-social-political synthesis" becomes a reality, individuals within that orbit tend to feel that its "circularity" provides ground for its absolute and coherent truth, which deserves and commands the devotion and loyalty of the individuals involved. For example, in most parts of the world if you ask people about their "religion," which presumably provides them with normative views of reality that authenticate their existence, people would most likely respond that their religion is what their families, communities, ethnic, or national groups accept "religion" to be. In these cases "religion" does not refer to any single area of human experience, be it feeling, thought, or need. It implies something akin to the "religious-cultural-social-political synthesis" that embraces a people's total life. Of course these features can be legitimately singled out and studied as "religious" (in a narrow sense), "cultural," "social," or "political" factors. But all of them have a predilection toward "adhesiveness." The seamlessness of the whole organism is such that theoretical distinctions among them elude individuals most of the time. To most people, these syntheses constitute their worlds of meaning and provide them with a sense of certainty. People are born into the "circularity" of this half-visible and half-invisible world; they grow up, live, and die in it. They learn the most sacred meaning of their lives from the religious-cultural-social-political synthesis that defines the nature of reality, the source of its order, and provides the authentification and justification of individuals' and society's beliefs, thoughts, convictions, and actions.

One of the most obvious characteristics of the religious-cultural-social-political synthesis is its characteristic mental outlook toward the recollection of past experiences, the delineation of the meaning of present existence, and the anticipation of the future. These three foci constitute a kind of "mental prism" that sorts out significant events from a mass of data and reenacts historical realities in the world of ideas and imagination. This prism also has the built-in self-protection of forgetfulness and optical illusion. All of us take this kind of prism for granted to the extent that we often assume that we were born with it. It is worth noting the close dialectic relations that exist between our mental prism and our concept of "progress." The notion of "progress," a word derived from *gressus* (step), implies an act of stepping forward to a better situation. It was Paul Tillich who made a helpful distinction between the "concept of progress," which is just a theoretical abstraction, and the "idea of progress," which is an interpretation of our historical experience in terms of the concept of progress, with or without a verifiable basis, most often based on speculation or affirmation. Our current concept of "progress" goes back to the belief of the ancient Hebrew community, which under the inspiration of Zoroastrianism eschatology affirmed that God had chosen a nation and a people and would fulfill his promise to move history toward a specific end. Christianity, born as a messianic movement within the Jewish fold, inherited the Zoroastrian-inspired Jewish eschatological faith in "progress."[75]

In summary, Western civilization, which developed by fusing Hellenism, Middle-Eastern religion and Roman jurisprudence, in the course of time successfully (1) transformed Christianity into a this-worldly religion, (2) tried to be religiously neutral, and eventually (3) became "secular" through the experiences of the Renaissance, Enlightenment, and scientific revolution. And yet—following Tillich's observation that "culture, even in the act of opposing 'religion,' . . . may bring forth new religious creation"[76]—the modern Western "religious-cultural-social-political synthesis," supported by such ideas as the Calvinistic notion of this-worldly asceticism, became *de facto* a pseudo-religion of secularized salvation. It was the "idea of progress" (and the idea of "modernization" in more recent years) that was trumpeted to the non-Western world as the goal of the true civilization during the era of "Western domination" (the nineteenth and the first half of the twentieth centuries). The impact of Western domination was such that westernized intellectuals and many rulers of the nations in the non-Western world "inhaled" the "idea of progress" (supported by non-Western religious and cultural notions) as well as the Western modes of demarcating human life and experience and of reshaping their societies and political orders.

I am always astonished to read the diaries of the intelligentsia in Asia during the early decades of our century and to learn that they idealized the modern Western "religious-cultural-social-political synthesis" as though it were an immortal creation. They were sincere in attempting to restructure Asia along the model of Northern Atlantic (British and Western European) nations and the United States, with the accompanying capitalism, democracy, technology, etc. Many non-Westerners, particularly farsighted and reform-minded leaders from various fields, had a genuine admiration for Westerners' accomplishments. This was especially true during the nineteenth century in arts, literature, music, philosophy, education, defense, technology, commerce, etc. They hoped that their compatriots would try to catch up with the "progressive Westerners" by emulating them.

It might surprise Westerners, to whom World War I is simply one of two great wars fought in our century, to discover that, to many non-Western leaders, who had earlier idealized the West, it signified an irrevocable event—the breakdown of the European (and American) moral community. Thus, to them, the Western "religious-cultural-social-political synthesis" no longer remained the paradigmatic model by which the non-Western world was to be guided. Their concern became how to be emancipated from the yoke of Westerners, how to be selective about Western features (some of which they needed or wanted), and how to eventually compete with the West.

There was a wide variety of reactions to the impact of the West in the non-Western world. Even in the world of Islam, very Western-oriented (on the whole) Turkey, and rather traditionally religious Pakistan show an interesting contrast in their reactions to the impact of the West.[77] (We should also not overlook a series of literary works by the Muslim mystics and their genuine effort in fostering human unity in the midst of the complex divisions of the global community.) In East Asia, Japan attempted to master the Western approaches in such a way that she would become in effect another colonial power in East Asia,[78] whereas China, which from the time of Sun Yat-sen's revolution in 1912 had attempted to straddle between the American form of political democracy and the economic democracy à la the USSR, eventually developed its own "religious-cultural-social-political synthesis" (which is independent of Moscow) under the leadership of Mao Tse-tung.[79] I am convinced of the necessity of understanding how the Chinese operate with their unique views of history, good and evil, and the meaning of life and the universe in order to appreciate their reactions to the West, or to the USSR. Chinese categories and concepts are very different from those outsiders identify. Even the views of Indian Buddhists and those of Chinese Buddhists show remarkable contrasts.[80] On this side of the Pacific, Latin America seems to face serious internal problems that complicate its response to the impact of its North American neighbors and the North Atlantic nations.[81] Also, although my knowledge of Africa is abysmally limited, I suspect that people in that continent are also in the process of developing a set of their own religious-cultural-social-political syntheses very different from Western models.[82]

The fascinating fact is that these non-Western religious-cultural-social-political syntheses are penetrating the Western world. For many Westerners, it is still a strange and new experience to encounter the encroachment of non-Western categories and worldviews. This is particularly true with Americans, who have long lived with the myth of the "melting pot," whereby they assumed that these alien thought forms would eventually be converted to the Europocentric American mode of thinking. Part of the misunderstanding is based on the fact that all the non-Western religious-cultural-social-political syntheses that are coming to Western shores have felt the impact of the West to the degree that they have embraced certain Westernized features. In fact, some Westerners might mistake these non-Western syntheses as extensions of Western ideologies. But the discerning minds in the West know how different these non-Western syntheses are, as illustrated by the observations of Henri de Lubac and Hendrik Kraemer on the "spiritual colonization by the Orient" (*pénétration pacifique*).

Yet the penetration of non-Western art, religion, philosophy, and literature has encouraged some Westerners' sense of *exotica* to deprecate things Western—from social custom, polity, and the educational system to art and religion. During the latter part of the last century some New England intelligentsia, to whom the Western spiritual tradition had lost its force, looked for quiet, solace, and escape—"in search of Nirvana," to quote John La Farge's favorite expression—in Eastern philosophies, religions, and cultures.[83] In our own time, a massive invasion of Eastern meditation practices, such as Zen, Yoga, and Transcendental Meditation, tends to create a one-sided impression that meditation is an Eastern phenomenon that is needed in a spiritually barren Western world. This viewpoint overlooks the historical fact that meditation is one of the most universally accepted religious practices, both in the East and in the West.

To complicate the matter further, the present-day "religious" components of various religious-cultural-social-political syntheses often detach themselves from their historical contexts and adroitly attach themselves to other syntheses. For example, the Black Muslims, Zen, Tibetan Buddhist, or Hare Krishna groups in North America or Europe have become just as common as Presbyterians in Korea or Methodists in India. The expansion of Eastern religions to the West, as much as Christian and Islamic expansions in Asia and Africa, have raised the perennial issue familiar in missionary circles as to how much cultural-social (and even political) baggage should accompany religious expansions. More fundamentally, we are confronted with the issue, dramatically articulated by Oswald Spengler, of in what sense the expansion of a religion from one context to the next is really possible; or as he phrased it: "What matters in all such cases is not the original meaning of the forms, but the forms themselves, as disclosing to the native sensibility and understanding of the observer potential modes of his own creativeness."[84]

In North America, we also face such knotty problems as the tension between the Roman Catholic laity's sexual practices and their church's official positions, or the Vatican's authority versus that of American universities' for indefinite tenure, to say nothing of the many Christian groups' criticisms of American foreign policies or the Roman Catholic bishops' evaluation of the American economic system.[85] American Jews also have their share of headaches in reference to the State of Israel and the American Middle East policy.[86]

Even a limited knowledge of history teaches two important facts. First, from the dawn of civilizations, human beings have been pulled in two diametrically opposed directions, by their inclination toward ethnocentrism or particularity, on the one hand, and by their visceral feeling and conscious aspiration for the universality and unity of humankind, on the other. Thoughtful men and women of this century, who have already experienced the horrors of two bloody world wars, are sensitive to the tragic state of the brokenness of humanity and are trying to make every effort to actualize their own visions of the unity of humankind. They know by bitter experience that the real problems that confront humanity are not soluble within the confines of the egocentric sovereign nations, or by creating more of the quarrelsome regional power blocks, or even through the current framework of the suspicion-ridden United Nations. The great powers, which still wield military or commercial power, are under the happy illusion that they can somehow forge the supernational communities needed for a unified or reunified humanity, but they are quickly losing their credibility and influence in this respect.[87]

Caught in this kind of untenable situation, some people are trying to retreat into their small worlds of complacent privacy, while others try to solve today's complex problems by yesterday's simple answers.[88] Others cling to the vision of "progress"—either in its Judeo-Christian sense or in its modern (antireligious) sense, including the Marxian approach to it.[89] Many people in the West, heirs of those who believed themselves to be the creators and transmitters of the only "true"—that is, "Western"—civilization, often fall into errors of assuming that the unity of humanity and human communities depends on the non-Westerners' acceptance of Western thoughts, beliefs, and technologies. Many Westerners are interested in finding their place in the universe, but they are fairly certain that they occupy central stage. Some of them feel that sooner or later their Western modes of thought and life might encounter their non-Western counterparts, but now they would rather look the other way. They tend to echo the feeble justification advanced by Robert Maynard Hutchins that we have enough to do in understanding ourselves. Hutchins's logic is perfectly clear: Westerners have to understand their own tradition well enough, because unquestionably, the Western tradition has to be the norm and yardstick to understand and evaluate non-Western traditions. Such a logic is a breeding ground for provincialism—and ultimately, for racism.

Many Westerners intellectually realize that a new world order is in the making and that they have to understand the dynamics of peoples and events in non-Western parts of the world. Yet they are not always emotionally prepared to encounter the strangeness of other peoples or are misled by their wishful thinking that minimizes the religious, cultural, and other differences of the peoples involved: Mircea Eliade, Romanian-American historian of religions and novelist, astutely observed that in Westerners' encounters with others they tend to depend on the more Westernized representatives of non-Western peoples or enter into relations with, say, the East only in such external spheres as economics and politics. In his opinion, "the Western world has not yet, or not generally, met with authentic representatives of the 'real' non-Western traditions."[90] Eliade, who throughout his life had unshakable convictions about the unity of humankind as well as great concern for the "new humanism" that would authenticate it, stressed in his last public lecture the necessity of better mutual understanding between contemporary *homo faber* (scientists and technologists) and *homo religiosus* (religious person), for both of them on different levels and perspectives have been motivated by the same fears, hopes, and convictions, even though by necessity their concepts, methods, and procedures seem to take different forms.[91] He was enough of a realist to know that such a mutual understanding and appreciation in depth would not come soon, or easily, but his basically optimistic stance was eloquently portrayed by his characteristic mood of "Waiting for the Dawn."[92]

Actually, most people are bound to experience separate historical and empirical religions before they discover "religion" *à la* Eliade, and opinions vary widely about the nature of empirical religions. (Curiously, numerous men and women who readily admit their ignorance of scientific, artistic, and other humanistic subjects are often convinced of the truth of their views on religious matters.) For example, there is a widespread feeling that the structure of the religious-cultural-social-political synthesis has been fixed permanently. Admittedly, most of those born in Ireland or the Philippines are likely to be Roman Catholics, and many of those born in Pakistan or Egypt grow up as Muslims. But religion is the most mobile component of the religious-cultural-social-political synthesis. Besides, the impact of non-Western syntheses is beginning to be strongly felt in the West.

The so-called interreligious or intercultural "dialogues" are becoming increasingly popular. Someone has pointed out that the idea of "dialogue" became acceptable as the Christian churches in the West lost missionary incentives. Whether or not such an observation is too cynical, at least one American scholar has the distinct impression that

> much of the external dialogue taking place today is by way of the initiative of Christian individuals and organizations. While it is true that many Asian philosophers and religious thinkers have studied in Europe and America, or spent years in the investigation of Western philosophy and theology, they have done so primarily to acquire a knowledge of Western skills and methods in order to reexamine their own traditions. Most of the openness to new levels of religious understanding . . . "mutual transformation" has been on the Western and Christian side. Certainly the motivation for external dialogue is primarily Western.[93]

Rightly or wrongly, the author of the above-quoted article is of the opinion that Europeans had originally regarded America as a stage for their "Westernization," that is, their revitalization. Americans have now joined the movement of Westernization in Asia, fostering and participating in the dialogue between Western Christian and Asian religious traditions.[94]

If the interreligious or intercultural dialogues were primarily Western-inspired affairs, it should not be surprising that it is the Western thinkers and scholars who, depending on Western concepts, methods, logics, and rhetorics, propose to get together with their non-Western counterparts. They are bound to have one-sided "Western" monologues with non-Western guests, who are expected to present their religious and cultural experiences and expressions primarily as "data" for the benefit of their Western hosts. This type of orientation was followed by the 1893 World's Parliament of Religions. Evidently, many of the

East-West interreligious dialogues are still Western-inspired, so that an American participant in a recent dialogue between Christianity and Buddhism felt that "much of the renewal of Buddhist interest in their own tradition [in the context of such a dialogue] may be the result of Western interest in them."[95] However, this is not a peculiar approach of Christian scholars in the West. It is equally tempting for many Western scholars of non-Western religion(s), including social scientists, even those who have little concern with the loss of religious self-confidence in the West or the revitalization of the Western tradition, to take the easy way out by pursuing non-Christian religions and cultures—as their predecessors dealt with the native American traditions—as "data" to be analyzed by means of Western scholarly methods.

If a more genuine "dialogue" should take place, it must be based on the sobering realization of the reality of the world's religious pluralism. Furthermore, we should have a more candid and realistic recognition that each of the religious-cultural-social-political syntheses is grounded in its own distinct manner of demarcating life and human experience. There is no short-cut by facile rhetoric to bypass these basic differences in our effort to inch along toward the common goal of the unity of humankind and the establishment of a truly global community. In this respect, I do not foresee, as some romantics do, the emergence of any new super-religion. I believe various religions will continue to develop according to their own dynamics, crisscrossing the face of the earth. Moreover, I am persuaded that modernity, despite its antireligious features, is tolerant of an infinite variety of religious forms, so that in the future we are destined to have more, and not less, religious traditions.

How will we be able to reconcile all these different religious, cultural sensitivities and temperaments in the meantime? We have to accept the fact that by mysterious dispensation all of us were born into particular religious, cultural, social, political, national, and racial orbits at a time of growing global pluralism, following an era of Western domination of the whole world. Inevitably, we react differently to our paradoxical and contradictory situations. We cannot artificially create unity by reaching down to our lowest common denominators—shortchanging our particularities.

It will not be feasible for one dominant religion or ideology to embrace all the others or for different traditions to give up their particularities in order to spawn the unity of humankind. We have to resort to the less glamorous but more realistic option of holding in balance both the "inner" and "outer" meanings of religion. For example, we might consider the plan pursued by the Buddhist King Aśoka in third-century B.C. India, by the Apostle Paul, and by eighteenth-century American Jewish and Christian groups. Briefly, King Aśoka was faithful to the Three Jewels (the Buddha, Dharma or the liberating law discovered by the Buddha, and Saṃgha or the Buddhist community) as the "inner" meaning of Buddhism, but, as a king reigning over a multireligious empire, he developed another triad (consisting of the sacred kingship, the Buddhist-inspired pan-Indian moral principle referred to as Dharma, and the state to be guided by Buddhist influence) as the "outer" meaning of Buddhism for the India of his time.[96] The Apostle Paul, who was convinced of the "inner" meaning of Christianity that paid supreme loyalty to Jesus Christ as the Son of God and the savior of humankind, nevertheless formulated his understanding of the "outer" meaning of Christianity as one of many competing religions, each claiming supreme adherence from the populace within the Roman Empire. Accordingly, as mentioned earlier, he stated: "For although there may be so-called gods in heaven or on earth— as indeed there are many 'gods' and many 'lords'—yet *for us* there is one God, the Father . . . and one Lord, Jesus Christ" (1 Cor. 8:5-6, italics mine).

In eighteenth-century America, none of the Jewish and Christian groups were willing to give up their "inner" meaning of religion—their absolute religious claims, but all of them recognized that other rival groups had similar claims, even though each group aspired to the freedom to hold its "inner" meaning. Thus, the principle of "religious liberty" that various Jewish and Christian groups recognized as the "outer"meaning of their religions enabled different religious traditions "to dwell together in relative peace—at first they learned to tolerate each other and eventually to think of [religious] freedom for all as an inherent or natural right."[97] Granted, the contemporary religious and cultural pluralism is infinitely more complex, but we should make similar efforts to differentiate the "outer" meaning of our religion from its "inner" meaning so that we can dwell together as *de facto* equal partners.

One of the salient features of all religions is their "imperialistic" temper and "missionary" spirit. This is not necessarily because each religion attempts to dominate other peoples, though this has happened throughout history, but because each religion *defines*, for the benefit of its religious-cultural-social-political synthesis, the nature and level of reality, including ultimate reality, which is the source of the cosmic, social, and human orders. In connection with history's different visions of the unity of humankind, it has been revealed that even the most broad-minded religious vision is usually anchored in the particular perspective of that religion and the way in which it defines the nature of reality, the world, and human destiny.

It is not my intention to conclude my observations with any ready-made and stereotyped pious rhetoric. The dilemmas and problems that confront us today are far too complex and ambiguous. Our difficulties are compounded by the fact that there seems to be a broad and deep gulf between our all-too-conventional expectations and historical realities in the latter end of the twentieth century. In that connection, I quote what Walter Lippmann stated over twenty years ago in his column, "Pull Out of Vietnam." He then said:

> President Johnson is a man who, having taken the wrong road, has lost his way. Until he corrects his . . . mistake he will not get to his destination by stepping on the accelerator and pushing on. The problem that we in America face is to find our way to the right road.[98]

What Lippmann was advocating in effect was for this country, instead of following the usual and familiar method of "revising" strategies, to pursue an option that is much more basic and probably risky, that is, to "re-vision" the world situation more realistically with a fresh outlook. Similarly, we as human beings living in the latter twentieth century may be compelled to "re-visioning" our situations rather than "revising" our tired old approaches to human experience, the world, and history—approaches that are equipped by the static and provincial, mostly West-centric perceptions of what the global order ought to be.

There was a time—and it was only yesterday—when many non-Western people felt they had no choice but to swallow Hegel's exaggerated assertion that Western thought was the "measure of all things," and that only "European thought [can] provide the context and categories for the exploration of all traditions" in the world.[99] No wonder many Eastern intelligentsia in those days took seriously such Western claims as objectivity, neutrality, and universality of its science and technology, global capitalism (commerce), eternal truth (religion), the psychic unity of humankind (social sciences),[100] and totality (Marxism).[101] Even today many Westerners, especially intellectuals, still assert that all-embracing, comprehensive intellectual disciplines—not only such obvious cases as metachemistry or metageometry but also metasociology, metaanthropology, and other inquiries pertaining to art, culture, and humanities—are possible only "in a Westernized world, under conditions shaped by Western ways of thinking."[102] Such overconfidence and self-assurance of Westerners about their civilization was no doubt at the bottom of the strange "success" of modern Western colonialism. According to Ashis Nandy:

> Modern colonialism won its great victories not so much through its military and technological prowess as its ability to create secular hierarchies incompatible with the traditional order [in the non-Western world]. These hierarchies opened up new vistas for many, particularly for those exploited or cornered within the traditional order. To them the new order looked like—and here lay its psychological pull—the first step towards a more just and equal world.[103]

Furthermore, during the nineteenth and twentieth centuries (at least before World War II) Western civilization promised two other anaesthetic by-products—progress and modernization—to the non-Western world.

Today we live in a vastly different world. Many people have already experienced two world wars, the emergence of Soviet Russia, the rise and decline of Fascism, Nazism, and Japanese militarism, Korean and Vietnamese wars, etc. *Pax Britannica* had been taken over by the aura of what some people call the "American empire," [104] which dominated the whole world economically, politically, and militarily. But, according to some pundits, the American empire began to decline, especially since the Tet Offensive. Even then some people still would like to believe that the impact of the modern West managed to create a single global network and point to technology, science, commerce, communication, and transportation systems as visible signs of such a global community in the making. But honesty requires us to admit that today's world is a fragmented one. Most people in rural areas in Europe or North America, living closely to their inherited values, beliefs, and mores, feel very differently from their counterparts in urban areas, especially in the ever-increasing "rainbow cities." Nowadays more and more men and women in every continent feel trapped by the tragedies of extreme poverty, drug wars, AIDS victims, environmental issues, etc. The stability of the old order, familiar to and idealized by people of the last generation, is crumbling in light of the revolutionary changes characterized by such new phenomena as glasnost, Perestroika, the Islamic revolution, demonstrations by Chinese students, and political changes in the Eastern bloc. It is ironic that European and North American societies have "graying populations," while many nations in the Third World have much younger populations. For example, Jinwung Kim records:

> Today, some 62% of eligible voters in South Korea fall between the ages of 20 and 39. The younger generation is increasingly well educated and mobile. University students constitute 2.27% of the population, compared with 2.0% in the U.S. and 1.47% in West Germany . . . [Also] young Koreans witnessed neither the American role in eliminating Japanese colonial rule in their country nor the American "sacrifice" in the Korean War. Accordingly, they feel that South Korea has no special bond with the U.S. and they bitterly criticize the older generation for being subserviently dependent upon America.[105]

All of us living in the last decade of the twentieth century
are compelled to "re-vision" our contemporary situation, especially if we are concerned with the perennial vision of the unity
of humankind. What is happening in the world before our eyes
may not appeal to various peoples for different reasons. It must
be especially difficult for people, who had believed in the reshaping of the whole world according to the Western image, to
come to terms with the reality of our rapidly changing situation.
Sadly, amazing numbers of people still affirm what Husserl advocated decades ago. In his words:

> Europe alone can provide other traditions with a universal frame-
> work of meaning and understanding. They will have to "Europe-
> anize themselves, whereas we . . . will never, for example,
> Indianize ourselves." The "Europeanization of all foreign parts of
> mankind" . . . is the destiny of the earth.[106]

However, much to their disappointment, the reality of today's
world has already "shifted gears" in this respect. "All foreign
parts of mankind," to use Husserl's phrase, are now far more
skeptical about the alleged promises of Western civilization—
justice, equality, fraternity, modernization, and progress—in the
way they are presented practically to them. Many people in the
Third World feel about "progress" as Octavio Paz states:

> . . . at last the philosophy of progress shows its true face: feature-
> less blank. We know now that the kingdom of progress is not of
> this world: the paradise it promises us is in the future, a future
> that is impalpable, unreachable . . . [The idea of progress] has given
> us things but not more being . . . How can we not turn away and
> seek another mode of development.[107]

Those of us who are concerned with spiritual welfare and
the vision of the unity of humankind have urgent tasks of "re-
visioning" our world situation, especially interreligious, intercultural, and interhuman relations. Above all, we need to
articulate both "inner" meanings of religion(s), particularly the
relationship between humankind and ultimate reality, as well as
"outer" meaning, relating our own and others' truth claims, as
different traditions are destined to dwell together on this planet.
Religions everywhere are bound to become parts of religious-
cultural-social-political syntheses. We must sadly recognize that

historically no one synthesis has shown a sufficient amount of wisdom to guide a divided humanity toward unity. But as religious persons, we hope and trust that various religious traditions possess sufficient religious resources to provide our divided humanity with the faith, courage, and hope necessary to endure and transcend the meaninglessness and ambiguity that envelop us.

APPENDIX

In Response

F. Stanley Lusby
University of Tennessee, Knoxville

As the author has indicated, this is not a work in his particular scholarly discipline of the history of religions. It is an incisive and richly illuminating exploration of "religious visions of the unity of humankind," fully informed by his far-ranging competence as a historian of religions as well as by his artful ability to understand "human being" as "religious being," however diverse the climes, times, and cultures in which human religiousness has been manifest.

Religious pluralism has been a historical reality for a long time; however, it never has been more permeative, globally and societally, than in the last decades of the twentieth century. There is a multiplicity of religious communities and traditions in most of the world's societies, and the events of history have brought about circumstances in which religious-cultural-social-political traditions are being hurled at one another incessantly.[1] Of all of the developments in our time—and there are many impressive ones (for example, space exploration, the development of nuclear power, advances in electronic communications and transportation, the impact of computer technology)—these other developments are likely, in the long run, to appear episodic in terms of their import for the future of humankind alongside the over-riding importance of the confrontation of religio-cultural traditions with one another.

As the author has discerned, a persistent motif of human religions and cultures is a yearning for the unity of humankind—a unity hoped to be manifest ultimately in the experience of human community. Ironically, the religious traditions of humankind have been both a resource sustaining, informing, and vitalizing that yearning and barriers to experiencing that unity beyond the boundaries of specific religious traditions. Those of us alert to the many tragic developments of our day are aware that religious commitments and loyalties are often foundational to the alienation of groups and societies from one another—even to the point of radical violence. A persistent yearning for the unity of humankind alongside the continuing experiences of alienation is the problem that the author is addressing by illuminating our present consideration by putting it in a historical perspective.

The distinction between the "inner" and the "outer" meanings of religion and religions is central to the author's discussion. "Because we are present to a world," observed Merleau-Ponty, "we are condemned to meaning."[2] Religion informs and sustains the life of a people by providing, through the various modes of religious expression,[3] a pervading sense of meaning that makes possible an affirmation of truth, an understanding of the nature of the human and of reality, and of the fulfilling relation between them. All of this is legitimized as being of salvific and cosmic import. So the "inner" meaning of a religious tradition is its symbolic center, that which is essential to it.

Equally important in discussing religious visions of the unity of humankind are the "outer" phenomenological meanings of religious traditions "that are derived from human experience as both human-in-a-particular-society-and-culture and human-in-the-global-community."[4] It is the "outer" meaning of a given religion that is most often neglected by religious persons and communities, with the result that the vision of a religious people becomes myopic. Thus, clarity with regard to the unity of humankind becomes eroded.

The "outer" meanings of religions involve an awareness that there is a plurality of religions and that there are others who are religious. Those selected moments in history when awareness of "inner" and "outer" meanings has informed constructive and exemplary endeavors to the enhancement of the quest for some realization of the unity of humankind are models. Those the author gives special attention include:

1. The "cultural colonialism" of Alexander the Great based on Hellenistic civilization during the last third of the 4th century B.C. The author observes that Alexander's vision of the unity of humankind, "was not readily understood by his contemporaries," but "upon his death his idea of the *oecumene* penetrated deeply into the psyches of many."[5]

2. The reign of Aśoka of the Maurya dynasty in India during the mid-third century B.C. Aśoka was "an energetic advocate of his new (Buddhist) faith," whose appropriation of the "humanitarian ethics of Buddhism"[6] and commendation of Buddhist practice throughout an expansive kingdom enriched his vision of the unity of humankind. Aśoka held in balance the "inner" meaning of Buddhism (the "Three Jewels" of the Buddha, the Dharma or the liberating law discovered by the Buddha, and the Saṃgha or Buddhist community) and the "outer" meaning (the sacred kingship, Buddhist-inspired pan-Indian moral principles based on the Dharma, and the Buddhist-inspired state with himself as the universal king).[7]

3. The Apostle Paul who affirmed "the 'inner' meaning of Christianity that paid supreme loyalty to Jesus Christ as the Son of God and the savior of humankind" and understood this in relation to "the 'outer' meaning of Christianity as one of many competing religions" in the Graeco-Roman world.[8]

4. The shaping of religious freedom during the colonial and constitutional eras in which the United States became a nation. The author observes an important factor contributing to the emergence and institutionalizing of religious freedom was the Jewish and Christian groups' awareness that, alongside the "inner" meaning of monotheistic affirmations of each theological tradition, was the "outer" meaning of "monolatry," in accordance

with which "each group believed in one supreme deity while tacitly acknowledging that other Christian and Jewish groups believed in their own kind of supreme deity."[9]

The fact and pervasiveness of religious pluralism present every religious community with problems. H. Richard Niebuhr, in his *The Meaning of Revelation*, suggests that, if science and the scientific worldview defined the basic problem for western theologians during the nineteenth century, the counterpart during the twentieth century is relativism, closely associated with an expanding awareness of religious pluralism.[10] Pluralism is characterized by Joseph L. Blau as "the religious manifestation that all starting points are equally valid."[11] For many, religious pluralism has been enervating, eroding definitive affirmations, and calling into question missionary endeavor. (Could it be that a resultant dis-ease and an accompanying failure to address the problems of pluralism have been factors in what the author decries as the loss of missionary incentive within Christianity?)

It is pertinent to suggest, in the spirit of H. Richard Niebuhr, that religious pluralism need not be so debilitating. The inappropriateness for anyone to proclaim, in this era of pluralism and its correlative relativism, that one has the full truth does not obviate the possibility—the responsibility—of one's proclaiming that, whatever the truth is in its fullness, that aspect of truth and reality that has been disclosed through the shared tradition and experience one has known is, at least, one aspect of "truth."[12]

The author's wide range of observations invite considerable reflection. It is impossible to do justice to all of them in these remarks, but perhaps the following comments will be suggestive.

First, whatever we do in our day to give expression to the deep yearning for the unity of humankind must be done with full awareness of the great, and increasing, variety of religions. The author is right in disallowing any expectation that there may emerge a global and universal new "super-religion."[13] Religious pluralism, global and societal, is the context within which our pilgrimage must continue. Ironically, modernity and secularism, whatever antithesis to religion they incorporate, actually enhance the emergence of additional new religions. This should not be surprising in view of W. C. Smith's observation, included in his discussion of Islam, that religion "is open at one end to the immeasurable greatness of the Divine, and . . . at the other end to the immeasurable diversity of the human."[14]

Second, religious freedom, certainly to be both cherished and celebrated, has seldom been more than partially realized. Generally it has not provided a context for the unrestrained development of particular religious traditions and peoples. The religious experiences of the peoples of the United States prove this point. The circumstances of history and the dimensions of faith contributed to the emergence of religious freedom in the U.S., which was later to be institutionalized constitutionally and manifested culturally. Religious freedom emerged in the crucible of our history; we are now fervently committed to it as a cherished value. Yet, even with the religious freedom we know in our society life has its tragic ambiguities—cultural, structural, linguistic, legal, social, economic, and religious. We who are Euro-Americans have regarded Euro-American culture as the predominant culture of our land and nation. The traditions, the languages, the symbolic "center," the *episteme* that have shaped our perception and our thinking were all derived from European and English roots. The ethos for most of our history has been predominantly Protestant Christian. One result has been the "hiddenness," "concealment," even the invisibility of entire groups of peoples of this land and their religions.[15] Tragic consequences have resulted from our failure to keep in balance the "inner" meaning of our Euro-American culture and the "outer" meaning that acknowledges the presence and multidimensionality of the experiences of all the peoples of the United States. The latent dialectic of the Native American, the manifest dialectic of the African-American, and the expanding dialectics of the Hispanic-American and Asian-American have become so clear in recent decades that we are at long last beginning to realize that we are an Aboriginal-African-Euro-Hispanic-Asian culture. We have yet to work out all of the implications of this for our societal life, but many of the ambiguities of our history were the result of a collapsing of the religious vision on the "inner" meaning of the Euro-American tradition to the neglect of the "outer" meaning of that tradition. The American rhetoric of equality, freedom, and the unity of humankind was seriously deficient at its base and in its structure. We realize anew that we have much to accomplish before the ideal of religious freedom will be more fully realized in the life of the nation.

The temptation to retreat to certainty, to focus exclusively on some "inner" meaning is understandable, given the complexities that religious pluralism and religious freedom address to us. But any vibrant vision of the unity of humankind should lead us to resist such a temptation. Resistance to the temptation to retreat should be reinforced by the dynamics of our own history and by the recent process of "Easternization," which the author discerns to be influenced by the 1893 World's Parliament of Religions in Chicago and the global perspective that was an inevitable aftermath of World War II.

Third, it needs to be said that neglect of the "outer" meaning of religions not only results in a diminishing of the vision of the unity of humankind, but also in the failure to develop fully the "inner" meaning of religions. The "inner" meaning of a tradition is foundational for any affirmation of religious truth; but that "inner" meaning is prompted to its fullest expression and development when understood in relation to an "other" or "others." It is then that a religious people experience the maturation of their sense of identity. So the Apostle Paul, aware of the other gods of the Graeco-Roman world, could make his Christian affirmation, "This God I proclaim unto you," the God, he affirmed, of Jesus Christ. So also Aśoka could commend the values and practices of Buddhism to citizens of diverse traditions in various regions.

Fourth, religious visions of the unity of humankind frequently suggest as a correlate the possibility of human community. We live in a time when events all too often include eruptions of violence as aspects of pulsating revolutions. Are violence and alienation to be the predominant and continuing human experience? Or is the religious vision of the unity of humankind to be manifest in nurturing the possibility of human community? I recall a dominant impression I had upon reading

Hannah Arendt's fine treatise, *On Revolution*; namely, that the opposite of violence in human affairs is not nonviolence, but, rather, human community.[16] To suggest this is certainly not to minimize the worth or importance of nonviolence as an appropriate procedure or strategy that may contribute to the shaping of human community and to the vision of the unity of humankind.

Finally, the importance of the author's discourse rests, in part, on the wisdom of his suggestion that religious persons should endeavor to keep in balance the "inner" and "outer" meanings of religion. If religious persons and communities can achieve the maturity to resist the temptation myopically to regard the "inner" meaning of a religion as the only meaning, can accept the responsibility to probe and express the deepest meaning of a given tradition in a manner consonant with its distinctive character and integrity, and, while doing so, become more fully aware of the "outer" meaning of that tradition in relation to other religions, then perhaps the religious pilgrimage of humankind can proceed in a manner that will nurture the unity of humankind.

It is notable that the author, a scholar in the history of religions, has also served as dean of the Divinity School at the University of Chicago. And this, in spite of the fact that, historically, the field of the history of religions has been regarded as being in tension with the work of theologians. The author's accomplishments as dean of a major divinity school and as a historian of religions are unique. The scholarly works of the author and his colleague historians of religion have illuminated our understanding of the "inner" meanings of religious traditions and made it unconscionable for any of us to overlook or neglect the "outer" meanings of religions. The theologian and the historian of religions are in a sort of symbiotic relationship; each needs to be informed by and to inform the work of the other.

I was recently able to participate in an inquiry concerning the relation of religious studies and theological studies in institutions of higher education. There was a tendency for the "outer" meanings of religion and religions to be neglected, and for the "internal" meanings to provide the focus of theological studies. This was particularly true of programs of study in theological seminaries, divinity schools, and in programs of clergy education. As I reflected on the thrust of this author's most recent manuscripts, I came to lament more strongly a "turning inward" that characterizes too many current programs of theological and clergy education. This fact underscores the importance of the author's work on religious visions of the unity of humankind.

Notes

PREFACE

1. Denis de Rougemont, *Man's Western Quest* (Westport, CT: Greenwood, 1973).

2. J. Donald Curless, *An Almanac for Moderns* (New York: A. Putnam's Sons, 1935), p. 367.

3. Arnold J. Toynbee, *Civilization on Trial* (New York: Oxford University Press, 1948), p. 90.

4. Ibid., p. v.

INTRODUCTION

1. Mircea Eliade, *The Quest: History and Meaning in Religion* (Chicago: The University of Chicago Press, 1969), Preface.

2. G. van der Leeuw, *Religion in Essence and Manifestation*, tr. by J. E. Turner (London: G. Allen and Unwin, 1938), pp. 242–43.

3. 1 Cor. 8:5-6. All Biblical quotations throughout the book are taken from *The Holy Bible - The Old Testament*, Revised Standard Version, 2 volumes (1952) and The New Covenant, commonly called The New Testament, Revised Standard Version (1901), all copyrighted by Thomas Nelson & Sons.

4. Sir Charles Eliot, *Hinduism and Buddhism* (New York: Barnes & Noble, 1954), vol. 1, p. 265.

5. Luke 24:13-35.

6. Paul Tillich, *Theology of Culture*, ed. by R. C. Kimball (New York: Oxford University Press, 1959), p. 204.

7. James W. Heisig, "Fore-Words," *Inter-Religio*, no. 14 (Fall 1988): p. 37.

8. See for example, Akizuki Ryōmin's article, "Christian-Buddhist Dialogue," *ibid.*, pp. 38–54.

CHAPTER 1: A VIEW OF UNITY

1. Gerardus van der Leeuw, *Sacred and Profane Beauty: The Holy in Art*, trans. David E. Green (New York: Rinehart and Winston, 1962), p. 11.

2. For more on Wach's view on this, see my article, "*Verstehen* and *Erlösung*: Some Remarks on Joachim Wach's Work," *History of Religions*, vol. 11, no. 1 (August 1971), pp. 31–53.

3. See especially the first two chapters of John E. Pfeiffer, *The Creative Explosion: An Inquiry into the Origins of Art and Religion* (Ithaca, NY: Cornell University Press, 1982), pp. 1–39.

4. See A. Irving Hallowell, "Bear Ceremonies in the Northern Hemisphere" (Ph.D. diss. The University of Pennsylvania, 1926), p. 134.

5. See Mircea Eliade, *A History of Religious Ideas*, trans. Willard R. Trask, vol. 1, chaps. 1 and 2 (Chicago: University of Chicago Press, 1978), pp. 3–55; and "Critical Bibliographies," pp. 376–78.

6. Thorkild Jacobsen, "Mesopotamia—Cosmos as a State," and "The Function of the State," in H. and H. A. Frankfort eds., *The Intellectual Adventure of Ancient Man* (Chicago: University of Chicago Press, 1946), pp. 125–201.

7. Ibid., p. 6.

8. Ibid., p. 213.

9. Jack Finegan, *Light from the Ancient East* (Princeton: Princeton University Press, 1946), p. 41.

10. Ibid., p. 61.

11. Ibid., p. 173.

12. R. C. Zaehner, "Zoroastrianism," in R. C. Zaehner ed., *The Concise Encyclopedia of Living Faiths* (New York: Hawthorne Books, 1959), p. 209.

13. Luigi Pareti, *The Ancient World: 1200 B.C. to A.D. 500*, trans. G. R. F. Chilver and S. Chilver, vol. 2: *History of Mankind* (New York: Harper and Row, 1965), p. 28.

14. Ibid., p. 23.

15. Ibid., p. 232.

16. Ibid., p. 236.

17. D. R. Cartlidge and D. L. Dungan, *Documents for the Study of the Gospels* (Philadelphia: Fortress Press, 1980), p. 144.

18. Finegan, *Light*, p. 206.

19. Pareti, *The Ancient World*, p. 339.

20. See Cartlidge and Dungan, *Documents*, pp. 13–22.

21. John A. Wilson, "Egypt," in Frankfort and Frankfort, *The Intellectual Adventure*, p. 35.

22. Ibid., p. 60.

23. Ibid., pp. 64–65.

24. Cited in George Foot Moore, *History of Religions*, vol. 1 (New York: Charles Scribner's Sons, 1948), p. 144.

25. Finegan, *Light*, p. 89.

26. For more on problems of dating the Exodus, see Finegan, *Light*, pp. 105–8.

27. S. G. F. Brandon, *Man and His Destiny in the Great Religions* (Toronto: University of Toronto Press, 1962), pp. 31–32.

28. S. A. B. Mercer, "The Religion of Ancient Egypt," in Vergilius Ferm ed., *Forgotten Religions* (New York: The Philosophical Library, 1950), p. 40.

29. Mircea Eliade, "*Homo Faber* and *Homo Religiosus*," in Joseph M. Kitagawa ed., *The History of Religions: Retrospect and Prospect* (New York: Macmillan, 1985), p. 6.

30. Moore, *History of Religions*, p. 159.

31. Wilson, "Egypt," p. 106.

32. See Finegan, *Light*, pp. 110–13.

33. Quoted in Wilson, "Egypt," pp. 114–15.

34. A stone honoring him in three languages—the ancient sacred hieroglyphics, the popular Egyptian of the second century B.C., and Greek—was found at Rosetta (Rashid) near the mouth of the Nile in 1799 during the Napoleonic expedition.

35. Wilson, "Egypt," p. 119.

36. Mercer, "The Religion of Ancient Egypt," p. 28.

37. See Wilson, "Egypt," p. 106.

38. Thomas J. Hopkins, *The Hindu Religious Tradition* (Encino: Dickenson, 1971), p. 3.

39. Eliade, *A History of Religious Ideas*, p. 126.

40. A. L. Basham, *The Wonder That Was India* (New York: Grove Press, 1954), p. 18.

41. Hopkins, *The Hindu Religious Tradition*, p. 9.

42. Basham, *The Wonder*, p. 25.

43. Two of Dumézil's studies are particularly important here: *Les dieux des Indo-Européens* (Paris: Presses Universitaires de France, 1952), and *L'ideologie tripartie des Indo-Européens* (Brussels: Latomus, 1958).

44. See Louis Renou ed., *Hinduism* (New York: George Braziller, 1961), pp. 15–25.

45. See Heinrich Zimmer, *Philosophies of India* ed. Joseph Campbell (New York: Pantheon Books, 1951), pp. 467–690.

46. See Clarence H. Hamilton, *Buddhism: A Religion of Infinite Compassion* (New York: The Liberal Arts Press, 1952), pp. xxv-xxvii.

47. There are a number of excellent introductory works on the Buddha, on Buddhist doctrines, and on Buddhist religion, among them Walpola Rahula's *What the Buddha Taught* (New York: Grove Press, 1959).

48. Basham, *The Wonder*, p. 54.

49. Cf. J. M. Kitagawa, "Buddhism and Social Change: An Historical Perspective," in *Buddhist Studies in Honor of Walpola Rahula*, ed. S. Balasooriya et al. (London: Gordon Frazer, 1980), pp. 84–102 and especially p. 91.

50. See Amulyachandra Sen, *Aśoka's "Edicts"* (Calcutta: The Indian Publicity Society, 1956).

51. T. R. V. Murti, *The Central Philosophy of Buddhism* (London: George Allen and Unwin Ltd., 1955).

52. See T. W. Rhys Davids, trans., *The Questions of King Milanda*, 2 vols. (New York: Dover, 1963); originally *The Sacred Books of the East*, ed. F. Max Müller (Oxford: Clarendon Press, 1890 and 1894), vols. 35, 36.

53. See Edward Conze, "Buddhism: The Mahayana," in Zaehner, *The Concise Encyclopedia*, p. 296.

54. Betty Heimann, *Indian and Western Philosophy: A Study in Contrasts* (London: George Allen and Unwin, 1937), pp. 13, 17.

55. See H. C. Warren, *Buddhism in Translation* (Cambridge, Mass.: Harvard University Press, 1896), p. 388.

56. Harold Isaacs, *Scratches on the Mind* (New York: John Day, 1958), p. 39.

57. D. L. Overmyer, *Religions of China* (San Francisco: Harper and Row, 1986), p. 3.

58. See I. Gunnar Andersson, *Children of the Yellow Earth: Studies in Prehistoric China* (London: Kegan Paul, Trench, Trubner, 1934; Cambridge: Massachusetts Institute of Technology Press, 1934), pp. 94–126.

59. Dun J. Li, *The Ageless Chinese: A History* (New York: Scribner's, 1965), p. 46.

60. Ibid., p. 88.

61. See Hyman Kublin ed., *China: Selected Readings* (Boston: Houghton Mifflin Co., 1968), pp. 43–48.

62. Laurence G. Thompson, *Chinese Religion: An Introduction* (Belmont: Dickenson, 1969), pp. 90–91.

63. K. S. Latourette, *The Chinese: Their History and Culture*, 2 vols. (New York: Macmillan, 1934), vol. 1, p. 109.

64. Frederick J. Taggert, *Rome and China: A Study of Correlations in Historical Events* (Berkeley: University of California Press, 1939), p. vii.

CHAPTER 2: HEBREW, GRECO-ROMAN AND CHRISTIAN VISIONS

1. Mircea Eliade, *The Myth of the Eternal Return* trans. W. R. Trask (New York: Pantheon Books, 1954), p. 110.

2. See Martin Buber's article, "The Suspension of Ethics," in *Moral Principles of Action*, ed. Ruth Nanda Anshen (New York: Harper, 1952), pp. 223–27.

3. See J. M. Kitagawa ed., *Understanding Modern China* (Chicago: Quadrangle Books, 1969), pp. 215-16.

4. The Hebrew Bible records both approaches to the Promised Land. On the one hand, it portrays Moses, who was no doubt representing the Israelites, on Mt. Pisgah praying to the Almighty for the privilege of physically stepping into the promised land, the good land beyond the Jordan. He was told, however, that he could only see it in his vision, in faith; he could not go beyond the Jordan (Deut. 3:27). On the other hand, biblical writers portray the accounts of the Israelites' military conquest of Canaan and the process of their physical settlement there, even though most historians believe that the invaders represented only a small segment of the Hebrew group. The Book of Judges and other biblical passages also tell us about the establishment of sanctuaries and the rise of the Levite priesthood, and about the heavy impact of Canaanite religion, especially the cult of Baal, on the Israelites who, as we have seen presumably belonged only to their national God, YHWH.

5. It was David's son, Solomon, who was instrumental in bringing pagan cults into the Hebrew community; and even then he was credited with dedicating the temple to the Lord.

6. This Old Testament book praises the Moabite woman and her loyalty to her deceased Jewish husband's mother and exemplifies her as the paragon of Jewish womanhood, enriching the line of King David.

7. Judah Goldin, "Early and Classical Judaism, in *A Reader's Guide to the Great Religions*, ed. C. J. Adams (New York: Macmillan-Free Press, 1965), p. 300.

8. Many Jews are reputed to have neglected the Oral Law (*halakha*) because of their belief in the divine inspiration of the Septuagint.

9. E. J. Bickerman, *The Maccabees* (New York: Schocken Books, 1947).

10. Goldin in Adams, *A Reader's Guide*, p. 302.

11. Goldin in Adams, *A Reader's Guide*, p. 310.

12. Because the Jewish community enjoyed *de facto* quasi-state status in Persia under the Sāsānian rulers (A.D. 224–651), some Jewish writers thought that the Persian Jewish community was preferable to its Palestinian counterpart.

13. *The New Encyclopaedia Britannica, Macropaedia*, 1985 ed., s.v. "Judaism," vol. 20, p. 413B.

14. See F. E. Peters, *Greek Philosophical Terms: A Historical Lexicon* (New York: New York University Press, 1967), s.v. "*logos*," pp. 110-12.

15. See Philo Judaeus, *Allegorical Interpretation of Genesis*, Loeb Classical Library (Cambridge, MA: Harvard University Press, 1949).

16. I use the usual Kantian distinction here.

17. See Peters, *Greek Terms*, s.v. "*nous*," pp. 132–39.

18. *The New Encyclopaedia Britannica, Macropaedia,* 1985 ed., s.v. "The Greco-Roman Civilization," vol. 20, p. 289A.

19. Charles A. Robinson, Jr., "The Inhabited World," in Ferm, *Forgotten Religions,* (New York: The Philosophical Library, 1950), p. 199.

20. Ibid., p. 201.

21. Cf. Harold C. Baldry, *Ancient Utopias* (Southhampton, England: University of Southhampton, 1956).

22. Pareti, *The Ancient World,* p. 470.

23. Robinson in Ferm, *Forgotten Religions,* p. 200.

24. This dual consulship often reverted to a dictatorship—usually for a period of six months—in times of national emergency.

25. "Greco-Roman Civilization," p. 235A.

26. Irach J. S. Taraporewala, "Mithraism," in Ferm, *Forgotten Religions,* p. 213.

27. Quoted in Pareti, *The Ancient World,* p. 549.

28. It is interesting that both Trajan and Hadrian came from Spain, that Antonius Pius was married to a Spanish woman, and that Marcus Aurelius was of part Spanish ancestry.

29. "Greco-Roman Civilization," p. 349B.

30. Pareti, *The Ancient World,* p. 702.

31. Sir Hamilton Gibb (I believe) said that to non-Muslims, Islam is the religion of the Muslims while to Muslims, Islam is the religion of truth.

32. I might add that the religion departments, or departments of religious studies, in many colleges and universities have done much for scholarship in the field by differentiating between the inner and outer meanings of the various religions. But even so, the old ways of thinking die hard and religious bigotry is a stubborn reality, especially since it is so often justified self-righteously in the name of religion.

33. Bertram Woolf, trans., *From Tradition to Gospel (Die Formsgeschichte des Evangelium* by Martin Dibelius) (London: I. Nicholson and Watson, 1934), p. 14.

34. Joachim Wach, *Sociology of Religion* (Chicago: University of Chicago Press, 1944), p. 134.

35. Edward J. Thomas, *The History of Buddhist Thought* (New York: Barnes and Noble, 1933, 1951).

36. D. D. Williams, *What Present-Day Theologians Are Thinking* (New York: Harper, 1952), p. 12; emphasis mine.

37. Leeuw, *Religion in Essence and Manifestation,* p. 264.

38. J. Muilenburg, "Ethics of the Prophet," in Anshen, *Moral Principles of Action,* p. 536.

39. Frederick C. Grant, *Ancient Roman Religion* (New York: Liberal Arts Press, 1957), p. 174; quoted in Cartlidge and Dungan, *Documents for the Study of the Gospels*, pp. 13–14.

40. Cartlidge and Dungan, *Documents*, pp. 17, 18, 21.

41. Peters, *Greek Terms*, p. 112.

42. Ernst Benz, "Theological Meaning of History of Religion," *Journal of Religion* 51, no. 1 (January 1961), p. 5.

43. Cartlidge and Dungan, *Documents*, p. 21.

44. Peter Brown, *Augustine of Hippo* (Berkeley: University of California Press, 1967), p. 214.

CHAPTER 3: VISIONS FROM EAST, WEST, AND ISLAM

1. See William S. Haas, *The Destiny of the Mind: East and West* (London: Faber and Faber, 1956).

2. Clifford Geertz, "Ritual and Social Change: A Javanese Example," in *The Reader in Comparative Religion: An Anthropological Approach*, ed. William A. Lessa and E. Z. Vogt (Evanston, IL: Row, Peterson, 1958), p. 501.

3. See Peter Brown, *The Cult of the Saints: Its Rise and Function in Latin Christianity* (Chicago: University of Chicago Press, 1981).

4. G. Gnoli, "Zoroastrianism," in M. Eliade ed., *The Encyclopedia of Religion*, (New York: Macmillan, 1987-88), vol. 15, p. 589.

5. Pareti, *The Ancient World*, p. 682.

6. Khosrow II was condemned to death in 628, and in 630 the cross was restored to the Church of the Holy Sepulcher in Jerusalem.

7. Muhammad took several wives over the course of his life after Khadījah's death.

8. The Muslim calendar is based on lunar months, and a twelve-month year is about 354 days. A complicated mathematical formula is needed to translate the common era calendar to the Muslim calendar, and vice versa.

9. See Sir William Muir, *The Life of Mohammed* (Edinburgh: John Grant, 1923), p. 118.

10. M. Mahdi, "Modernity and Islam," in J. M. Kitagawa (ed.), *Modern Trends in World Religions* (LaSalle, IL: The Open Court, 1959), pp. 11–12.

11. G. E. von Grunebaum, *Medieval Islam* (Chicago: University of Chicago Press, 1946), p. 3.

12. Ibid., p. 43.

13. Ibid., p. 44.

14. Sir Hamilton A. R. Gibb, *Mohammedanism: An Historical Survey* (London: Oxford University Press, revised edition, 1953), p. 6.

15. G. E. von Grunebaum ed., *Unity and Variety in Muslim Civilization* (Chicago: University of Chicago Press, 1955), p. 21.

16. Reuben W. Smith, *Islamic Civilization in the Middle East: Course Syllabus* (Chicago: University of Chicago, 1965), p. 27.

17. Muhammed left no male heir, although some of the early caliphs were related to him by marriage.

18. Mahdi, "Modernity and Islam," pp. 12–13.

19. Grunebaum, *Medieval Islam*, pp. 11–12.

20. Philip K. Hitti, *The Arabs: A Short History* (Princeton: Princeton University Press, 1949), p. 39.

21. Hendrik Kraemer, *World Cultures and World Religions* (Philadelphia: Westminster Press, 1960), p. 38.

22. Some scholars also suggest the possible influences of Zoroastrianism, Judaism, Monophysite Christianity, Hinduism, and Buddhism on the development of Sufism.

23. Kraemer, *World Cultures*, p. 46.

24. Earlier, during the ninth century, Islamic forces attacked Rome and conquered Sicily, which then belonged to the Byzantine empire. The Carolingians fought the Islamic forces in Italy, while the Greek emperor, Basil, finally ousted the Muslims from Italy. Thus the direct contacts between the Islamic community—which had welcomed many Jewish scholars—and the Latin West during the Middle Ages were confined to the Iberian peninsula and Sicily. In comparison with the Latin West's contacts with Spain and Sicily, the Crusaders' contacts with Palestinian and Syrian elements of the Islamic community were culturally less significant.

25. Grunebaum, *Medieval Islam*, p. 42.

26. Ibid., pp. 234–35.

27. Kraemer, *World Cultures*, pp. 46–47.

28. This is in contradistinction to the Augustinians' emphasis of the primacy of the will, which has to be illuminated by God to attain certainty in faith and knowledge.

29. Cf. Helene Wieruszowski, *The Medieval University* (Princeton: van Norstrand, 1966).

30. Toward the end of the twelfth century, the cultural creativity of the Islamic community came to a sudden end.

31. The Seljūq Turks captured the Byzantine emperor, Romanus IV Diogenes (died 1072). Their mistreatment of Christian pilgrims in Jerusalem offered Latin Christendom an easy excuse to initiate the Crusades.

32. Hichem Djait, *Europe and Islam* (Berkeley: University of California Press, 1985), p. 109.

33. Frederick I considered himself the divinely ordained successor to the Caesars, Justinian, Charlemagne, and Otto the Great. He did not need a pope to add a sacred aura to his monarchy.

34. Urban II established the *curia* and strengthened the centralization of the Latin church.

35. Significantly, Frederick's Holy Roman Empire was threatened in 1241 by the invasion of the Mongol forces that later captured the capital of the Islamic community, Baghdad.

36. "Byzantine Empire," in *The New Encyclopaedia Britannica, Macropaedia*, 1985 ed., vol. 15, p. 404.

37. Marshall Hodgson, *The Venture of Islam* (Chicago: University of Chicago Press, 1974), vol. 2, p. 3.

38. Saladin's forces conquered Jerusalem, thus provoking the Third Crusade.

39. Hopkins, *Hindu Religious Tradition*, p. 82.

40. Heimann, *Indian and Western Philosophy*, pp. 29–30.

41. The *Ṛg Veda* affirmed four *varṇas*—*Brahmins*, or priests; *Kṣatriyas*, or warriors; *Vaiśyas*, or traders; and *Śūdras*, or outcastes, as the original divisions of society.

42. Hopkins, *Hindu Religious Tradition*, p. 85.

43. See Zimmer, *Philosophies of India*.

44. Ibid., p. 155.

45. Ibid., p. 44.

46. *Sāṁkya, Yoga, Vedānta, Nyāya, Vaiśeṣika,* and *Pūrva Mīmāṁsā* are known as the six "orthodox" philosophical viewpoints (see S. Radhakrishnan and C. A. Moore eds., *A Source Book in Indian Philosophy* (Princeton: Princeton University Press, 1957), pp. 349–571.

47. Ibid., pp. 181ff.

48. Heimann, *Indian and Western Philosophy*, p. 53; my italics.

49. William T. de Bary, et al., compl., *Sources of Indian Tradition* (New York: Columbia University Press, 1958), p. 307.

50. Basham, *The Wonder*, p. 333.

51. Murti, *The Central Philosophy*, p. 10.

52. Ibid., p. 11.

53. Basham, *The Wonder*, p. 344.

54. Hopkins, *Hindu Religious Tradition*, p. 86.

55. John A. Hutchison, *Paths of Faith* (New York: McGraw-Hill, 1969), p. 475.

56. See Haas, *The Destiny of the Mind*.

57. See Melford E. Spiro, *Buddhism and Society: A Great Tradition and Its Burmese Vicissitudes* (New York: Harper and Row, 1970).

58. Ibid., p. 12.

59. H. G. Creel, *Chinese Thought from Confucius to Mao Tse-tung* (Chicago: University of Chicago Press, 1953), p. 181.

60. G. B. Sansom, *A History of Japan to 1334* (Stanford: Stanford University Press, 1958), p. 72.

61. Ibid., p. 98.

62. See Arthur Waley, "The Fall of Lo-yang," *History Today*, no. 4 (1951), pp. 7–10.

63. Arthur F. Wright, *Buddhism in Chinese History* (Stanford: Stanford University Press, 1959), p. 52.

64. K. Ch'en, *Buddhism in China: A Historical Survey* (Princeton: Princeton University Press, 1946), p. 66.

65. See E. Zürcher, *The Buddhist Conquest of China* (Leiden: E. J. Brill, 1959), Text Volume, pp. 204–39, especially p. 238.

66. Ibid., pp. 217–19.

67. See Wright, *Chinese History*, p. 48.

68. Ibid., p. 58.

69. See René Grousset, *Chinese Art and Culture* (New York: Grove Press, 1959), p. 130, FN 41.

70. *The Cambridge Encyclopedia of China*, Brian Hook, ed. (Cambridge: Cambridge University Press, 1982), p. 321.

71. Grousset, *Chinese Art and Culture*, p. 150.

72. Zenryū Tsukamoto, *Shina Bukkyō-shi Kenkyū: Hokugi-hen* (Studies of Chinese Buddhist History: Section on Northern Wei) (Tokyo: Kōbundō, 1942), pp. 364–84.

73. Wright, *Chinese History*, pp. 61–62.

74. See A. F. Wright, "The Formation of Sui Ideology, 581–604," in J. K. Fairbank ed., *Chinese Thought and Institutions* (Chicago: University of Chicago Press, 1957), pp. 71–104.

75. Grousset, *Chinese Art and Culture*, p. 185.

76. I-Tsing (I-Ching), *A Record of the Buddhist Religion as Practiced in India and the Malay Archipelago* (A.D. 671–695), translated by Junjiro Takakusu (Oxford: Oxford University Press, 1896).

77. Etienne Balazs, *Chinese Civilization and Bureaucracy: Variations on a Theme* (New Haven: Yale University Press, 1964), p. 282.

78. Cited in ibid., p. 288.

79. Ibid., p. 289.

80. Quoted in Yu-lan Fung, *A Short History of Chinese Philosophy* (New York: Macmillan, 1950), p. 297.

81. Li, *The Ageless Chinese*, p. 224.

82. Balazs, *Chinese Civilization and Bureaucracy*, p. 80.

83. René Grousset, *The Rise and Splendor of the Chinese Empire* (Berkeley: University of California Press, 1952), p. 247.

84. Hook, *Cambridge Encyclopedia*, p. 218.

85. L. Warner, *The Enduring Art of Japan* (Cambridge: Harvard University Press, 1952), p. 6; my italics.

CHAPTER 4: ENCOUNTERS OF PEOPLES, CIVILIZATIONS, AND RELIGIONS

1. Bryan Wilson, *Contemporary Transformation of Religion* (Oxford: Clarendon Press, 1976), p. 10.

2. Arnold Toynbee, *A Study of History*, abridged by D. C. Somerwell (New York: Oxford University Press, 1947), p. 249.

3. Wieruszowski, *Medieval University*, p. 40.

4. J. O. Thorne & T. C. Collocott eds., *Chambers Biographical Dictionary* (Cambridge: Cambridge University Press, 1984), p. 47.

5. Francis Oakley, *The Western Church in the Later Middle Ages* (Ithaca, NY: Cornell University Press, 1979), p. 17.

6. See ibid., pp. 19–20.

7. Wach, *Sociology* p. 326.

8. Ernst Troeltsch, *The Social Teachings of the Christian Church* (Glencoe: Free Press, 1949), vol. 1, p. 251.

9. Charles A. Beard, *The Idea of National Interest* (New York: Macmillan, 1934), p. 8.

10. Edward Westermarck, *The Origin and Development of Moral Ideas* (London: Macmillan, 1908), vol. 2, p. 179.

11. Troeltsch, *Social Teachings*, vol. 2, p. 479.

12. Wilhelm Pauck, *The Heritage of the Reformation* (Glencoe: The Free Press, 1950), p. 26.

13. Ibid., p. 50.

14. Wach, *Sociology*, p. 328.

15. Edgar M. Carlson, "Luther's Conception of Government," *Church History*, vol. 15, no. 4 (1946), p. 260.

16. Troeltsch, *Social Teachings*, vol. 2, p. 479.

17. Nils Ehrenström, *Christian Faith and the Modern State: An Ecumenical Approach*, (New York: Willett, Clarke & Co., 1937), p. 99.

18. Troeltsch, *Social Teachings*, vol. 2, p. 591.

19. Lars P. Qualbem, *A History of the Christian Church* (New York: Thomas Nelson and Sons, 1936), p. 271.

20. Ehrenström, *Christian Faith*, p. 116.

21. Ibid., p. 129.

22. Troeltsch, *Social Teachings*, vol. 1, p. 652.

23. Stephen Neill, *The Christian Society* (New York: Harper and Brothers, 1952), p. 134.

24. Burnett H. Streeter, *The Buddha and the Christ* (London: Macmillan, 1932), p. 137.

25. Edward G. Selwyn ed., *A Short History of Christian Thought* (London: Geoffrey Bles, 1949), p. 106.

26. F. S. C. Northrop, *The Meeting of East and West* (New York: Macmillan, 1946), p. 173.

27. Quoted in Joachim Wach, *Types of Religious Experience: Christian and Non-Christian* (Chicago: University of Chicago Press, 1951), pp. 193–94.

28. See "Christian Councils," in M. Eliade ed., *Encyclopedia of Religion*, vol. 4, pp. 129–30.

29. "Charles V," in *The New Encyclopaedia Britannica: Micropaedia*, 1985 ed., vol. 3, p. 111.

30. de Bary, *Sources of Indian Tradition*, p. 438.

31. Hodgson, *Venture of Islam*, vol. 3, pp. 59–60.

32. K. M. Panikkar, *Asia and Western Dominance* (London: G. Allen and Unwin, 1953), p. 31.

33. Grousset, *Chinese Art and Culture*, p. 290.

34. Li, *Ageless Chinese*, p. 386.

35. Paul E. Eckel, *The Far East Since 1500* (New York: Harcourt, Brace and World, Inc., 1949), pp. 53–54.

36. See J. M. Kitagawa, *On Understanding Japanese Religion* (Princeton: Princeton University Press, 1987), pp. xiii–xiv.

37. William Earle, *Public Sorrows and Private Pleasures* (Bloomington: Indiana University Press, 1976), p. 75.

38. Panikkar, *Western Dominance*, p. 24.

39. Hodgson, *Venture of Islam*, vol. 2, p. 430.

40. Panikkar, *Western Dominance*, p. 27.

41. "Judaism in the Middle East and North Africa since 1492," in M. Eliade ed., *Encyclopedia of Religion*, vol. 8, p. 158a.

42. "Marranos," in M. Eliade ed., *Encyclopedia of Religion*, vol. 9, p. 217.

43. "Portugal," *Encyclopedia Britannica*, 1971 ed., vol. 18, p. 279a.

44. "European Overseas Exploration and Empires," *The New Encyclopuedia Britannica: Macropaedia*, 1985 ed., vol. 18, p. 868a.

45. "Spain," *Encyclopaedia Britannica*, 1971 ed., vol. 20, p. 1094b.

46. William W. Sweet, "Christianity in the Americas," in A. G. Baker ed., *A Short History of Christianity* (Chicago: University of Chicago Press, 1940), p. 227.

47. D. F. Lach, *Asia in the Making of Europe* (Chicago: University of Chicago Press, 1965), vol. 1, pp. 246–48.

48. See ibid., p. 242.

49. See ibid., vol. 2, p. 709.

50. Ibid., vol. 1, p. 302.

51. See Charles H. Robinson, *History of Christian Missions* (New York: Charles Scribner's, 1915), pp. 42–43.

52. See ibid., p. 44.

CHAPTER 5: THE SEARCH FOR A NEW SYNTHESIS

1. Henry W. Littlefield, *New Outline-History of Europe, 1815–1949* (New York: Barnes and Noble, 1949), p. 145.

2. Ibid., p. 137.

3. R. Drinnon, *Keeper of Concentration Camps* (Berkeley: University of California Press, 1987), p. xxvii.

4. Quoted in Panikkar, *Western Dominance*, p. 166.

5. Ibid., p. 104.

6. See Milton R. Konvitz, *Alien and the Asiatic in American Law* (Ithaca: Cornell University Press, 1946), and J. M. Kitagawa, ed., *American Refugee Policy: Ethical and Religious Reflections* (Minneapolis: Winston Press, 1984).

7. Quoted by Peter I. Rose, "The Politics and Morality of United States Refugee Policy," *The Center Magazine* (Santa Barbara: R. M. Hutchins Center, September/October, 1958), p. 3.

8. N. E. Fehl, *History and Society* (Hong Kong: Chung Chi College, 1964), p. 18.

9. A. J. Macdonald, *Trade Practice and Christianity in Africa and the East* (London: Longman, Green and Company, 1916), p. 270.

10. J. H. Randall, Jr., *The Making of the Modern Mind* (Boston: Houghton Mifflin Co., 1940), p. 283.

11. Fehl, *History and Society*, pp. 14–15. See also Bernard McGinn, *The Calabrian Abbot: Joachim of Fiore in the History of Western Thought* (New York: Macmillan, 1985).

12. C. Dawson, *Enquiries into Religion and Culture* (London: Sheed and Ward, 1933), p. 150.

13. Randall, *Making of Modern Mind*, p. 403.

14. Dawson, *Enquiries into Religion*, p. 150. See also Peter France's small but helpful book, *Rousseau's Confessions* (New York: Cambridge University Press, 1987).

15. Leeuw, *Religion in Essence*, 1938, pp. 691–94.

16. See Klaus-Peter Koepping, *Adolf Bastian and the Psychic Unity of Mankind* (St. Loucia: University of Queensland Press, 1983).

17. Haas, *Destiny of The Mind*, p. 303.

18. "Pietism," in M. Eliade ed., *Encyclopedia of Religion*, vol. 11, pp. 324–26.

19. Bengt Sundkler, *The World Mission* (Grand Rapids: Eerdmans, 1965), p. 105.

20. Macdonald, *Trade Practice*, pp. ix–x.

21. Neill, *The Christian Society*, p. 203.

22. Haas, *Destiny of the Mind*, p. 301.

23. Daniel J. Boorstin, *The Genius of American Politics* (Chicago: University of Chicago Press, 1953), pp. 70, 133.

24. Sweet, "Christianity in the Americas," p. 207.

25. Quoted in A. E. Christy, ed., *The Asian Legacy and American Life* (New York: John Day Co., 1942), p. 22.

26. Glenn Miller, *Piety and Intellect*, (Atlanta: Scholars Press, forthcoming), Chapter 6, "Old England in the New Republic," p. 4.

27. F. J. Turner, *The Frontier in American History* (Chicago: Henry Holt, 1948).

28. Boorstin, *Genius of American Politics*, p. 157.

29. C. A. and Mary Beard, *The Rise of American Civilization* (New York: Macmillan, 1945), vol. 2, p. 480.

30. Wach, *Types of Religious Experience*, 1951, p. 189.

31. Troeltsch, *Social Teachings*, 1949, vol. 2, p. 461.

32. Ibid.

33. See L. von Wiese, *Systematic Sociology*, adapted and amplified by H. Becker (New York: J. Wiley and Sons, 1932), pp. 624 ff.

34. On this question, consult Wach, *Types of Religious Experience*, 1951, chapter 9, "Church, Denomination and Sect," pp. 187–208.

35. Boorstin, *Genius of American Politics*, p. 136.

36. Quoted in ibid., p. 146.

37. Ibid., p. 141.

38. S. E. Mead, "Theological School Address," Commencement, Meadville Theological School, Chicago, June 8, 1954.

39. Quoted in Boorstin, *Genius of American Politics*, p. 145.

40. E. T. Clarke, *The Small Sects in America* (Nashville: Abingdon-Cokesbury Press, 1949), p. 9.

41. Ibid., pp. 7–8.

42. Mead, S. E. "Christendom, Enlightenment, and the Revolution," in J. C. Brauer, ed. *Religion and the American Revolution*, p. 30.

43. S. E. Mead, "The American People: Their Space, Time, and Religion," *Journal of Religion*, vol. 34, no. 4 (October 1954), p. 253.

44. Wilhelm Pauck, "Theology in the Life of Contemporary American Protestantism," *Shane Quarterly*, vol. 13 (April 1952), p. 49.

45. Mead, "The American People," 1954, p. 245.

46. See J. M. Kitagawa, "The 1893 World's Parliament of Religions and Its Legacy," (Chicago: University of Chicago, 1984).

47. The World's Religious Congress, *General Programme*, Preliminary Edition (Chicago, 1893), p. 20.

48. Hendrik Kraemer, *The Christian Message in a Non-Christian World* (London: The Edinburgh House, 1938), p. 36.

49. C. S. Goodspeed, ed., *The World's First Parliament of Religions* (Chicago: Hill and Schuman, 1895), p. 56.

50. Arnold Toynbee, *The World and the West* (New York: Oxford University Press, 1953), p. 4.

51. Jawaharlal Nehru, *The Discovery of India* (New York: John Day, 1956), p. 579.

52. Irving Kristol, "The 20th Century Began in 1945," *The New York Times Magazine*, May 2, 1965, p. 25.

53. See Nasir Shansab, *Soviet Expansion in the Third World: Afghanistan, A Case Study* (Silver Spring: Bartleby Press, 1987).

54. W. MacMahon Ball, *Nationalism and Communism in East Asia* (Melbourne: Melbourne University Press, 1952), p. 2.

55. N. Mansergh, "The Impact of Asian Membership," *The Listener*, December 8, 1954, p. 1001.

56. Ball, *Nationalism*, p. 198.

57. P. D. Devanandan and M. M. Thomas, eds., *Communism and Social Revolution in India* (Calcutta: YMCA, 1953), p. 7.

58. W. E. Hocking, "Living Religions and a World Faith," in A. E. Christy, ed., *The Asian Legacy and American Life* (New York: John Day, 1942), p. 197.

59. Ibid., p. 207.

60. C. H. Robinson, *History of Christian Missions*, p. 134.

61. H. Richard Niebuhr, *Christ and Culture* (New York: Harper and Brothers, 1951), p. 207.

62. Neill, *The Christian Society*, p. 250.

63. IMC, *The Relation Between the Younger and the Older Churches*, The Jerusalem Meeting of the IMC, vol. 3 (New York: International Missionary Council, 1928), p. 167.

64. IMC, *The Growing Church*, Madras Series, vol. 2 (London: International Missionary Council), 1939, p. 276.

65. "Responsible Society," *The Indian Journal of Theology*, vol. 1, no. 2 (November 1952), p. 55.

66. "Christian Hope," ibid., p. 48.

67. IMC, *The Christian Life and Message in Relation to Non-Christian Systems of Thought and Life* (New York: International Missionary Council, 1928), pp. 71–73.

68. Robert Maynard Hutchins, *The Great Conversation* (Chicago: Encyclopaedia Britannica, 1952), pp. 71–73.

69. H. de Lubac, *La recontre du Bouddhism et de l'Occident* (Paris: Aubier Editions Montaigne, 1952), p. 274.

70. Kraemer, *World Cultures and World Religions*, p. 18.

71. Christy, *The Asian Legacy*, p. 43.

72. See "Gloucester Fears Moonies Seek to Net Fish Industry," *Chicago Sun-Times*, 1979 April 1, p. 24.

73. See my discussion of "The Asian's World of Meaning" in Gerhard Müller and W. Zeller, eds., *Glaube, Geist, Geschichte* (Leiden: E.J. Brill, 1967), pp. 470–71.

74. The concluding essay by James Luther Adams (who also translated) Paul Tillich, *The Protestant Era* (Chicago: University of Chicago Press, 1948), p. 195.

75. Paul Tillich, *The Future of Religion*, ed. by J. C. Brauer (New York: Harper and Row, 1966), pp. 64, 68.

76. Tillich (trans. Adams), 1948, p. 295.

77. See W. C. Smith, *Islam in Modern History* (Princeton: Princeton University Press, 1957).

78. See Kitagawa, *On Understanding Japanese Religion*, 1987, especially chapter 16, "The Religious Ethos of Present-Day Japan," pp. 273–85.

79. See Kitagawa, *Understanding Modern China*, 1969.

80. See Zimmer, *Philosophies of India*, 1951 and Heimann, *Indian and Western Philosophy*, 1937.

81. See E. Bradford Burns, *The Poverty of Progress* (Berkeley: University of California Press, 1980) and Julio de Santa Ana's informative article, "The Common Struggle of Christians and Marxists in Latin America," in S. J. Samartha, ed., *Living Faiths and Ultimate Goals* (Geneva: World Council of Churches, 1974), pp. 90–107.

82. See Peter Worsley, *The Third World*, 2nd ed. (Chicago: University of Chicago Press, 1964); for Africa south of the Sahara, consult Adda B. Bozeman, *Conflict in Africa* (Princeton: Princeton University Press, 1976).

83. Cited in Christy, *The Asian Legacy*, pp. 43–44.

84. O. Spengler, *The Decline of the West* (New York: A.A. Knopf, 1930), vol. 2, p. 57.

85. See particularly Thomas M. Gannon, ed., *The Catholic Challenge to the American Economy* (New York: Macmillan, 1987).

86. See Howard A. Berman's perceptive sermon entitled "The Pollard Affair—Has American Jewry Learned the Lesson?" *Sinai Congregation Bulletin*, 16, June 1, 1987.

87. See Walter Lippmann, "Why the Mighty Fail to Prevail," *Chicago Sun-Times*, 20 August 1964.

88. See the proposed solution of American Evangelicals in an article entitled "Evangelists Seek Political Clout," *Chicago Sun-Times*, 13 January 1980.

89. See John Fountain's observation in his article, "NU President Urges Grads to Use Optimism as a Lever for Progress," *Chicago Sun-Times*, 21 June 1987.

90. M. Eliade, *Myths, Dreams and Mysteries* (New York: Harper and Brothers, 1960), pp. 8–9.

91. Eliade, "*Homo Faber* and *Homo Religiosus*," p. 11.

92. *Waiting for the Dawn* was the title of the book on "Mircea Eliade in Perspective," edited by David Carrasco and Jane Marie Swanberg (Boulder: Westview Press, 1985).

93. R. S. Wentz, "The Prospective Eye of Interreligious Dialogue," *Japanese Journal of Religious Studies*, vol. 14, no. 1 (March 1987), p. 6.

94. Ibid., p. 15.

95. Quoted in ibid., p. 11.

96. Kitagawa (in the volume edited by Balasooriya et al.), 1980, pp. 84–102.

97. Mead, "The American People," 1954, p. 245.

98. Walter Lippmann, "Pull Out of Vietnam," *Chicago Sun-Times*, 22 October 1967.

99. See Wilhelm Halbfass, *India and Europe* (Albany: SUNY Press, 1986), pp. 84, 96.

100. See Klaus-Peter Koepping, *Adolf Bastian and the Psychic Unity of Mankind* (St. Lucia: University of Queensland Press, 1983).

101. Martin Jay, *Marxism and Totality* (Berkeley: University of California Press, 1984).

102. Halbfass, *India and Europe*, p. 440.

103. Ashis Nandy, *The Intimate Enemy: Loss and Recovery of Self Under Colonialism* (Delhi: Oxford University Press, 1983), p. ix.

104. See Walter Russell Mead, *Moral Splendor: The American Empire in Transition* (Boston: Houghton Mifflin, 1987).

105. Jinwung Kim, "Recent Anti-Americanism in South Korea: The Causes," *Asian Survey*, vol. 29, no. 8 (August 1989), p. 752.

106. Quoted in Halbfass, *India and Europe*, p. 437.

107. Quoted in Burns, *The Poverty of Progress*, front page. See, as one possible alternative, Robert S. Ozaki, "The Humanistic Enterprise System in Japan," *Asian Survey*, vol. 28, no. 8 (August 1988), pp. 830–48.

APPENDIX: "IN RESPONSE"

1. Huston Smith, "Accents of the World's Philosophies," *Philosophy East and West*, April-July 1957, p. 7.

2. Merleau-Ponty, as quoted in Huston Smith, *Condemned to Meaning* (New York: Harper and Row, 1965), p. 17.

3. Wach, *Types of Religious Experience*, pp. 30–47.

4. Joseph M. Kitagawa, *The Quest for Human Unity* (Minneapolis: Fortress Press, 1990), "Introduction," pp. 2–4.

5. Ibid., chapter 2, p. 69.

6. Ibid., chapter 1, p. 40, quoting A. L. Basham, *The Wonder That Was India* (New York: Grove Press, 1954), p. 18.

7. Kitagawa, op. cit., chapter 5, p. 233; chapter 1, p. 40.

8. Ibid., chapter 5, p. 233.

9. See ibid., "Introduction," p. 6; cf. p. 4.

10. H. Richard Niebuhr, *The Meaning of Revelation* (New York: The Macmillan Company, 1941), chapter 1, especially pp. 7ff.

11. Joseph L. Blau, *Judaism in America: From Curiosity to Third Faith* (Chicago: University of Chicago Press, 1976), p. 8.

12. Niebuhr, op. cit., especially chapters 2 and 3.

13. Kitagawa, op. cit., chapter 5, p. 232.

14. Wilfred Cantwell Smith, *Islam in Modern History* (Princeton: Princeton University Press, 1957), p. 17.

15. See Vine Deloria, Jr., *God Is Red* (New York: Grosset and Dunlap, 1973); Ralph Ellison, *Invisible Man* (New York: Random House, 1952); and Charles H. Long, "A New Look at American Religion," *Anglican Theological Review*, July 1973, no. 1, pp. 117–25 and "The Study of Religion in the United States of America: Its Past and Its Future," *Religious Studies and Theology*, vol. 5, no. 3, September 1985, pp. 30–44.

16. See Hannah Arendt, *On Revolution* (New York: Viking Press, 1965 edition).

Bibliography

A. BOOKS

Adams, Charles J. ed., *A Reader's Guide to the Great Religions* (New York: Macmillan-Free Press, 1965).

Andersson, I. Gunnar, *Children of the Yellow Earth: Studies in Prehistoric China* (London: K. Paul, Trench, Trubner, 1934; also Cambridge: MIT Press, 1934).

Anshen, Ruth Nanda ed., *Moral Principles of Action* (New York: Harper, 1952).

Arendt, Hannah, *On Revolution* (New York: Viking Press, 1965).

Baker, A. G. ed., *A Short History of Christianity* (Chicago: University of Chicago Press, 1940).

Balasooriya, S., et al., eds., *Buddhist Studies in Honor of Walpola Rahula* (London: Gordon Frazer, 1980).

Balazs, Etienne, *Chinese Civilization and Bureaucracy: Variations on a Theme* (New Haven: Yale University Press, 1964).

Baldry, Harold C., *Ancient Utopias* (Southampton: University of Southhampton, 1956).

Ball, W. MacMahon, *Nationalism and Communism in East Asia* (Melbourne: Melbourne University Press, 1952).

Basham, A. L., *The Wonder That Was India* (New York: Grove Press, 1954).

Beard, Charles A., *The Idea of National Interest* (New York: Macmillan, 1934).

Beard, C. A. and Mary, *The Rise of American Civilization*, vol. 2 (New York: Macmillan, 1945).

Bickermann, E. J., *The Maccabees* (New York: Schocken Books, 1947).

Blau, Joseph L., *Judaism in America: From Curiosity to Third Faith* (Chicago: University of Chicago Press, 1976).

Boorstin, Daniel J., *The Genius of American Politics* (Chicago: University of Chicago Press, 1953).

Bozeman, Adda B., *Conflicts in Africa* (Princeton: Princeton University Press, 1976).

Brandon, S. G. F., *Man and His Destiny in the Great Religions* (Toronto: University of Toronto Press, 1962).

Brauer, Jerald C. ed., *Religion and the American Revolution* (Philadelphia: Fortress Press, 1976).

Brown, Peter, *Augustine of Hippo* (Berkeley: University of California Press, 1967).

——————— , *The Cult of the Saints: The Rise and Function in Latin Christianity* (Chicago: University of Chicago Press, 1981).

Buber, Martin, "The Suspension of Ethics" in R. N. Anshen ed., *The Moral Principles of Action*.

Burns, E. Bradford, *The Poverty of Progress* (Berkeley: University of California Press, 1980).

Carrasco, David and Jane Marie Swanberg eds., *Waiting for the Dawn* by M. Eliade (Boulder: Westview Press, 1985).

Cartlidge, D. R. and D. L. Dungan, *Documents for the Study of the Gospels* (Philadelphia: Fortress Press, 1980).

Ch'en, Kenneth, *Buddhism in China: A Historical Survey* (Princeton: Princeton University Press, 1946).

Christy, Arthur E. ed., *The Asian Legacy and American Life* (New York: John Day, 1942).

Clarke, E. T., *The Small Sects in America* (Nashville: Abingdon-Cokesbury, 1949).

Conze, Edward, "Buddhism: The Mahayana" in Zaehner, *The Concise Encyclopedia of Living Faiths*.

Creel, H. G., *Chinese Thought from Confucius to Mao Tse-tung* (Chicago: University of Chicago Press, 1953).

Curless, J. Donald, *An Almanac for Moderns* (New York: A. Putnam's Sons, 1935).

Dawson, C., *Enquiries into Religion and Culture* (London: Sheed and Ward, 1933).

de Bary, William T. et al. compl., *Sources of the Indian Tradition* (New York: Columbia University Press, 1958).

Deloria, Vine, Jr., *God Is Red* (New York: Grosset and Dunlap, 1973).

Devanandan, P. D. and M. M. Thomas, eds., *Communism and Social Revolution in India* (Calcutta: YMCA, 1953).

Djait, Hichem, *Europe and Islam* (Berkeley: University of Califorina Press, 1985).

Drinnon, R., *Keeper of Concentration Camps* (Berkeley: University of California Press, 1987).

Dumézil, G., *Les dieux des Indo-Européens* (Paris: Presses Universitaires de France, 1952).

———————, *L'ideologie tripartie des Indo-Européens* (Brussels: Latomus, 1958).

Earle, William, *Public Sorrow and Private Pleasures* (Bloomington: Indiana University Press, 1976).

Eckel, Paul E., *The Far East Since 1500* (New York: Harcourt, Brace and World, 1949).

Ehrenström, Nils, *Christian Faith and the Modern State: An Ecumenical Approach* (Chicago: Willett, Clark & Co., 1937).

Eliade, Mircea, *The Myth of the Eternal Return* (New York: Pantheon Books, 1954).

———————, *Myths, Dreams and Mysteries* (New York: Harper, 1960).

———————, *The Quest: History and Meaning in Religion* (Chicago: University of Chicago Press, 1969).

———————, *A History of Religious Ideas*, vol. 1 (Chicago: University of Chicago Press, 1978).

———————, *Waiting for the Dawn*, ed. by David Carrasco and Jane Marie Swanberg (Boulder: Westview Press, 1985).

——————— ed., *The Encyclopedia of Religion* (16 vols.; New York: Macmillan, 1987–88).

———————, "*Homo Faber* and *Homo Religiosus*" in J. M. Kitagawa (ed.), *The History of Religions: Restrospect and Prospect.*

Eliot, Sir Charles, *Hinduism and Buddhism* (New York: Barnes & Noble, 1954).

Ellison, Ralph, *Invisible Man* (New York: Random House, 1952).

Fairbank, J. K. ed., *Chinese Thought and Institutions* (Chicago: University of Chicago Press, 1957).

Fehl, Noah E., *History and Society* (Hong Kong: Chung Chi College, 1964).

Ferm, Virgillus ed., *Forgotten Religions* (New York: Philosophical Library, 1950).

Finegan, Jack, *Light from the Ancient East* (Princeton: Princeton University Press, 1946).

France, Peter, *Rousseau's Confessions* (New York: Cambridge University Press, 1987).

Frankfort, H. and H. A. eds., *The Intellectual Adventure of Ancient Man* (Chicago: University of Chicago Press, 1946).

Fung, Yu-lan, *A Short History of Chinese Philosophy* (New York: Macmillan, 1950).

Gannon, Thomas M. ed., *The Catholic Challenge to the American Economy* (New York: Macmillan, 1987).

Geertz, Clifford, "Ritual and Social Change: A Javanese Example" in W. A. Lessa and E. Z. Vogt eds., *The Reader in Comparative Religion: An Anthropological Approach* (Evanston: Row, Peterson, 1958).

Gibb, Sir Hamilton A. R., *Mohammedanism: An Historical Survey* (London: Oxford University Press, rev. ed., 1953).

Goldin, Judah, "Early and Classical Judaism" in C. J. Adams (ed.), *A Reader's Guide to the Great Religions*.

Goodspeed, C. S. ed., *The World's First Parliament of Religions* (Chicago: Hill and Schuman, 1895).

Grant, Frederick C., *Ancient Roman Religion* (New York: Liberal Arts Press, 1957).

Grant, Robert M., *Religion and Politics at the Council of Nicaea* (Chicago: University of Chicago Press, 1974).

Grousset, René, *The Rise and Splendor of the Chinese Empire* (Berkeley: University of California Press, 1952).

_____ , *Chinese Art and Culture* (New York: Grove Press, 1959).

Grunebaum, G. E. von, *Medieval Islam* (Chicago: University of Chicago Press, 1946).

_____ ed., *Unity and Variety in Muslim Civilization* (Chicago: University of Chicago Press, 1955).

Haas, William S., *The Destiny of the Mind: East and West* (London: Faber and Faber, 1956).

Halbfass, Wilhelm, *India and Europe* (Albany: SUNY Press, 1986).

Hallowell, A. Irving, "Bear Ceremonials in the Northern Hemisphere" (Ph.D. dissertation, University of Pennsylvania, 1926).

Hamilton, Clarence H., *Buddhism: A Religion of Infinite Compassion* (New York: The Liberal Arts Press, 1952).

Heimann, Betty, *Indian and Western Philosophy: A Study in Contrasts* (London: G. Allen and Unwin, 1937).

Hitti, Philip K., *The Arabs: A Short History* (Princeton: Princeton University Press, 1949).

Hocking, William E., "Living Religions and a World Faith" in Arthur E. Christy ed., *The Asian Legacy and American Life* (New York: John Day, 1942).

Hodgson, Marshall, *The Venture of Islam* (3 vols.; Chicago: University of Chicago Press, 1974).

Hook, Brian ed., *The Cambridge Encyclopedia of China* (Cambridge: Cambridge University Press, 1982).

Hopkins, Thomas J., *The Hindu Religious Tradition* (Encino: Dickenson, 1971).

Hutchins, Robert Maynard, *The Great Conversation* (Chicago: Encyclopaedia Britannica, 1952).

Hutchison, John A., *Paths of Faith* (New York: McGraw-Hill, 1969).

International Missionary Council, *The Relation Between the Younger and Older Churches*, The Jerusalem Meeting of the IMC (New York: International Missionary Council, 1928).

——————— , *The Christian Life and Message in Relation to Non-Christian Systems of Thought and Life*, The Jerusalem Meeting of the IMC (New York: International Missionary Council, 1928).

——————— , *The Growing Church*, Madras Series, vol. 2 (London: International Missionary Council, 1939).

Isaacs, Harold, *Scratches on the Mind* (New York: John Day, 1958).

I-Tsing (I-Ching), *A Record of the Buddhist Religion as Practised in India and the Malay Archipelago (A.D. 671–695)*, trans. by Junjiro Takakusu (Oxford: Oxford University Press, 1896).

Jacobsen, Thorkild, "Mesopotamia—Cosmos as a State" and "The Function of the State" in H. and H. A. Frankfort, eds., *The Intellectual Adventure of Ancient Man*.

Jay, Martin, *Marxism and Totality* (Berkeley: University of California Press, 1984).

Kitagawa, Joseph M., "The 1893 World's Parliament of Religions and Its Legacy" (Chicago: University of Chicago Press, 1984).

——————— , *On Understanding Japanese Religion* (Princeton: Princeton University Press, 1987).

——————— ed., *Modern Trends in World Religions* (Lasalle, Ill.: The Open Court, 1959).

——————— ed., *Understanding Modern China* (Chicago: Quadrangle Books, 1969).

——————— ed., *American Refugee Policy: Ethical and Religious Reflections* (Minneapolis: Winston Press, 1984).

——————— ed., *The History of Religions: Retrospect and Prospect* (New York: Macmillan, 1985).

——————— , "The Asian's World of Meaning," in Gerhard Müller and W. Zeller eds., *Glaube, Geist, Geschichte*.

——————— , "Buddhism and Social Change: An Historical Perspective," in Balasooriya, S., et al. *Buddhist Studies in Honor of Walpola Rahula*.

——————— , "Reflections on the Work Ethic in the Religions of East Asia," in *Comparative Work Ethics* (Washington, D.C.: Library of Congress, 1985).

Koepping, Klaus-Peter, *Adolf Bastian and the Psychic Unity of Mankind* (St. Lucia: University of Queensland Press, 1983).

Konvitz, Milton R., *Alien and the Asiatic in American Law* (Ithaca: Cornell University Press, 1946).

Kraemer, Hendrik, *The Christian Message in a Non-Christian World* (London: The Edinburgh House, 1938).

——————— , *World Cultures and World Religions* (Philadelphia: Westminster Press, 1960).

Kublin, Hyman ed., *China: Selected Readings* (Boston: Houghton Mifflin, 1968).

Lach, Donald F., *Asia in the Making of Europe* (2 vols.; Chicago: University of Chicago Press, 1965).

Latourette, K. S., *The Chinese: Their History and Culture* (2 vols.; New York: Macmillan, 1934).

Leeuw, G. van der, *Religion in Essence and Manifestation* (London: G. Allen and Unwin, 1938).

——————— , *Sacred and Profane Beauty: The Holy in Art* (New York: Rinehart and Winston, 1962).

Li, Dun J., *The Ageless Chinese: A History* (New York: Scribner's, 1965).

Littlefield, Henry W., *New Outline-History of Europe, 1815–1949* (New York: Barnes and Noble, 1949).

Lubac, H. de, *Le recontre du Bouddhism et de l'Occident* (Paris: Aubier Editions Montaigne, 1952).

Macdonald, A. J., *Trade Practice and Christianity in Africa and the East* (London: Longman, Green and Co., 1916).

Mahdi, M. "Modernity and Islam," in J. M. Kitagawa ed., *Modern Trends in World Religions*.

McGinn, Bernard, *The Calabrian Abbot: Joachim of Fiore in the History of Western Thought* (New York: Macmillan, 1985).

Mead, Sidney E., "Christendom, Enlightenment, and the Revolution," in Jerald C. Brauer ed., *Religion and the American Revolution*.

Mead, Walter Russell, *Moral Splendor: The American Empire in Transition* (Boston: Houghton Mifflin, 1987).

Mercer, S. A. B., "The Religion of Ancient Egypt," in V. Ferm ed., *Forgotten Religions*.

Miller, Glenn T., *Piety and Intellect* (Atlanta: Scholars Press, forthcoming), esp. chap. 6, "Old England in the New Republic."

Moore, George Foot, *History of Religions*, vol. 1 (New York: Scribner's, 1948).

Muilenberg, J., "Ethics of the Prophet," in Anshen, *Moral Principles of Action*.

Muir, Sir William, *The Life of Mohammed* (Edinburgh: John Grant, 1923).

Müller, Gerhard and W. Zeller eds., *Glaube, Geist, Geschichte* (Leiden: E. J. Brill, 1967).

Murti, T. R. V., *The Central Philosophy of Buddhism* (London: G. Allen and Unwin, 1955).

Nandy, Ashis, *The Intimate Enemy: Loss and Recovery of Self Under Colonialism* (Delhi: Oxford University Press, 1983).

Neill, Stephen, *The Christian Society* (New York: Harper, 1952).

Nehru, J., *The Discovery of India* (New York: John Day, 1956).

Niebuhr, H. Richard, *The Meaning of Revelation* (New York: Macmillan, 1941).

——————— , *Christ and Culture* (New York: Harper, 1951).

Northrop, F. S. C., *The Meeting of East and West* (New York: Macmillan, 1946).

Oakley, Francis, *The Western Church in the Later Middle Ages* (Ithaca: Cornell University Press, 1979).

Overmyer, D. L., *Religions of China* (San Francisco: Harper, 1986).

Panikkar, K. M., *Asia and Western Dominance* (London: G. Allen and Unwin, 1953).

Pareti, Luigi, *The Ancient World: 1200 B.C. to A.D. 500*, vol. 2 of *History of Mankind* (New York: Harper, 1965).

Pauck, Wilhelm, *The Heritage of the Reformation* (Glencoe: The Free Press, 1950).

Peters, F. E., *Greek Philosophical Terms: A Historical Lexicon* (New York: New York University Press, 1967).

Pfeiffer, John E., *The Creative Explosion: An Inquiry into the Origins of Art and Religion* (Ithaca: Cornell University Press, 1982).

Philo Judaeus, *Allegorical Interpretation of Genesis* (Loeb Classical Library; Cambridge: Harvard University Press, 1949).

Qualbem, Lars P., *A History of the Christian Church* (New York: Thomas Nelson and Sons, 1936).

Radhakrishnan, S. and C. A. Moore eds., *A Source Book in Indian Philosophy* (Princeton: Princeton University Press, 1957).

Rahula, Walpola, *What the Buddha Taught* (New York: Grove Press, 1959).

Randall, J. H., Jr., *The Making of the Modern Mind* (Boston: Houghton Mifflin Co., 1940).

Renou, Louis ed., *Hinduism* (New York: George Braziller, 1961).

Rhys Davids, T. W. trans., *The Questions of King Milanda* (2 vols.; New York: Dover, 1963); originally in *The Sacred Books of the East*, vols. 35 and 36, ed. by F. Max Müller (Oxford: Clarendon Press, 1890 and 1894).

Robinson, Charles A., Jr., "The Inhabited World," in V. Ferm ed., *Forgotten Religions*.

Robinson, Charles H., *History of Christian Missions* (New York: Scribner's, 1915).

Rougemont, Denis de, *Man's Western Quest* (Westport, Conn.: Greenwood, 1973).

Samartha, S. J. ed., *Living Faiths and Ultimate Goals* (Geneva: World Council of Churches, 1974).

Sansom, George B., *A History of Japan to 1334* (Stanford: Stanford University Press, 1958).

Santa Ana, Julio de, "The Common Struggle of Christians and Marxists in Latin America," in S. J. Samartha ed., *Living Faiths and Ultimate Goals*.

Selwyn, Edward G. (ed.), *A Short History of Christian Thought* (London: Geoffrey Bles, 1949).

Sen, Amulyachandra, *Aśoka's "Edicts"* (Calcutta: The Indian Publicity Society, 1956).

Shansab, Nasir, *Soviet Expansion in the Third World: Afghanistan, A Case Study* (Silver Spring: Bartleby Press, 1987).

Smith, Huston, *Condemned to Meaning* (New York: Harper, 1965).

Smith, Reuben W., *Islamic Civilization in the Middle East: Course Syllabus* (Chicago: University of Chicago Press, 1965).

Smith, W. C., *Islam in Modern History* (Princeton: Princeton University Press, 1957).

Spengler, O., *The Decline of the West* (2 vols.; New York: A. A. Knopf, 1930).

Spiro, Melford E., *Buddhism and Society: A Great Tradition and Its Burmese Vicissitudes* (New York: Harper, 1970).

Streeter, Burnett H., *The Buddha and the Christ* (London: Macmillan, 1932).

Sundkler, Bengt, *The World of Mission* (Grand Rapids: Eerdmans, 1965).

Sweet, William W., "Christianity in the Americas," in A. G. Baker ed., *A Short History of Christianity*.

Taggert, Frederick J., *Rome and China: A Study of Correlations in Historical Events* (Berkeley: University of California Press, 1939).

Taraporewala, Irach J. S., "Mithraism," in V. Ferm ed., *Forgotten Religions*.

Thomas, Edward J., *The History of Buddhist Thought* (New York: Barnes and Noble, 1951).

Thompson, Laurence G., *Chinese Religion: An Introduction* (Belmont: Dickenson, 1969).

Thorne, J. O. and T. C. Collocott eds., *Chambers Biographical Dictionary* (Cambridge: Cambridge University Press, 1984).

Tillich, Paul, *The Protestant Era*, trans. by J. L. Adams (Chicago: University of Chicago Press, 1948).

———————, *Theology of Culture* (New York: Oxford University Press, 1959).

———————, *The Future of Religion*, ed. by J. C. Brauer (New York: Harper, 1966).

Toynbee, Arnold, *A Study of History*, abridged by D. C. Somerwell (New York: Oxford University Press, 1947).

———————, *Civilization on Trial* (New York: Oxford University Press, 1948).

———————, *The World and the West* (New York: Oxford University Press, 1953).

Troeltsch, Ernst, *The Social Teachings of the Christian Church* (2 vols.; Glencoe: The Free Press, 1949).

Tsukamoto, Zenryū, *Shina Bukkyō-shi Kenkyū: Hokugi-hen* (Studies of Chinese Buddhist History: Section of Northern Wei) (Tokyo: Kōbundō, 1942).

Turner, F. J., *The Frontier in American History* (Chicago: Henry Holt, 1948).

Wach, Joachim, *Sociology of Religion* (Chicago: University of Chicago Press, 1944).

———————, *Types of Religious Experience: Christian and Non-Christian* (Chicago: University of Chicago Press, 1951).

Warner, Langdon, *The Enduring Art of Japan* (Cambridge: Harvard University Press, 1952).

Warren, H. C., *Buddhism in Translation* (Cambridge, Mass.: Harvard University Press, 1896).

Westermarck, Edward, *The Origin and Development of Moral Ideas* (London: Macmillan, 1908).

Whitehead, Alfred North, "Appeals to Sanity," in *Essays in Science and Philosophy* (New York: Philosophical Library, 1948).

Wieruszowski, Helene, *The Medieval University* (Princeton: van Nostrand, 1966).

Wiese, L. von, *Systematic Sociology*, adapted and amplified by H. Becker (New York: J. Wiley and Sons, 1932).

Williams, Daniel Day, *What Present-Day Theologians Are Thinking* (New York: Harper, 1952).

Wilson, Bryan, *Contemporary Transformation of Religion* (Oxford: Clarendon Press, 1976).

Wilson, John A., "Egypt," in Frankfort and Frankfort, *The Intellectual Adventure of Ancient Man*.

Woolf, Bertram L. trans., *From Tradition to Gospel* (*Die Formsgeschichte des Evangelium* by Martin Dibelius) (London: I. Nicholson and Watson, 1934).

The World's Religious Congress, *General Programme*, Preliminary Edition (Chicago: The World's Religious Congress, 1893).

Worsley, Peter, *The Third World* (Chicago: University of Chicago Press, 2nd ed., 1964).

Wright, Arthur F., *Buddhism in Chinese History* (Stanford: Stanford University Press, 1959).

—————————, "The Formation of Sui Ideology, 581–604," in J. K. Fairbank ed., *Chinese Thought and Institutions*.

Zaehner, R. C. ed., *The Encyclopedia of Living Faiths* (New York: Hawthorne Books, 1959).

—————————, "Zoroastrianism," in his ed., *The Concise Encyclopedia of Living Faiths*.

Zimmer, Heinrich, *Philosophies of India* (New York: Pantheon Books, 1951).

Zürcher, E., *The Buddhist Conquest of China* (2 vols.; Leiden: E. J. Brill, 1959).

B. ARTICLES

Berman, Howard A., "The Pollard Affair—Has American Jewry Learned the Lesson?" (Sermon; Chicago: *Sinai Congregation Bulletin*, 16, June 1, 1987).

Carlson, Edgar M., "Luther's Conception of Government," *Church History*, vol. 15, no. 4 (1946).

Chicago Sun-Times
  Lippman, Walter, "Why the Might Fail to Prevail," 20 August 1964.
  "Glouster Fears Moonies Seek to Net Fish Industry," 1 April 1979.

"Evangelists Seek Political Clout," 13 January 1980.

Fountain, John, "NU President Urges Grads to Use Optimism as a Lever for Progress," 21 June 1987.

"Pull Out of Vietnam," 22 October 1967.

Encyclopaedia Britannica, 1971 ed.
"Portugal," vol. 18.
"Spain," vol. 20.

Encyclopedia of Religion, ed. by M. Eliade (1987–1988)
"Christian Councils," vol. 4.
"Judaism in the Middle East and North Africa," vol. 8.
"Marranos," vol. 9.
"Pietism," vol. 11.
"Zoroastrianism," vol. 15.

Hess, John L., "French Anthropologist at Onset of '70's Deplores the 20th Century," *New York Times*, 31 December 1969.

Indian Journal of Theology
"Christian Hope," vol. 1, no. 2 (November 1952).
"Responsible Society," vol. 1, no. 2 (November 1952).

Inter-Religio
Akizuki, Ryōmin, "Christian-Buddhist Dialogue," no. 14, Fall 1988.
Heisig, James W., "Fore-Words," no. 14, Fall 1988.

Journal of Religion
Benz, Ernst, "Theological Meaning of History of Religion," vol. 51, no. 1 (January 1961).
Mead, Sidney E., "The American People: Their Space, Time, and Religion," vol. 34, no. 4 (October 1954).

Kitagawa, Joseph M., "*Verstehen* and *Erlösung:* Some Remarks on Joachim Wach's Work," *History of Religions*, vol. 11, no. 1 (August 1971).

Kim, Jinwung, "Recent Anti-Americanism in South Korea: The Causes," *Asian Survey*, vol. 29, no. 8 (August 1989).

Kristol, Irving, "The 20th Century Began in 1945," *The New York Times Magazine*, 2 May 1965.

Long, Charles H., "A New Look at American Religion," *Anglican Theological Review*, no. 1 (July 1973).

————————, "The Study of Religion in the United States of America: Its Past and Its Future," *Religious Studies and Theology*, vol. 5, no. 3 (September 1985).

Mansergh, N., "The Impact of Asian Membership," *The Listener*, Dec. 8, 1954.

Mead, Sidney E., "Theological School Address," Commencement Talk (Chicago: Meadville Theological School, June 8, 1954).

——————— , "The American People: Their Space, Time, and Religion," *The Journal of Religion*, vol. 34, no. 4 (October 1954).

The New Encyclopaedia Britannica: Macropaedia, 1985 ed.
"Charles V," vol. 3.
"Byzantine Empire," vol. 15.
"European Overseas Exploration and Empires," vol. 18.
"Greco-Roman Civilization," vol. 20.
"Judaism," vol. 20.

Ozaki, Robert S., "The Humanistic Enterprise System in Japan," *Asian Survey*, vol. 28, no. 8 (August 1988).

Pauck, Wilhelm, "Theology in the Life of Contemporary American Protestantism," *Shane Quarterly*, vol. 13 (April 1952).

Rose, Peter I., "The Politics and Morality of United States Refugee Policy," *The Center Magazine* (Santa Barbara: R. M. Hutchins Center, September/October, 1958).

Smith, Huston, "Accents of the World's Philosophies," *Philosophy East and West*, April-July 1957.

Waley, Arthur, "The Fall of Lo-yang," *History Today*, no. 4 (1951).

Wentz, Richard S., "The Prospective Eye of Interreligious Dialogue," *Japanese Journal of Religious Studies*, vol. 14, no. 1 (March 1987).

Index

Abraham, 19, 29, 55–56, 61–62, 85–87
  and Islamic legacy, 105, 106
Acts, Book of, 83–85, 88–89
Adam, 89
Afterlife. *See* Reincarnation; Immortality
Ahura Mazda, 21–22
Ājīvikas, 39, 43
Akbar, 161–62
Akhnaton, 30, 33
Albertus Magnus, 115, 149
Alexander the Great, 23, 243
  and the Romans, 73
  as savior, 25–26, 34, 41, 53, 69–70, 75
  compared with Akbar, 162
  conquests of, 24–25, 51, 63, 69
Al-Ghazālī, 113
Amenemope, Wisdom of, 33
America
  churches in, 198–204
  cults in, 204
  early Jews in, 171

Jews in, 205–6
missionaries from, 199–201
religious freedom in, 205–8
Amitābha, 44, 136
Analects of Confucius, 48, 141
Anemhotep IV, 30, 33
Angra Mainyu, 22
Apostles, 82, 84
Aquinas, Thomas, 115, 149
Arendt, Hannah, 246
Aristotle, 24, 69, 70, 149
  and Islam, 113, 115
Artaxerxes, 63
Asceticism, Hindu, 123–24
Ashkenazim, 170–73
Asia
  Christianity in, 215–19
  Europeans in, 210, 219
  modernization of, 220
  revolutions in, 211–14
  social class in, 211–14, 257 n.41
Asia Minor. *See* Mesopotamia
Aśoka, 7–8, 41–44, 53, 124, 130, 234, 243, 246